THE ALTERNATIVE RIGHT

Edited by

GREG JOHNSON

Counter-Currents Publishing Ltd.
San Francisco
2018

Cover image:
Emanuel Leutze, *Washington Crossing the Delaware*, 1851
Metropolitan Museum of Art, New York

Cover design by Kevin I. Slaughter

Published in the United States by
COUNTER-CURRENTS PUBLISHING LTD.
P.O. Box 22638
San Francisco, CA 94122
USA
http://www.counter-currents.com/

Hardcover ISBN: 978-1-940933-94-8
Paperback ISBN: 978-1-940933-95-5
E-book ISBN: 978-1-940933-96-2

Library of Congress Cataloging-in-Publication Data

Names: Johnson, Greg, 1971- editor.
Title: The alternative right / edited by Greg Johnson.
Description: San Francisco : Counter-Currents Publishing Ltd., 2018. |
   Includes bibliographical references and index.
Identifiers: LCCN 2017057286 (print) | LCCN 2018001770 (ebook) | ISBN
   9781940933962 (e-book) | ISBN 9781940933948 (hbk : alk. paper) | ISBN
   9781940933955 (pbk : alk. paper) | ISBN 9781940933962 (ebk)
Subjects: LCSH: Right-wing extremists--United States.
Classification: LCC HN90.R3 (ebook) | LCC HN90.R3 .A663 2018 (print) |
DDC
   303.48/4--dc23
LC record available at https://lccn.loc.gov/2017057286

CONTENTS

Art, Religion, & Politics

Sexual Politics & the Alt Right

The End of the Alt Right

EDITOR'S PREFACE

I first conceived this collection of essays in the latter half of 2016, when the Alternative Right was at the peak of its potency and popularity. Then, the volume was to be just a collection of snapshots of a living movement written by participants, fellow travelers, and sympathetic critics. Two years later, however, the book has a sense of completeness, for these pages encompass both the rise and the fall of the Alt Right and offer many lessons for the next phase of white identity politics.

I wish to thank John Morgan and Michael Polignano for helping bring this book to press; Kevin Slaughter for his work on the cover; James O'Meara and Alex Graham for their help with the index; James O'Meara for creating the eBook; the authors for their work and their patience; and, as always, the readers, writers, and supporters of *Counter-Currents* who make everything possible.

I wish to dedicate this book to the memory of Louis Andrews, one of the wisest, most practical, and most hard-working people I have ever known. He embodied the aristocratic ethos of "Talk little, do much, and be more than you appear to be." The movement sorely misses his adult supervision.

Budapest
November 19, 2018

WHAT IS THE ALTERNATIVE RIGHT?

GREG JOHNSON

The Alternative Right does not have an essence, but it does have a story, a story that begins and ends with Richard Spencer. The story has four chapters.

First the term "Alternative Right" was coined in 2008. Then the *Alternative Right* webzine was launched on March 1, 2010 and ran until December 25, 2013. When it was first coined, the Alternative Right simply referred to an alternative to the American conservative mainstream. When it became the name of a publication, it functioned as a broad umbrella term encompassing such schools of thought as paleoconservatism, libertarianism, race-realism, the European New Right, Southern Nationalism, and White Nationalism. By the time the *Alternative Right* webzine was shut down, however, the term Alt Right had taken on a life of its own. It was not just the name of a webzine, but a generic term for Right-wing alternatives to the conservative mainstream.

The second chapter is the emergence in 2015 of a vital, youth-oriented, largely online Right-wing movement. This movement encompassed a wide range of opinions from White Nationalism and outright neo-Nazism to populism and American civic nationalism. Thus this movement quite naturally gravitated to the broad generic term Alt Right. The new Alt Right threw itself behind Donald Trump's run for the presidency soon after he entered the race in 2015 and became increasingly well-known as Trump's most ferocious defenders in online battles, to the point that Hillary Clinton actually gave a speech attacking the Alt Right on August 25, 2016.

The third chapter is the Alt Right "brand war" of the fall of 2016. The Alt Right "brand" had become so popular that it was being widely adopted by Trumpian civic nationalists, who rejected the racism of White Nationalists. White Nationalists began to worry that their brand was being coopted and started to push back against the civic nationalists. The brand war ended on November 21, 2016 at a National Policy Institute conference with the incident known as Hailgate, in which Richard Spencer uttered the words "Hail Trump, hail our people, hail victory!" and raised his whiskey glass in a toast, to which some of some of the audience responded with Hitler salutes. When video of this went public, civic nationalists quickly abandoned the Alt Right brand, and the "Alt Lite" was born.

The fourth chapter is the story of the centralization and decline of the Alt Right, largely under the control of Richard Spencer. This period was characterized by polarization and purges, as well as the attempt to transform the Alt Right from an online to a real-world movement, which culminated at the Unite the Right rally in Charlottesville, Virginia on August 11–12, 2017. Both trends led the Alt Right to shrink considerably. Some abandoned the brand. Others abandoned the entire movement. The remnant has retreated back to its strongholds on the internet. As of this writing, there is no fifth chapter, and the Alt Right's future, if any, remains to be seen. Like cancer, there may be no stage five.

THE INVENTION OF A BRAND

The Alternative Right brand first emerged in the fuzzy space where the paleoconservative movement overlaps with White Nationalism. The term "paleoconservatism" was coined by Paul Gottfried, an American Jewish political theorist and commentator. Paleoconservatism defined itself as a genuinely conservative opposition to the heresy of neoconservatism.

The paleoconservative movement was a safe space for the discussion and advocacy of everything that neoconservatism sought to abolish from the conservative movement: Christianity, tradition, America's white identity, an America-first foreign policy, immigration restriction, opposition to globalization and free trade, the defense of traditional/biological sexual roles and institutions, and even—although mostly behind closed doors—biological race differences and the Jewish question.

Aside from Gottfried, the leading paleocons included Samuel Francis, who openly associated with White Nationalists; Joseph Sobran, who was purged from *National Review* for anti-Semitism and who also openly associated with White Nationalists; and Patrick Buchanan, who stayed closer to the political mainstream but was eventually purged from MSNBC for "racism" because his book *Suicide of a Superpower* defended the idea of the United States as a normatively white society.

William H. Regnery II (b. 1941) is a crucial figure in the rise of the Alt Right because of his work in creating institutional spaces in which paleoconservatives and White Nationalists could exchange ideas. Lazy journalists repeatedly refer to Regnery as a "publishing heir." In fact, his money came from his grandfather William H. Regnery's textile business. The conservative Regnery Publishing house was founded by Henry Regnery, the son of William H. Regnery and the uncle of William H. Regnery II. (In 1993, the Regnery family sold Regnery Publishing to Phillips Publishing International.)

In 1999–2001, William H. Regnery II played a key role in founding the Charles Martel Society, which publishes the quarterly journal *The Occidental Quarterly*, currently edited by Kevin MacDonald. In 2004–2005, Regnery spearheaded the foundation of the National Policy Institute, which was originally conceived as a vehicle for Sam Francis, who died in February of 2005. NPI was run by Louis R. Andrews until 2011, when Richard Spencer took over. Both the Charles Martel Society and the National Policy Institute are White Nationalist in orientation. *The Occidental Quarterly* is also openly anti-Semitic.

But at the same time Regnery was involved with CMS and NPI, he was also working with Jewish paleocon Paul Gottfried to create two academic Rightist groups that were friendly to Jews. First, there was the Academy of Philosophy and Letters,[1] of which Richard Spencer was reportedly a member.[2] But Regnery and Gottfried broke with the Academy of Philosophy and Letters over the issue of race, creating the H. L. Mencken Club, which Gottfried runs to this day.[3] The Mencken Club, like the

---

[1] https://philosophyandletters.org/

[2] Aram Roston and Joel Anderson, "The Moneyman Behind the Alt Right," *BuzzFeed.News*, July 23, 2017.

[3] http://hlmenckenclub.org/

Charles Martel Society and NPI, is a meeting ground for paleoconservatives and White Nationalists, although it is also friendly to Jews.

Richard Spencer began as a paleoconservative, entered Regnery's sphere of influence, and emerged a White Nationalist. In 2007, Spencer dropped out of Duke University, where he was pursuing a Ph.D. in modern European intellectual history. From March to December of 2007, Spencer was an assistant editor at *The American Conservative*, a paleoconservative magazine founded in 2002 by Scott McConnell, Patrick Buchanan, and Taki Theodoracopulos in opposition to the neocon-instigated Iraq War. By the time Spencer arrived, however, Buchanan and Taki had departed. After being fired from *The American Conservative*, Spencer went to work for Taki, editing his online magazine *Taki's Top Drawer*, later *Taki's Magazine*, from January of 2008 to December of 2009. Taki thought his magazine was stagnant under Spencer's editorship, so they parted ways. With money raised through Regnery's network, Richard Spencer launched a new webzine, *Alternative Right* (alternativeright.com) on March 1, 2010.

The phrase "alternative right" first appeared at *Taki's Magazine* under Spencer's editorship. On December 1, 2008, Spencer published Paul Gottfried's "The Decline and Rise of the Alternative Right," originally given as an address at that year's H. L. Mencken Club conference in November.[4] Spencer claims credit for the title and thus the phrase "alternative right," while Gottfried claims that they co-created it.[5] The Alternative Right in decline is, of course, the paleoconservative movement. The Alternative Right on the rise is the more youthful post-paleo movement crystallizing at the Mencken Club and allied forums. The *Alternative Right* webzine was to be their flagship.

---

[4] Paul Gottfried, "The Decline and Rise of the Alternative Right," *Takimag*, December 1, 2008.

[5] Thomas J. Main, *The Rise of the Alt-Right* (Washington, D.C.: Brookings Institution Press, 2018), p. 63; see also my review, "Thomas J. Main's *The Rise of the Alt-Right*," *Counter-Currents*, September 13, 2018.

The *Alternative Right* webzine had an attractive design and got off to a strong start. I particularly respected Spencer's decision to publish Steve McNallen and Jack Donovan, important writers who were anathema to Christians and paleocons. But after about six months, the site seemed to lose energy. Days would go by without new material, which is the key to building regular traffic, and matters were not helped by the site layout. Instead of simply putting new material at the top of a blog roll, the site had a host of departments, so one had to click six or eight links to discover that there was no new material. After doing this for a couple of weeks, readers would stop coming, waiting to hear about new material by email or on social media. By the beginning of 2012, Spencer had lost interest in editing the webzine. On May 3, 2012, he stepped down and handed the editorship to Andy Nowicki and Colin Liddell.

However, in 2013, Spencer was embarrassed by negative press coverage of one of Liddell's articles and realized that he would always be linked to *Alternative Right*, even though he no longer had control of its contents. On Christmas day of 2013, Spencer shut *Alternative Right* down without consulting or warning Nowicki and Liddell. The domain address was repointed to Spencer's new webzine, *Radix Journal*, which would never become a household name. Then, after another strong start, *Radix* too slumped into a low-energy site.

Nearly four years of articles and comments at *Alternative Right*—the collective contributions of hundreds of people—simply vanished from the web. Nowicki and Liddell salvaged what they could and carried on with the *Alternative Right* brand at BlogSpot.com, although their site had few readers and little influence. In 2018, embarrassed by the decline of the Alt Right brand, they changed the name to *Affirmative Right*.

Spencer's greatest mistake in shutting down *Alternative Right* was not his high-handed manner, which caused a good deal of bitterness, but the fact that he pulled the plug after its name had become a generic term. Just as the brand "Xerox" became a term for photocopying in general, the brand "Hoover" became a verb for vacuuming in general, Sony's "Walkman" became a generic term for portable cassette players, and "iPod" became a generic term for portable mp3 players, the Alt Right had become a generic term for a whole range of radical alternatives to mainstream conservatism. Imagine Xerox rebranding with a weird-sounding Latinate name like Effingo once it had become synonymous with its entire industry.

The beauty of the Alt Right brand is that it signaled dissidence from the mainstream Right, without committing oneself to such stigmatized ideas as White Nationalism and National Socialism. As I put it in an article hailing *Alternative Right* to my readers at *TOQ Online*:

> I hope that *Alternative Right* will attract the brightest *young* conservatives and libertarians and expose them to far broader intellectual horizons, including race realism, White Nationalism, the European New Right, the Conservative Revolution, Traditionalism, neo-paganism, agrarianism, Third Positionism, anti-feminism, and Right-wing anti-capitalists, ecologists, bioregionalists, and small-is-beautiful types. . . . The presence of articles by Robert Weissberg and Paul Gottfried indicates that *Alternative Right* is not a clone of *TOQ* or *The Occidental Observer*. (Not that anybody expected that, although some might applaud it.) But that is fine with me. It is more important to have a forum where our ideas interface with the mainstream that to have another Occidental something-or-other.com.[6]

Obviously, a term as useful as Alternative Right was going to stick around, even after being abandoned by its creator. Writers at *Counter-Currents*, the *Alternative Right* BlogSpot site, and even *Radix* kept the concept of the Alt Right in circulation in 2014 and the early months of 2015, after which it caught on as the preferred name of a new movement.

THE EMERGENCE OF A MOVEMENT

The second phase of the Alt Right was quite unlike the first.

---

[6] Greg Johnson, "Richard Spencer Launches *Alternative Right*," *TOQ Online*, March 2, 2010.

The new Alt Right had different ideological origins, different platforms, and a radically different ethos. But it rapidly converged on White Nationalism and carried off some of its best ideas, as well as the term Alt Right. Then it became an international media phenomenon.

In terms of ideology, the first Alt Right was heavily influenced by White Nationalism and paleoconservatism. But the new Alt Right emerged largely from the breakdown of the Ron Paul movement, specifically the takeover of the libertarian movement by cultural Leftists, which drove culturally more conservative libertarians to the Right.[7] Other factors driving the emerging racial consciousness of this group were the Trayvon Martin and Michael Brown controversies, the rise of the Black Lives Matter movement, and the beginning of the migrant crisis in Europe.

The first Alt Right emerged from a milieu of dissident book publishers and print journals, quasi-academic conferences where speakers wore coats and ties, and middle to highbrow webzines. The new Alt Right emerged on social media, discussion forums, image boards, and podcasts, with the webzines coming later. The most influential incubators of the new Alt Right were 4chan and 8chan, *Reddit*, and *The Right Stuff*, especially its flagship podcast, *The Daily Shoah*, and affiliated discussion forums.

The new Alt Right also had a very different ethos and style. While the first Alt Right published reasonable and dignified articles on webzines, the new Alt Right's ethos was emerging from flame wars in the comment threads below. Whereas the first Alt Right cultivated an earnest tone of middle-class respectability, avoiding racial slurs and discussing race and the Jewish question in terms of biology and evolutionary psychology, the new movement affected an ironic tone and embraced obscenity, ste-

---

[7] In 2009, I predicted that people in the Ron Paul movement would start moving toward white identity politics, so I sponsored an essay contest on Libertarianism and Racial Nationalism at *The Occidental Quarterly*, which I edited at the time, to develop arguments to ease the conversion of libertarians. The essays appeared in *The Occidental Quarterly*, vol. 11, no. 1 (Spring 2011).

reotypes, slurs, and online trolling and harassment.

There were also generational differences between the two Alt Rights. The first Alt Right was the product of a Gen-Xer under the patronage of people born in the Baby Boom and before, who actually had memories of America before the cultural revolution of the 1960s and the massive demographic shifts after 1965, when America opened its borders to the non-white world. The new Alt Right consisted primarily of Millennials and Gen-Zs, some of them as young as their early teens, who were products of a multicultural America with rampant social and familial decay, sexual degeneracy, and drug and alcohol abuse. The first group tended to be conservative, because they had memories of a better country. The latter group had no such memories and tended toward radical rejection of the entire social order.

In 2013, I argued that White Nationalists needed to reach out to significant numbers of white Millennials who had graduated from college during the Obama years, often with crushing debts, and who found themselves unemployed or underemployed, and frequently ended up living at home with their parents.[8] I believed that White Nationalists had better explanations for and solutions to their plight than the Occupy Movement, and this "boomerang generation" could be an ideal "proletariat," because they were highly educated; they were from middle and upper middle class backgrounds; they had a great deal of leisure time, much of which they spent online; and they were angry and disillusioned with the system, and rightly so.

As is so often the case, our movement's outreach gestures went nowhere, but the logic of events drove these people in our direction anyway. Boomerang kids became a core group of the new Alt Right known as the "NEETs" — an acronym for Not in Education, Employment, or Training. When these NEETs and their comrades focused their wit, intelligence, anger, tech savvy, and leisure time on politics, a terrible beauty was born.

The Gamergate controversy of 2014 was an important trial

---

[8] Greg Johnson, "The Boomerang Generation: Connecting with Our Proletariat," in *Truth, Justice, & a Nice White Country* (San Francisco: Counter-Currents, 2015).

run and tributary to what became the new Alt Right in 2015. Gamergate was a leaderless, viral, online populist insurrection of video gaming enthusiasts against arrogant Leftist SJWs (Social Justice Warriors) who were working to impose political correctness on gaming. Gamergate activists turned the tables on bullying SJWs, brutally trolling and mocking them and relentlessly exposing their corruption and hypocrisy. Gamergate got some SJWs fired, provoked others to quit their jobs, and went after the advertisers of SJW-dominated webzines, closing some of them down.[9]

Gamergate is important because it showed how an online populist movement could actually roll back Leftist hegemony in a specific part of the culture. Although not everyone involved in Gamergate went on to identify with the Alt Right, many of them did. A leading Gamergate partisan, for instance, was Milo Yiannopoulos of *Breitbart*, who later gave favorable press to the Alt Right and is now a prominent Alt-Lite figure. Moreover, Alt Rightists who had nothing to do with Gamergate eagerly copied and refined its techniques of online activism. Indeed, I would argue that Gamergate was the moral and organizational model for the Disney Star Wars boycott of 2018, which tanked the movie *Solo* and cost Disney hundreds of millions of dollars in lost revenue.

One of the best ways to understand the evolution of the new Alt Right is to read *The Right Stuff* and listen to *The Daily Shoah* from its founding in 2014 through the summer of 2015, when Donald Trump declared his candidacy for the President of the United States. The members of *The Daily Shoah* Death Panel began as ex-libertarians and "edgy Republicans" and educated themselves about race realism and the Jewish question week after week, bringing their ever-growing audience along with them. In February of 2015, Mike Enoch attended the American Renais-

---

[9] For a fuller account of Gamergate, see Vox Day's *SJWs Always Lie: Taking Down the Thought Police* (Castalia House, 2015). See also my review, "Defeating the Left: Vox Day's SJWs Always Lie," in *Confessions of a Reluctant Hater*, second, expanded ed. (San Francisco: Counter-Currents, 2016).

sance conference and afterwards started calling himself a White Nationalist.

By the spring of 2015, this new movement was increasingly comfortable with the term Alt Right.

When Donald Trump declared his candidacy for the US Presidency on June 16, 2015, most White Nationalist currents found common cause in promoting his candidacy. Trump advocacy encouraged cooperation and collegiality within the movement and provided a steady stream of new targets for creative memes and trolling, and as Trump's candidacy ascended, the new Alt Right ascended with him.

In July of 2015, in the runup to the Republican Primary debates, the new Alt Right scored a major victory by injecting a meme that changed the mainstream political conversation: "cuckservative." The inception of this meme was at *Counter-Currents* when on May 2, 2014, Gregory Hood referred to "cuck-old conservatives like Matt Lewis."[10] At this point, many in the media and political establishment realized that a genuine alternative to the mainstream Right had arrived.

The new Alt Right became skilled in using social media to solicit attention and promote backlashes from mainstream media and politicians. This attention caused the movement to grow in size and influence, reaching its peak when Hillary Clinton gave her speech denouncing the Alt Right on August 25, 2016.

An older generation of white advocates saw the notoriety of the Alt Right as an opportunity to reach new audiences. Jared Taylor, who was never thrilled with the Alt Right label, wrote about "Race Realism and the Alt Right."[11] Kevin MacDonald wrote about "The Alt Right and the Jews."[12] Peter Brimelow spoke at National Policy Institute conferences. David Duke began circulating memes.

Although I prefer to describe myself with much more specific

---

[10] Gregory Hood, "For Others and their Prosperity," in his *Waking Up from the American Dream* (San Francisco: Counter-Currents, 2016).

[11] Jared Taylor, "Race Realism and the Alt Right," reprinted below.

[12] Kevin MacDonald, "The Alt Right and the Jews," reprinted below.

terms like White Nationalism and the New Right, I always appreciated the utility of a vague term like Alt Right, so I allowed its use at *Counter-Currents* and occasionally used it myself. But whenever I use "we" and "our" here, I am referring to White Nationalism and the New Right, not the fuzzy-minded civic nationalists and Trumpian populists who also came to use the term Alt Right.

Some have dismissed the Alt Right as a Potemkin movement because it was small, existed largely online, and grew by provoking reactions from the mainstream. But this ignores the fact that America is ruled by a tiny elite employing soft power propagated by the media. So if the Alt Right is somehow illegitimate, so is the entire political establishment. The new Alt Right was a perfect mirror image of the establishment media: it was a metapolitical movement that promoted political change by transforming values and perceptions, but it was promoting change in the opposite direction by negating the establishment's values and worldview.

The Alt Right's particular tactics were dictated by the asymmetries between itself and the mainstream media. They had billions of dollars and armies of professional propagandists. We had no capital and a handful of dedicated amateurs. But new software gave us the ability to create quality propaganda at home, and the internet gave us a way to distribute it, both at very little cost. The establishment's vast advantages in capital and personnel were also significantly negated by the facts that the multicultural consensus it promotes is based on falsehoods and can only cause misery, and the people who control it are weakened by arrogance, smugness, and degeneracy. They are easily mocked and triggered into self-defeating behavior. Our great advantage was telling the truth about liberalism and multiculturalism and proposing workable alternatives. As long as we could stay online, and as long as we attacked from our strengths to their weaknesses, we went from success to success.

But many in the movement were not psychologically ready for success.

BRAND WARS & POLARIZATION

The Alt Right was winning debates and changing minds. Even more significantly, it was also changing the parameters of political debate. It was increasingly capable of driving the news cycle and forcing the political establishment to respond to it. It was also funny, creative, and cool. Naturally, people wanted to join the movement and embrace the brand.

But that presented some problems.

First of all, the Alt Right was a decentralized, largely anonymous, largely online network of individuals, webzines, and small organizations. Because of its online nature, there were no barriers to the movement's viral growth—but by the same token, there were no barriers to entry either.

Second, the Alt-Right brand was effective because of its vagueness. But the flip side of that vagueness was that nobody could control how it was used. Anyone who dissented from the Republican establishment could call himself Alt Right, and as the Trump campaign gained momentum, increasing numbers of young Trumpian populists and civic nationalists wanted to use the term. However, many of these newcomers were ideologically naïve and half-baked.

The main bone of contention was race. The core and vanguard of the Alt Right were White Nationalists. They believed that whiteness is a necessary condition for being a member of any European or European-derived society like the United States. Many newcomers rejected this idea. They were ignorant of the problems of multiracial, multicultural societies. They believed the widespread dogma that being an American is a matter of a civic creed, to which people of any race can adhere. Many of them greeted White Nationalist ideas with indifference or downright hostility.

The utility of the Alt Right brand was as a tool of reaching out to people who were closer to the political mainstream, the "normies." The normies were now coming in droves, and some of them wanted to define the Alt Right in more comfortable civic nationalist terms. This led to a crisis in the Alt Right.

For years, people in our movement had complained about only "preaching to the choir." But now that White Nationalists had a vast audience of people who didn't *already* agree with them, they did not feel elated; they felt threatened. Many people were worried that their movement was going to be "coopted" by "entryists" and started thinking in terms of how to repulse new-comers.

I thought this was self-defeating. I urged people to see the situation as an opportunity to convert a vastly expanded audience to White Nationalism. The reason we had come so far is that we had the best arguments and propaganda. We just needed to have faith in ourselves and our message, then we needed to get back in the battle and continue winning new converts.

We also needed to be realistic about the limits of our ability to control a decentralized, grass-roots, online social movement with anything less than the best memes. It is empty to talk of entryism and purges when one is dealing with an online movement with fuzzy boundaries. We cannot prevent people from going online, nor can we throw them off the internet. Finally, we needed to develop an ethos that would allow us to collaborate productively with people closer to the center, whose links to the mainstream were channels for our ideas and influence.

These arguments, however, were rendered moot on November 21, 2016, when Hailgate allowed the mainstream media to forever tie the Alt Right to neo-Nazism. At this point, many civic nationalists rejected the Alt Right brand entirely. This was the birth of the so-called "Alt Lite." It was "lite" only in one sense: it had tossed White Nationalists overboard. The Alt Lite remained a potent force, while the Alt Right became significantly weaker. The Alt Lite commanded a large audience, which White Nationalists could no longer reach. The Alt Lite retained an enormous social network, from which we were now cut off. White Nationalists could accomplish less, because a lot of highly competent and creative people on the Alt Lite would no longer cooperate with us.

Perhaps the worst loss, however, was in the ideological realm. The most important intellectual battle White Nationalists face is to destroy the taboo against white identity politics. After Hailgate, the Alt Lite differentiated itself from White Nationalism by drawing a firm line against white identity politics and digging in behind it, strengthening the taboo among the very people who were most receptive to questioning it.

It was a disaster. But it did get high marks from Andrew Anglin, who had been at the forefront of the effort to identify the Alt Right with Nazism: "Basically, Richard Spencer did something at NPI that was needed exactly right now in the post-victory period: he separated the Alt-Right from the Alt-Cuck and the Alt-Kike. We are better off without these people."[13] We were better off only if one's goal was to assert control over a marginal, subcultural political movement. We were significantly worse off if one's goal was to interface with the cultural and political mainstream and move it in our direction.

Some figures on the Alt Lite have speculated that Spencer engineered Hailgate precisely to drive off civic nationalists by identifying the Alt Right with racial nationalism in its most stigmatized and toxic form. For what it is worth, I ran this theory by someone who socialized and worked closely with Spencer over the years, and he rejected it as "giving him too much credit" for Machiavellian strategizing. Instead, he chalked Hailgate up to a mix of impulsiveness, drunkenness, and unfathomable bad judgment.

Whether Hailgate was intentional or not, however, it became the pattern for what came next: a drive to centralize the Alt Right under the leadership of Richard Spencer, which led to further division and dysfunction.

CENTRALIZATION, PURGES, & BREAKDOWN

It was quite natural for Richard Spencer to regret dropping a brand that had been adopted by a potent political force and an international media sensation. So he attempted to reassert ownership. But there was a problem: the new movement that emerged in 2014 to 2015 owed little to Spencer except the name that it eventually adopted. Spencer acknowledged this in an October 12, 2016 interview he gave to political scientist George Hawley who was doing research for his book *Understanding the*

---

[13] Andrew Anglin, "Jared Taylor Throws Richard Spencer Under the Bus," *Daily Stormer*, November 27, 2016.

Alt-Right, where Spencer says, "The Alt-Right is what it is today not because of me; it is what it is today because I let it go."[14] This is correct.

But from the point of view of 2018, it is also true to say that the Alt-Right is the mess it is today—largely but certainly not entirely—because Spencer tried to take it back.

On September 9, 2016, NPI held a "What is the Alt Right?" press conference in Washington D.C. The speakers were Richard Spencer, Jared Taylor, and Peter Brimelow. At the conference, Spencer unveiled his "Alt-Right logo," which never really caught on.[15] Clearly Spencer wanted to get out ahead of the new Alt Right, redefine it in his terms, and put his stamp on it.

After Hailgate, Richard Spencer and Persian-American academic Jason Reza Jorjani, who also spoke at NPI 2016, began a series of meetings to create what became the Altright Corporation. The main shareholders were Richard Spencer, Jason Jorjani, Daniel Friberg of Arktos Media, and Red Ice TV.[16]

The Altright Corporation launched the *AltRight.com* webzine on January 16, 2017. Spencer's plan was to elevate himself to movement leadership by *looking like* the leader. He was going to "fake it till you make it"[17] by coaxing as many important voices as possible onto his platform; by coopting organizations like

---

[14] George Hawley, *Making Sense of the Alt-Right* (New York: Columbia University Press, 2017), p. 68.

[15] See Margot Metroland, "The NPI Presser: 'What is the Alt Right?,'" *Counter-Currents*, September 12, 2016.

[16] On some of the shady, deep-state connected operators who encouraged the formation of the Altright Corporation, see Greg Johnson, "The Alt Right Corporation and the American Deep State," *Counter-Currents*, October 18, 2017.

[17] In Josh Harkinson's "Meet the White Nationalist Who Wants to Ride the Trump Train to Lasting Power," *Mother Jones*, October 27, 2016, Spencer is quoted as follows: "'I still feel like we are faking it until we make it,' he confesses. 'I mean, in some ways, you've got to fucking fake it. You have to project success and project power and kind of make it a self-fulfilling prophecy . . .'" Spencer has never disputed the accuracy of this quote, and it coheres with his pickup artist *schtick* that the model for political persuasion is "seduction."

Identity Evropa; by schmoozing with the players who were too big to be coopted (TRS, Jared Taylor, Kevin MacDonald, Peter Brimelow); by maligning and purging those who were immune to his charms (Milo, Mike Cernovich, me); and, above all, by giving interviews to the mainstream media on the cynical but unfortunately correct assumption that *many people in our movement will accept whoever the enemy media anoints as their leader.*

The new webzine followed the same pattern as Spencer's other webzines: a strong start and then a slump. Only in this case, the start was much weaker and the slump came much sooner. *AltRight.com* also differed from Spencer's earlier webzines in the gutter vulgarity of its writing, which was clearly an attempt to curry favor with chan kids and *Daily Stormer* readers. For instance, this is how Vincent Law concludes his article "Daniel Borden Did Literally Nothing Wrong":

> . . . in the case of Daniel, inside sources say that he is holding up well. He has already received hundreds of nude photos and marriage proposals from girls solidly in 7–8 HB range. There is even a smattering of 9s as well.
>
> Daniel is worried though.
>
> He says he doesn't know how to swim and has no idea how he won't drown once he gets out [of jail] from swimming in all that pussy. Don't worry, Daniel. We'll be waiting with some water wings once you get out.[18]

Serious writers were not exactly clamoring to share the same platform.

Spencer's efforts at polarization and purges were no more successful. It is a classic White Nationalist rookie move for a new, would-be leader to set up his PO Box and webzine and then to try to recruit followers and donors by launching attacks on his rivals. The underlying assumption of the polarization

---

[18] Vincent Law, "Daniel Borden Did Literally Nothing Wrong," *Altright.com*, July 9, 2017.

strategy is that a certain percentage of followers will come over to the attacker's camp, while the rest will remain with the target. But the movement as a whole will not suffer. The deck will simply be reshuffled.

In fact, such tactics are profoundly damaging to the movement as a whole. To use arbitrary numbers, the attacker might gain 15% of the target audience, and the target might retain 40 to 50%, depending on his response. But the rest become disgusted and demoralized and refuse to have anything to do with either party. Some simply quit entirely. Polarization, therefore, brings some benefits to the aggressor but harms the movement as a whole, which is why we should shun anyone who uses this strategy as a selfish self-promoter.

One can argue that subjecting a movement like the Alt Right to any kind of centralized leadership is a bad idea. The Alt Right—and White Nationalism as a whole—is a decentralized, non-hierarchical network. The nodes of this network are individuals—most of them anonymous—and small hierarchical organizations. These nodes are largely linked by the internet, especially social media platforms.

The drivers of the movement are creative individuals who produce memes in the form of articles, podcasts, videos, and images. When a particularly potent meme is created, the network propagates and augments it until the meme is exhausted and something new comes along. When it works well, the movement is endlessly stimulating and fun, and it has genuine transformative effects on the public mind.

Because the network makes possible the creative collaboration of countless anonymous individuals, one can argue that the network itself is actually smarter, more creative, and more powerful than any of the nodes. There are differences between the nodes. Some create memes; others merely propagate them. Some individuals and organizations have larger audiences, greater impact, and more moral and intellectual credibility than others. I would like to see many large, well-funded, and highly influential companies, think tanks, and political parties emerge from this network. But even the biggest nodes are smaller than the network as a whole.

What would happen to the overall effectiveness of the network if a would-be leader tried to subject it to his control? Even a small networked movement like the Alt Right is more complex and creative than any individual node. Thus if an individual were to try to assume leadership of the movement, he would inevitably have to simplify its structure, which would inevitably dampen its creativity and power. This is why centralization is always accompanied by polarization and purges. The size and complexity of the movement has to be reduced to what can be comprehended and controlled by an individual mind. The smaller the mind, the greater the damage. Those who are unimpressed with the would-be leader must, furthermore, be driven out.

The quest for centralization might promise immense ego gratification for a would-be leader. But the net result is a smaller, dumber, less creative movement. It is also less active, because formerly independent agents must now wait around for orders from above. Or they have to wrangle to gain the agreement of others, whereas formerly they could just act on their own judgment. Thus centralization inevitably makes the movement weaker. This would be true even if the centralizer were the kind of organizational genius capable of founding a large corporation or a government. It is especially the case when the would-be leader can't even run a successful webzine.

Spencer's attempts to purge rivals from the movement were also unsuccessful but created a great deal of lasting collateral damage. In the fall of 2016, Spencer's polarization and purge tactics consisted largely of whispering campaigns. After Hailgate, he unleashed a barrage of transparently envious and embittered tweets against Milo, Cernovich, and other Alt-Lite figures.

But on June 1, 2017, Spencer tried something much bolder. Spencer launched an attack against me and *Counter-Currents* with a lame and dishonest article co-authored by Daniel Friberg, "Greg Johnson's Attacks and How to Deal with Them."[19] He did not, however, reckon any blowback into his

---

[19] See Greg Johnson, "Reply to Daniel Friberg," *Counter-Currents*,

plans. *Counter-Currents* is still here, but the Altright Corporation began to unravel at that point, first losing Jason Jorjani then Red Ice. Eventually even Friberg quietly severed ties.

But nobody really wins such battles. In this case, many relationships of friendship, comradeship, and collegiality were replaced by enmity, bitterness, and distrust that persist to this day. Connections that allowed productive collaborations were severed, leaving the movement less effective and more dysfunctional.

Spencer's use of the media to elevate him to leadership status was ultimately unsuccessful as well. The media attention Spencer received came at a price. All Spencer had to do was help the media advance its anti-white agenda by conforming to one of its negative stereotypes, in Spencer's case the smug, snobbish, amoral WASP plutocrat.[20] The media loved Spencer, because he helped them make White Nationalism look bad. Spencer loved the media, because he hoped it would elevate him over his rivals in the movement. Neither party to this cynical transaction had any interest in representing White Nationalism in a way that might actually connect with the white majority.

As I have already argued, there is no way to be the leader of this movement as a whole. But one can still aspire to be a leader *within* the movement. There are basically two ways to do this: the grassroots way and the AstroTurf way. The grassroots way is to build a solid platform from the ground up, based on a record of achievements, whether they be in political activism or propaganda work. But the grassroots way is also the hard way, requiring many years of sustained and patient labor.

Thus it is tempting to take the easy way, the AstroTurf way: give an interview, or pull a publicity stunt, in the hope that the

---

June 18, 2017; Omar Filmersson, "Greg Johnson Told the Truth," *Counter-Currents*, June 22, 2017; Aedon Cassiel, "Friberg Falls Back," *Counter-Currents*, June 25, 2017; John Morgan, "The Truth About Daniel Friberg," *Counter-Currents*, June 27, 2017.

[20] For more on the press engagement strategy of Spencer and Matt Heimbach/Matt Parrott, see Greg Johnson, "In Bed with the Press," in Greg Johnson, *Toward a New Nationalism* (San Francisco: Counter-Currents, 2018).

enemy media will anoint you leader. But even if you pull it off, you can't remain a *virtual* leader forever. You have to start delivering *actual* results, *positive* results. Spencer has done things of value over the years: NPI conferences, *Radix*, and Washington Summit Publishers. But these were all sidelined for rallies and a college speaking tour that turned out to be net negatives.

At this point, most of Spencer's followers have abandoned him, even his inner circle, and he has gone silent except for an occasional Tweet or YouTube livestream. The establishment, then, got the better deal. Whether Spencer ultimately fades away or makes a comeback, the media will be trotting out footage of Hailgate and other cringe-inducing gaffes to stigmatize Trump and White Nationalism for decades to come.

Those of us who are trying to present a morally coherent and historically accurate case for white self-determination will be forever dogged with clips of Spencer defending imperialism and white supremacism, attacking freedom of speech, calling for the genocide of Turks, dismissing the relevance of morality, and playing "agree and amplify" with outrageous anti-white canards like "Part of your greatness is the exploitation of other people."[21] It would be one thing if these were sincere but mistaken convictions. But with Spencer they are simply half-baked postures and provocations.

One cannot, however, entirely blame Richard Spencer for the declining fortunes of the Alt Right. Again, the movement that emerged in 2014 and 2015 owed little to Spencer except its name. And even though Spencer damaged the Alt Right by trying to assert control over it, the movement — including its problems — was always bigger than him. Which means that he cannot bear sole blame for its downfall. In particular, it is unjust to blame Spencer for the disastrous Unite the Right Rally of August 11–12, 2017, since he played little role in planning it. There were broader forces at work, in which Spencer himself was caught up, and which can be summed up as *the return of White Nationalism 1.0.*

---

[21] https://youtu.be/h6N4VNxDT24

WHITE NATIONALISM 1.0 & 2.0

In 2015, when the new Alt Right became more comfortable with the idea of White Nationalism, most of its members had only the vaguest acquaintance with an earlier generation of White Nationalist figures. Lawrence Murray, for instance, claimed, "I myself had never heard of [William] Pierce and [David] Duke . . . until becoming involved with the Alt-Right."[22] Murray's experience is typical of Millennial and Gen-Z Alt Rightists.

The Alt Right began calling the White Nationalism of their fathers' generation "White Nationalism 1.0." The dubbed the Alt Right "White Nationalism 2.0." Built into this framework was a dismissive attitude toward White Nationalism 1.0 and an assumption that the Alt Right was a marked improvement. I agreed with the latter judgment. But more often than not, Alt Rightists dismissed figures like Pierce and Duke based simply on impressions gleaned from the mainstream media. I thought it was shameful to parrot enemy propaganda. Thus when such attitudes appeared in various private forums, I urged Alt Rightists to become better informed and learn what they could from White Nationalism 1.0. As a movement, it was largely a failure, but learning from failure is part of success. Unfortunately, some people learned the wrong lessons.

By the beginning of 2017, I began to notice a definite shift toward 1.0 ideas and attitudes:

❖ The assumption that German National Socialism is the only authentic form of White Nationalism

❖ Advocating the mass extermination of non-whites, race-mixers, and homosexuals, straight from the pages of *The Turner Diaries*

❖ A marked upsurge attitudes toward women that can legitimately be labeled misogyny, including the toxic "white *sharia*" meme and a push to bully female voices into silence

❖ A revival of the skinhead subculture of binge drink-

---

[22] Quoted in Hawley, *Making Sense of the Alt-Right*, p. 80.

          ing and hard drugs
❖ The return of costumed demonstrations and street brawls with Leftists

The entirely negative consequences of these attitudes and behaviors were easy to predict. But they were nevertheless tolerated, given platforms, and even advocated and encouraged by leading Alt-Right voices.

First and foremost, WN 1.0 ideas are self-marginalizing and self-defeating.

The best possible way to advocate White Nationalism is to emphasize that it is a political philosophy based in human nature, confirmed by social science and political experience, and rooted in the political traditions of all white nations. The worst possible way to advocate White Nationalism is to claim that every form of ethnonationalism is fake—except the German form that was defeated in 1945 and has been execrated continuously since then.[23]

As I argue in *The White Nationalist Manifesto*, the white race is currently being subjected to genocide, and White Nationalism is the best political system to end white genocide and restore healthy white communities.[24] The worst possible way to rally our people against the genocide directed at us is to advocate genocide against others.

One of the self-evident axioms of politics is that a movement has a better chance of winning if more people fight for it and fewer people fight against it. There are two ways to do this. First, we must rally our own people to our banner. Second, we can try to split the enemy bloc by converting some of them to allies, sympathizers, or simply neutral parties.

But if we have exterminationists among us, our own people will not side with us, because such morally repugnant positions only attract psychopaths to the movement while repulsing normal people. Indeed, exterminationists actually reinforce the

---

[23] See Greg Johnson, "The Relevance of the Old Right," in *The White Nationalist Manifesto* (San Francisco: Counter-Currents, 2018).

[24] See Part 1, White Nationalism, encompassing chapters 2–7.

white guilt propaganda that asserts that whites are a uniquely evil race whose disappearance would not be a great loss to the cosmos. Furthermore, exterminationists ensure that the enemy bloc will be larger and more unified simply because no non-white in his right mind could sympathize with or be indifferent to our movement—much less aid it.

Just as egalitarians label simple realism about racial differences "hate," they label simple realism about the differences between the sexes "misogyny," i.e., the hatred of women. That said, however, there are quite a few race realists who genuinely hate other races, many of them gleefully, without reluctance or reservations.[25] Likewise, there are quite a lot of people in our circles who simply hate women.

Many of the race haters don't understand that the fundamental purpose of our movement is to drain the multicultural swamp in which racial hatred breeds, rather than to self-indulgently wallow in it. Indeed, the more the movement is simply a platform for expressing hate, the less likely it is to actually create a society that is free of racial hatred.

Likewise, many of the woman haters don't understand that another fundamental aim of our movement is to drain the cultural swamp that breeds distrust and hatred between the sexes, rather than just to provide a platform for misogynists to vomit bile into the void. Indeed, the more the movement is simply a safe space for damaged people to vent, the less likely it is to actually create a society with healthy families and sexual norms.

Politics is not therapy. The more our movement resembles a group therapy session—with the lunatics running the asylum—the less likely it is to achieve its political goals.

The idea of "white *sharia*" took wholesome and salutary truths about the differences between the sexes and their appropriate roles in the family and society at large and self-defeatingly packaged them in terms that bring to mind child brides, arranged marriages, rape gangs, sex slavery, polygamy, clitoridec-

---

[25] See, by way of contrast, Greg Johnson, "Confessions of a Reluctant Hater," in *Confessions of a Reluctant Hater*.

tomies, acid attacks, *purdah*, and dressing in drop cloths.[26]

Again: the White Nationalist movement has a better chance of winning if more people fight for us and fewer people fight against us. Thus it is self-defeating for a movement that is already small and marginal to launch bullying campaigns against entire classes of white people who want to help—including the more than 50% of the white race that happens to be female.

As I argue in my essays "Redefining the Mainstream"[27] and "Against Right-Wing Sectarianism,"[28] White Nationalism will win when it becomes the common sense of the whole cultural and political mainstream. There is nothing inherently Right-wing about the essential ideas of White Nationalism: for instance, that being white is a necessary condition of European identity; that the white race is being subjected to slow genocide due to policies that promote low white fertility and non-white immigration; that creating sovereign white homelands with pro-natal, pro-family values is the solution to white genocide; and that Jews have played a leading role in promoting white genocide and blocking whites from stopping it. At present, though, White Nationalism is a movement of the Right. But that presents us with a tricky problem.

To transform the mainstream in a White Nationalist direction, we need to let our message emerge from its current Right-wing cocoon and spread its wings. It would be self-defeating to change any of our essential principles to conform to the mainstream. The whole point is to get the mainstream to conform to us. Thus the only thing we can change is how we *package* and *communicate* our message. We need to craft versions of the essential White Nationalist message that can convert every white constituency. We even need to convert some non-whites into allies and sympathizers, or at least convince them they have nothing

---

[26] See Donald Thoresen, "Whigger *Sharia*," *Counter-Currents*, June 7, 2017, reprinted below.

[27] Greg Johnson, "Redefining the Mainstream," in *Toward a New Nationalism*.

[28] Greg Johnson, "Against Right-Wing Sectarianism," in *Toward a New Nationalism*.

to lose from our victory.

That is a tall order, and we are just beginning to figure out how to make it work. It is, however, easy to determine what won't work, namely insisting that the White Nationalist idea must be accepted with a long list of Right-wing add-ons. Right-wing sectarianism is the path to self-marginalization and self-defeat, and in this game, White Nationalism 1.0 is the undisputed champion.

But we know that victory is possible, because it was not too long ago that pro-white ideas were culturally and politically dominant. Furthermore, the present hegemony of anti-white ideas was created through the exact same metapolitical strategies by which we aim to reverse it. The sooner stop doing things that don't work—and start doing things that do work—the sooner we win.

We need to take a nuanced stance on drinking, drugs, and other unhealthy habits. On the one hand, our movement aims at the creation of a better society. On the other hand, the people in our movement are the products of the profoundly sick society that we wish to overcome. Thus young audiences find it real and relatable to watch Millennial Woes chain-smoking his way through his YouTube videos, or to listen to the countless podcasts whose hosts and guests are obviously drunk or stoned.

But imagine tuning back in ten years from now and finding them doing the exact same thing. Obviously, something would have gone terribly wrong. Obviously, an important opportunity would have been lost. For the whole point of being real and re-latable is to establish a connection to one's audience in order to *lead* them. Not just to lead them, to *better* them. But we cannot better people if we do not better ourselves. Thus an ethos that celebrates or merely tolerates chemical dependencies is self-defeating. It turns the movement into just another dead-end of modern decadence rather than an exit from it. How can we overcome the downward plunge of the whole modern world if we can't even overcome the downward pull of our own petty vices?

Imagine, for a moment, that the movement adopted Harold Covington's General Order Number 10: for the duration of the struggle, no White Nationalist will use alcohol and drugs.[29] We would gain much and lose nothing. First, drugs and alcohol impair judgment and effectiveness, leading to bad decisions and clumsy execution with predictably self-defeating consequences. Second, drugs and alcohol get people into trouble with the law, which is one way they are turned into informants and saboteurs. Third, drugs and alcohol consume time and money that could be better spent on the cause. Fourth, demanding people give up drugs and alcohol communicates that our cause is serious and demands personal sacrifices but also makes us better and nobler people. Finally, adopting a zero-tolerance policy for drugs and alcohol weeds out unserious people who prize personal self-indulgence over racial salvation. Now imagine if the Alt Right had adopted this sort of ethos at the beginning of 2016. Think of everything we could have avoided.

We also need to take a nuanced stance on the return of costumed protests and brawls with Communists. The Old Right began by battling Communists in the streets of Europe. For a while after Trump's election, it looked like those days were back as masked Communists ("antifa") attacked Trump supporters in the streets. Naturally, Trump supporters, including White Nationalists, wanted to fight back. It was only natural to test the waters and see what was possible.

At a certain point, however, caution and prudence were tossed to the winds. People got giddy, grandiose, and delusional. For instance, in the midst of the Unite the Right rally in Charlottesville, Richard Spencer declared, "The Alt-Right is finished debating, negotiating, surrendering. We're ready to close ranks and fight for what is ours. . . . We stand poised to conquer the continent."[30] In fact, the Alt Right stood poised for a fall: a wave

---

[29] See Greg Johnson, "Birth of a Nation," in *In Defense of Prejudice* (San Francisco: Counter-Currents, 2017) a review of Harold Covington's first four Northwest novels, and "Drug Legalization in the White Republic," in *Confessions of a Reluctant Hater*, a libertarian position that I have abandoned because of the catastrophic consequences of drugs on white communities.

[30] Quoted in Brett Barrouquere, "Judge upholds bulk of lawsuit against alt-righters in Charlottesville after 'Unite the Right,' dismisses

of doxing, deplatforming, and criminal and civil trials, the costs of which will continue to mount for years to come.

Charlottesville offered valuable lessons that many of us took to heart. Don't hold rallies in enemy strongholds. Don't announce our events months in advance, giving the enemy time to prepare. Don't trust the enemy media to convey our message. Don't trust police to enforce the laws if they benefit us. White Nationalists will be fired from their jobs, demonized by the press, deplatformed from the web, and prosecuted by the anti-white establishment, while antifa will be coddled. We don't have the numbers, money, institutions, and public sympathy to engage in demonstrations like Unite the Right. The Left has effectively bottomless reserves of lawyers and money to harass us with frivolous lawsuits, the aim of which is to exhaust and bankrupt us, and to expose the identities of our activists and donors through the "discovery" process. But we don't have comparable resources to defend ourselves.

The great lesson of Charlottesville was simply to take stock of the strengths and weaknesses of both the establishment and our movement, then focus on doing what works. The enemy's strengths include vast numbers of people, effectively infinite amounts of money, and control over the leading institutions of society. The same can be said, however, of any establishment right up to the point that it was overthrown. The enemy's chief weaknesses are promoting morally heinous and socially destructive policies based on lies, as well as being corrupt, decadent, vicious, and silly.

Our weaknesses are the mirror image of our enemies' strengths. Our movement has tiny numbers and scarce funds. We control almost no institutions of our own and are at the mercy of the institutions controlled by our enemies. Again, this is true of practically every revolutionary movement at one time or another, including those that go on to win.

Our strengths too are the mirror image of our enemies' weaknesses. They are promoting policies based on lies about human nature that are leading to hatred, conflict, and eventually

---

Peinovich," *Hatewatch*, July 10, 2018.

genocide. We promote policies based on truths about human nature that will minimize ethnic conflict, hatred, and genocide. They promote bad arguments and double standards, and we are masters of deconstructing them. They are laughable, and we are masters of mocking and shaming them.

As long as we attacked the enemy's weaknesses from our strengths, we were making remarkable metapolitical gains. But as soon as some attacked the enemy's strongest points from a position of relative weakness, they were destroyed. Those of us who are still in the struggle either never got involved with street activism or have returned to doing what works: metapolitics — which means community organizing and the propaganda war, including the low-risk, high-reward propaganda of the deed strategies pioneered by the Identitarian Movement and adopted by Identity Evropa in the United States.

Is the story of the Alt Right over, or will there be a next chapter? At this point, we shouldn't really care. Even if the Alt Right is dead, White Nationalism and white identity politics are very much alive, and it is the issues not the symbols that really matter. The Alt Right was just a brand. It was a useful umbrella term that created a discursive space in which White Nationalists could network with and convert people who are closer to the mainstream. But Richard Spencer collapsed that discursive space with Hailgate. The much-reduced Alt Right movement that Spencer created under his leadership met its Waterloo at Charlottesville. At this point, the Alt Right movement is dead, and the brand has been irreparably tarnished. There will always be some people who will choose to call themselves Alt Right — just as there are people who call themselves Nazis — but it will be little more than a defiant gesture of self-marginalization. Those who are serious about creating a future for white people need to look beyond the Alt Right toward a new nationalism.

Counter-Currents, October 10, 18, & 22 & November 15, 2018

RACE REALISM & THE ALT RIGHT

JARED TAYLOR

What is the Alt Right? It is a broad, dissident movement that rejects egalitarian orthodoxies. These orthodoxies require us to believe that the sexes are equivalent, that race is meaningless, that all cultures and religions are equally valuable, and that any erotic orientation or identification is healthy. These things we deny. The Alt Right is also skeptical of mass democracy. It opposes foreign aid and foreign intervention—especially for "nation building."

Given the loose nature of the movement, there are people who consider themselves "Alt Right" but who disagree on one or more of these points—except one. The entire Alt Right is united in contempt for the idea that race is only a "social construct." This is an idea that is so wrong and stupid that only very intelligent people can convince themselves it is true.

Race is a biological fact. Does anyone think that the differences between Danes and Pygmies are a sociological illusion? A barely socialized two-year-old can tell races apart at a glance. There are countless race differences in such things as skull structure, twinning rates, and susceptibility to disease. It is even possible to tell a person's race from the varieties of bacteria that live in his mouth!

Human races have been evolving separately for perhaps as long as 100,000 years, and evolution has marked their temperaments and mental abilities just as it has their physical characteristics. Different races have different average IQs, and the evidence is overwhelming that these differences are, to a substantial degree, genetic.

Orthodoxy insists that this is "pseudo-science" that has been "discredited." Nonsense. No one has discredited Arthur Jensen, Richard Herrnstein, Charles Murray, Linda Gottfredson, Richard Lynn, Michael Levin, Michael Woodley, Philippe Rushton, and Robert Plomin.

Orthodoxy on race leads to endless folly. There are approximately 13,500 school districts in the United States. In every one, test results fit the pattern for IQ: Asians get the best scores, followed by whites, then Hispanics, then blacks. Is this because every district is biased and prejudiced? Of course not. This pattern reflects biology.

Those who deny biology always try to "narrow the gaps" in test scores. That was the purpose of the 2002 No Child Left Behind Act, which *required* schools to bring racial averages up to the same level. No school could. This silliness consumed huge amounts of time and money, and required so many exemptions it was finally set aside as meaningless. It was crushed by the reality of race.

The world makes no sense without an understanding of race. Why is black Africa poor? Why is Haiti—populated by the same people but with a completely different history—equally poor? Why do blacks in America, Canada, and Britain—likewise with very different histories—show exactly the same patterns of crime, poverty, illegitimacy, and school failure? Why, on the other hand, are Asians ahead of whites on all these measures? Because race is real.

No coherent social policy can be based on egalitarian dogmas about race. That is why everything from education to welfare to housing to policing to immigration policy yields deformed results. If you cannot understand race you cannot understand anything else.

Is it harsh to explain black and Hispanic failure in terms of inherent racial differences? Whites *must* speak in these terms in self-defense. Since orthodoxy has decreed that all groups are precisely equal, it permits only one explanation for non-white failure: white oppression. An entire industry has risen up to stoke white guilt and purge whites of "unearned privilege." We are not responsible for the shortcomings of others, and we despise those who claim we are.

Race is not just real: it is central to group and individual identity. All other racial groups take this for granted; only whites must pretend that their race means nothing to them. Question: What do you call a black person who prefers to be around other black people, and likes black music and culture? A black person. What do you call a white person who listens to classical music, likes European culture, and prefers to be around white people? A Nazi. All non-whites are expected to have a strong racial identity; only whites must not.

And yet, even if they do not admit it to themselves, whites act on the basis of race all the time. When the neighborhood turns black or Hispanic, they move away. When their children's school fills up with non-whites, they change schools. This is as true of "liberals" as it is of "conservatives." As the late Joseph Sobran used to say, "In their mating and migratory habits, liberals are no different from members of the Ku Klux Klan."

People of all races prefer to be with people like themselves, and church congregations prove it. Ninety-five percent are at least 80-percent one race, and many are 100-percent one race. This is because churches—unlike neighborhoods, companies, private clubs, and schools—are not yet required by law to integrate. Congregations reflect complete freedom of choice, and when Americans are free to choose they gravitate to people like themselves.

Finally, the Alt Right recognizes that whites have legitimate interests as a people. One of the most obvious is to resist the waves of non-white immigration that are dispossessing us. We refuse to stand with arms folded and watch our children become a minority; if current ideological trends continue, they will be a hated minority.

Virtually all whites everywhere in the world face the same crisis of dispossession. The only exceptions are a few Eastern European countries that refuse to accept immigrants or refugees. Ironically, whites who lived behind the "Iron Curtain" were protected from the mental poisons that paralyze whites and keep them from taking the most elementary steps to remain masters in their own houses.

The Alt Right is a necessary alternative to a "respectable" right that has completely capitulated. In the 1960s, *National Review* defended South African apartheid and Southern segregation. It accepted the reality of race and discussed racial differences in average IQ. Today, no publication outside the Alt Right dares discuss the implications of low black and Hispanic IQ or the need for whites to act in the name of their race and culture. "Conservatives" no longer try to conserve *what is most important*: their own people.

The Alt Right laughs at the idea that "diversity is a strength." Diversity of language, religion, but especially of race bring conflict and tension. The worship of diversity leads to idiotic statements like that of General George Casey, who commanded the American troops in Iraq: "I firmly believe the strength of our Army comes from our diversity."

Does General Casey really believe that the army is strong because of black and Mexican and Filipino soldiers? Do equipment and training have something to do with it? Has General Casey forgotten the murderous racial tensions in the Vietnam-era army? Doesn't he remember Major Nidal Hassan, who killed 13 soldiers and wounded 30 more at Fort Hood? Does he think the all-white armies that fought at Gettysburg or on Iwo-Jima were pitiful bands of defectives? Does General Casey believe his own rubbish? Even our generals are eunuchs, taught to believe that dispossession is wonderful.

We are told over and over that it is the duty of all Americans to "celebrate diversity." It really is a celebration for non-whites, because diversity means greater numbers and growing influence — for them. But to ask whites to "celebrate diversity" means asking them to rejoice in their own declining numbers and dwindling influence. Only whites, only a thoroughly denatured people could ever be browbeaten into celebrating impending oblivion.

As waves of non-white immigrants sweep over us it is common to say that diversity is Americas "greatest strength." Does anyone realize what that really means? It means that the 90-percent white America of the 1950s and '60s was about to choke to death on its own homogeneity but was saved by Mexicans and Haitians. It means whites were a moribund people brought back to life only by the lucky arrival of people unlike ourselves.

Nothing is more grating than when non-white immigrants themselves throw "diversity" in our faces — as if they came for the sole purpose of bringing us this precious gift. They came, of course, because we built a wonderful society. People who have made their own countries miserable come to take advantage of a society they could never have created—and if they come in large enough numbers they will turn our country into something completely alien. And we are supposed to thank them for this.

Imagine the shoe on the other foot. Imagine going to China and saying, "It's not a bad country you have here, but it's got a real problem: too many Chinese. You need to ginger the place up with a couple of million Iraqis, a stiff dose of Haitians, and enough Venezuelans to set up 'little Caracases' in all your big cities. Diversity is a strength!" The Chinese would call for the men in white coats.

When the Alt Right dissents from racial orthodoxy, it can count on being called names. The liberals' favorite is "white supremacist," which is the most emotionally charged way to try to discredit a white person. "White supremacy" implies nostalgia for slavery, Jim Crow, and lynchings, and suggests we want to rule over people of other races. This is foolishness. I have never met anyone who wants to rule other races. We want to be left alone so we can be the people we were meant to be. The expression "white supremacist" should be dropped from current use, but the more it is used the more ridiculous it sounds.

Our opponents call us names because they cannot refute us, and calling us names is the most graceless way of admitting they have no argument. It means no more to call us racists than to call us giraffes. Our opponents must instead explain why we are illogical or mistaken—which they cannot do. They know that "conservatives" scurry into dark corners when they are called names; not us. We are proud to stand up for our people, and names will never frighten us.

Liberals now call so many things "racist" the word has practically no meaning. Whatever it means, though, it implies moral inferiority, that we dissidents are not just mistaken but bad. What nonsense. There is no higher morality than to work for the survival and prosperity of one's people. We spit on the idea that all other groups may advance their rights while only we—only white people—may not.

What we ask for ourselves is nothing more nor less than what we want for people of all races: the right to pursue their destinies free from the unwanted embrace of others, to seek a future that is uniquely theirs within neighborhoods, institutions, regions, and ultimately nations in which they are the permanent and undisputed majority.

It is we who are the champions of true diversity. Imagine the whole world becoming the multi-culti mix to which orthodoxy condemns white countries. Could the delicate culture of Japan survive mass immigration? Would India still be India if millions of foreigners moved there? Of course not. And yet Europe, America, Australia, Canada—all white nations are to welcome aliens and we are to smile as we are submerged.

What whites are expected to do is without precedent in human history. We have the power to keep our lands for ourselves, but we are throwing them open to aliens, aliens who despise us as they take what is ours. Many nations have been overrun by powerful invaders. Never has any people or nation let itself be pillaged by the weak. This is a mental sickness unique to whites and unique to our era.

The media have tried to attack Donald Trump by blaming him for our support. This is deeply dishonest; the American Communist Party endorses Mrs. Clinton, but no one says that discredits her. But the media attention has backfired. It has introduced our ideas to millions of people, many of whom we are winning over to our side.

Donald Trump may win or lose, but we will grow, with him or without him. We will not only grow; we will prevail. Our vision of mankind, of society, of history, of right and wrong is deeply rooted in morality and human nature. We are right, and our enemies are wrong. The folly that has seized our people will pass, and we will come through this crisis a wiser, stronger people.

American Renaissance, October 11, 2016

JEWS & THE ALT RIGHT

KEVIN MACDONALD

Certainly the most basic issue of the Alt Right is that it is entirely legitimate for whites to identify as whites and to pursue their interests as whites, such as resisting attempts to make white Americans a minority.

Ethnic and racial identities are common among all other groups, and, despite constant propaganda emanating from centers of media and academic power, whites should be no exception. Voluntarily ceding political and cultural power is the ultimate foolishness, particularly in an atmosphere of non-white grievance and the hostility towards whites, their history, and their culture, that is so apparent today.

However, another issue that is central to the world view of many on the Alt Right (but by no means unanimous) is the issue of Jewish power and influence. Ultimately, this stems from an understanding of the role of Jews in white dispossession, both historically and in the contemporary West. Accounting for around 2% of the US population, Jews have never had much power as a result of sheer numbers. What counts is Jewish power in the media, in the academic world, and in government.

It must be made clear at the outset that the Jewish community is not monolithic, and, as discussed below, there may be some Jews who are wholeheartedly opposed to the de-Europeanization of America. As an obvious example of the lack of unanimity among Jews on important issues, neoconservatism is a Jewish movement, led by and dominated by Jews since its inception. Most Jews are not neocons, but neoconservatism has had a huge influence on American foreign policy, successfully dominating the George W. Bush administration and promoting the Iraq War. And long before that, during the Reagan administration, neoconservatives were instrumental in expelling more traditional conservatives from power in the GOP and in general moving it to the Left on critical issues like immigration.

Samuel Francis recounts the catalog of neoconservative efforts not merely to debate, criticize, and refute the ideas of traditional conservatism but to denounce, vilify, and harm the careers
of those Old Right figures and institutions they have targeted.

There are countless stories of how neoconservatives have
succeeded in entering conservative institutions, forcing
out or demoting traditional conservatives, and changing
the positions and philosophy of such institutions in neoconservative directions. . . . Writers like M. E. Bradford, Joseph Sobran, Pat Buchanan, and Russell Kirk, and institutions like *Chronicles,* the Rockford Institute, the Philadelphia Society, and the Intercollegiate Studies Institute have
been among the most respected and distinguished names
in American conservatism. The dedication of their neoconservative enemies to driving them out of the movement
they have taken over and demonizing them as marginal
and dangerous figures has no legitimate basis in reality. It
is clear evidence of the ulterior aspirations of those behind
neoconservatism to dominate and subvert American conservatism from its original purposes and agenda and turn
it to other purposes. . . . What neoconservatives really dislike about their "allies" among traditional conservatives is
simply the fact that the conservatives are conservatives at
all—that they support "this notion of a Christian civilization," as Midge Decter put it, that they oppose mass immigration, that they criticize Martin Luther King and reject
the racial dispossession of white Western culture, that they
support or approve of Joe McCarthy, that they entertain
doubts or strong disagreement over American foreign policy in the Middle East, that they oppose reckless involvement in foreign wars and foreign entanglements, and that,
in company with the Founding Fathers of the United
States, they reject the concept of a pure democracy and the
belief that the United States is or should evolve toward it.[1]

---

[1] Samuel Francis, "The Neoconservative Subversion," in Brent
Nelson, ed., *Neoconservatism. Occasional Papers of the Conservative Citi-*

The result is that the GOP has become the party of the Chamber of Commerce and the Israel Lobby. They are entirely on board with massive non-white immigration, and this is in no small part due to neoconservative influence. Neoconservatives have been staunch supporters of arguably the most destructive force associated with the Left in the 20th century — massive non-European immigration. Support for massive non-European immigration has spanned the Jewish political spectrum throughout the 20th century to the present and, as noted below, Jewish organizations and activism were responsible for the sea change in immigration policy resulting from the 1965 immigration law. A principal motivation of the organized Jewish community for encouraging such immigration has involved a deeply felt animosity toward the people and culture responsible for the immigration restriction of 1924–1965 — "this notion of a Christian civilization" as Samuel Francis characterized it. The comment of neoconservative Ben Wattenberg indicates the emotional commitment that many Jews have to the ethnic transformation of America: "The non-Europeanization of America is heartening news of an almost transcendental quality."

Even Daniel Pipes, who is known as an "Islamophobic" critic of the Muslim community, is not supporting Donald Trump because of his stance on immigration- and diversity-related issues. This may seem surprising because one of Trump's signature proposals has been a moratorium on Muslim immigration, while Hillary Clinton wants to ramp up the number of refugees and other immigrants from Muslim countries.

Actually, it should not be surprising that Pipes is anti-Trump given that he favors a "house-broken Islam" in Western countries. What neocons like Pipes want is continued immigration of Muslims and the creation of Muslim communities that do not threaten the *status quo* on Israel. They are quite content with the demographic decline of white populations, whether in Europe or the US.

Indeed, Pipes just quit the GOP over this issue, complaining about Trump's "pro-fascistic tendencies":

The United States, the world's oldest democratic republic, faces an internal danger unlike any in the past 1½ centuries, one with the potential to degrade domestic life and reduce the country's standing in the world. Nothing is as important as resisting and defeating Donald J. Trump and the neo-fascist virus he wishes to bring to the White House.[2]

Needless to say, this is especially hypocritical given Pipes' status as a pro-Israel activist, since Trump's proposals parallel the policies of Prime Minister Benjamin Netanyahu in Israel. A consistent theme on the Alt Right is that diaspora Jews have advocated very generous immigration and refugee policies in the West and the idea that Western countries have no ethnic core (the proposition nation idea) while supporting Israel as a Jewish ethnostate. This should be infuriating to anyone who advocates white interests.

But most Jews are not neocons and remain Democrats. Most Jews did not support the Iraq invasion. Nevertheless, Jewish power was very much a part of the Iraq War story. Besides neocons, other prominent elements of the organized Jewish community were intimately involved in the Iraq invasion as well, especially AIPAC. Moreover, the ADL was involved because it called people "anti-Semites" if they said true things about the role of the Israel Lobby in promoting the war; also, the Conference of Presidents of Major American Jewish Organizations and the American Jewish Congress made comments encouraging President Bush to engage in some kind of military action in Iraq. The role of the Jewish lobby and neocons in the Iraq War has been noted by many, including John Mearsheimer and Steven Walt in *The Israel Lobby and U.S. Foreign Policy*.

Another example was bombing Syria in 2013 ("Wall-to-Wall Support for a Strike on Syria") when the entire organized Jewish community (including the Simon Wiesenthal Center, the ADL, and the Conference of Presidents of Major American Jewish Or-

---

[2] Daniel Pipes, "There's a Name for Trump's Brand of Politics: Neo-Fascism," *Philadelphia Inquirer*, April 8, 2016.

ganizations) advocated the strike—a view that was out of step with "record opposition" to the strike noted by many Congressmen but entirely in line with Israeli policy.

Every American, and especially anyone with any sense of American nationalism and sympathetic to the Alt Right, should be furious at Jewish involvement in this disastrous war—thousands dead, tens of thousands grievously wounded, trillions of dollars, with no end in sight. The instability caused by these wars is a main cause of the refugee crisis that is engulfing Europe (abetted by treasonous elites in Europe), and as usual, the entire organized Jewish community in Europe and the US is encouraging generous refugee policies.

Given Jewish influence over the political process, their opinion matters, so that it is vitally important for those of us attempting to reverse white dispossession to understand this, to call attention to it, and to combat it.

The special role of Jewish organizations in the 1965 law was also noted by historians Hugh Davis Graham and Otis Graham. This is how Hugh Davis Graham summarized it in his 2002 book *Collision Course*:

Most important for the content of immigration reform, the driving force at the core of the movement, reaching back to the 1920s, were Jewish organizations long active in opposing racial and ethnic quotas. These included the American Jewish Congress, the American Jewish Committee, the Anti-Defamation League of B'nai B'rith, and the American Federation of Jews from Eastern Europe. Jewish members of the Congress, particularly representatives from New York and Chicago, had maintained steady but largely ineffective pressure against the national origins quotas since the 1920s. . . . Following the shock of the Holocaust, Jewish leaders had been especially active in Washington in furthering immigration reform. To the public, the most visible evidence of the immigration reform drive was played by Jewish legislative leaders, such as Representative Celler and Senator Jacob Javits of New York. Less visible, but equally important, were the efforts of key advisers on presidential and agency staffs. These included senior policy advisers such as Julius Edelson and Harry Rosenfield in the Truman administration, Maxwell Rabb in the Eisenhower White House, and presidential aide Myer Feldman, assistant secretary of state Abba Schwartz, and deputy attorney general Norbert Schlei in the Kennedy-Johnson administration.[3]

This unanimity across the Jewish organizational spectrum continues today. For example, a wide range of Jewish organizations advocate a path to citizenship for illegals. And in 2013 during debate over the immigration amnesty/surge bill, a letter organized by the Hebrew Immigrant Aid Society and sent by over 100 Jewish organizations to President Obama and Congress notes that "American Jews know too well the impact of restrictive immigration policies." This bill was bitterly opposed by the grassroots Republican base and didn't make it through the House. There were no Jewish organizations that came out against the bill.

JEWISH ACTIVISM ON BEHALF OF BLACKS
Activist Jews and the organized Jewish community had a critical role in changing the racial landscape of America. Given that Alt Righters tend strongly to be race realists (i.e., they accept research findings that there are real average differences between races that are important for success in the contemporary world, such as IQ and impulse control), they realize that these actions of the Jewish community have compromised legitimate white interests in a creating a culture of grievance and white guilt in which the genetically based tendencies of blacks are ignored.

The role of the Jewish community in the transformation of racial attitudes and institutions during the 1950s and 1960s is well known and often commented on with pride by Jewish intellectuals. As I noted in my chapter titled "Jews, Blacks, and Race":

---

[3] Hugh Davis Graham, *Collision Course: The Strange Convergence of Affirmative Action and Immigration Policy in America* (New York: Oxford University Press, 2003), pp. 56–57.

Jews contributed from two thirds to three quarters of the money for civil rights groups during the 1960s. The AJCongress, the AJCommittee, and the ADL worked closely with the NAACP to write legal briefs and raise money in the effort to end segregation. Jewish groups, particularly the AJCongress, played a leading role in drafting civil rights legislation and pursuing legal challenges related to civil rights issues mainly benefiting blacks. "Jewish support, legal and monetary, afforded the civil rights movement a string of legal victories. . . . There is little exaggeration in an American Jewish Congress lawyer's claim that "many of these laws were actually written in the offices of Jewish agencies by Jewish staff people, introduced by Jewish legislators and pressured into being by Jewish voters."[4]

This Jewish role in the racial reconstruction of the US should certainly be something that should be of deep concern to people who identify with the Alt Right.

JEWS & THE MEDIA

Because of their very powerful role in the media, Jews are also important for the cultural transformations in the areas of promoting a public culture of homosexuality, premarital sex, pornography, and adultery. Survey data continue to show that Jewish attitudes on these issues are well to the Left of most Americans. The fact that Jewish attitudes depart from traditional American attitudes on these issues has therefore had a huge effect on American culture and certainly not in a direction supported most of those associated with the Alt Right. And although Jewish activists like Abe Foxman claim that the large number of Jews with positions of power in Hollywood makes no difference, it makes a very large difference. Even Joe Biden thinks (correctly) that Jews were behind the gay marriage movement.

---

[4] Kevin MacDonald, "Jews, Blacks, & Race," *Counter-Currents*, February 15, 2012.

42   *The Alternative Right*

In general, television portrays Jewish issues "with respect, relative depth, affection and good intentions, and the Jewish characters who appear in these shows have, without any doubt, been Jewish — often depicted as deeply involved in their Judaism" (Pearl & Pearl 1999, 5). For example, *All in the Family* (and its sequel, *Archie Bunker's Place*) not only managed to portray working class Europeans as stupid and bigoted, it portrayed Jewish themes very positively. By the end of its 12-year run, even archenemy Archie Bunker had raised a Jewish child in his home, befriended a black Jew (implication: Judaism has no ethnic connotations), gone into business with a Jewish partner, enrolled as a member of a synagogue, praised his close friend at a Jewish funeral, hosted a Sabbath dinner, participated in a *bat mitzvah* ceremony, and joined a group to fight synagogue vandalism. . . .

Television presents images of Jewish issues that conform to the views of mainstream Jewish organizations. Television "invariably depicts anti-Semitism as an ugly, abhorrent trait that must be fought at every turn" (p. 103). It is seen as metaphysical and beyond analysis. There is never any rational explanation for anti-Semitism; anti-Semitism is portrayed as an absolute, irrational evil. Positive, well-liked, non-Jewish characters, such as Mary Tyler Moore, often lead the fight against anti-Semitism — a pattern reminiscent of that noted in [*The Culture of Critique*] in which non-Jews become high-profile spokespersons for Jewish dominated movements. There is also the implication that anti-Semitism is a proper concern of the entire community.[5]

JEWISH INVOLVEMENT IN CENSORSHIP & PUNISHING THOUGHT CRIMES

Another issue that concerns many Alt Righters is that Jewish groups have been in the forefront of penalizing thought crimes

---

[5] http://www.kevinmacdonald.net/PrefacePPB.pdf, pp. xlvi–lvi, especially p. I (50) ff.

related to white identity. Groups like the ADL and the SPLC (funded mainly by Jews) have successfully gotten people fired from their jobs for criticizing Jews or dissenting from other multicultural orthodoxies. This is true in other Western countries as well. The general picture is that Jewish groups were enthusiastic defenders of free speech during the 1950s when Jewish communists were being called up before Congressional committees and forced to sign loyalty oaths, but this is definitely not the case now. Even within the Jewish community, there have been campaigns to silence Jewish critics of Israel and thus present a united front (reviewed in Mearsheimer and Walt's *The Israel Lobby and U.S. Foreign Policy*).

JEWS & THE ALT RIGHT

Although I certainly believe that it's important for the Alt Right to be aware of the Jewish involvement in white displacement, I think it's fine that some organizations and Alt Right figures do not discuss Jewish issues. Many people are more open to that approach, and we have to recognize that there are different audiences that can be reached with different messages. My general impression in talking to Alt Righters is that many begin with an awareness of white decline, race differences in traits like IQ, and minority hostility, and then progress toward an understanding of Jewish influence as they read more widely. I would love it if there could be an Alt Right mass movement with significant Jewish support. But at the same time, it is also legitimate for others to discuss Jewish issues in a critical manner.

At the same time, I am often dismayed by how some people associated with the Alt Right express their views on Jewish issues. I have often thought that anyone who hasn't read a lot in the area and has an IQ of less than 120 should not be allowed to discuss Jewish issues in public.

It is certainly possible that individual Jews may be attracted to work in concert with the Alt Right. This attraction may come because of a genuine concern that a non-white America would not be good for Jews. Indeed, we are already seeing in some European countries that Muslim immigration has resulted in anti-Jewish and anti-Israel attitudes being increasingly common on the Left, and that some parties on the Left (e.g., the Labour Party in the UK) depend on Muslims votes. Jews have no problem in being friendly with non-Jews, such as Christian Zionists, whenever doing so is "good for the Jews." We can do the same: whatever is good for European-Americans.

However, as Andrew Joyce has noted, there is a historical pattern where Jews have entered putatively nationalist movements and directed them towards positions that make them "safe for the Jews," at the expense of developing a true sense of ethnic interests.

> That Jews would try to co-opt, or attempt to derail, a potentially damaging movement does have many historical precedents. In one of the most pertinent, Steven Beller writes that during the rise of German nationalism in 1860–1880, Jews attempted to take key roles in the movement with a view to re-directing it from its roots in *völkisch* philosophy and an antagonism towards Jewish influence, and towards a mission of "cultural and social revolution." Media promotion and careful networking even led to two Jews, Victor Adler and Heinrich Friedjung, vying for leadership of the German nationalist movement in Austria. Indeed, Adler and Friedjung were two of the five framers of the famous Linz Program of 1882, a political platform that called for the complete Germanization of the Austrian state. It was only due to the continued insistence of the non-Jewish movement leaders, particularly Georg Schönerer, that an ethnic version of German nationalism was eventually adhered to. On Schönerer's insistence, and to the dismay of the erstwhile Jewish "leaders," the movement adopted an "Aryan clause." Their attempt to co-opt the movement having failed, Beller adds, "the Jewish reaction was to look elsewhere for their goals of social and cultural change." For example, Adler became an out-and-out Marxist overnight.
>
> Similarly in Germany, historian Gordon Mork notes that Jews were also "prominent" among the early leading advocates of German nationalism. In particular, Jews were

concentrated in the National Liberal Party, and then formed an influential clique around Bismarck himself. This diversionary clique within German nationalism may be regarded as a key reason why it was more stunted, in terms of an ethnic expression, than its Austrian counterpart until after World War I.[6]

Moreover, Jews who align themselves with organizations or publications that explicitly promote the interests of European-Americans should be willing to acknowledge the role of the organized Jewish community in the dispossession of European America. They should also acknowledge that the policies of the organized Jewish community at the present time are definitely opposed to the interests of European Americans.

Jews who want to be considered our allies should direct most of their activism to changing the direction of the organized Jewish community. Just as Joe Lieberman was the emissary of the McCain campaign to the traditionally Democratic Jewish community, there is every reason to think that Jews would be far more effective in producing change in the organized Jewish community than non-Jews. Such efforts, especially if they were successful, would be the surest sign of their sincerity and good will.

On the other hand, the absence of a commitment to change the Jewish community or refusing to acknowledge the historical role of the organized Jewish community in producing our present malaise invites the skepticism that the Jews involved in pro-European-American movements are simply trying to make these movements safe for Jews in the event that such movements gain traction. It's a fallback plan and an escape hatch if things start to get sticky.

Moreover, when pro-European-American groups feel it judicious to be silent about the role of the organized Jewish community in our current malaise, this must be seen as an expression of Jewish power. Much of our task on behalf of European-

---

[6] Andrew Joyce, "Jews Versus the Alt Right: Lessons from History," *The Occidental Observer*, September 10, 2016.

American civilization and our people is the promotion of historical understanding. Many Jews will inevitably find an honest discussion of the history of European dispossession threatening because of the prominent role of Jews revealed by any objective account of that history. However, silence on the role of Jews in our current malaise forces these groups to live in a sort of a-historical present—avoiding a realistic discussion of the past and preventing any attempt to understand this past in an objective manner.

This forces these pro-European movements into a major departure from all other ethnic activist movements we are aware of, including Judaism: ethnic identity and commitment are deeply interwoven with an understanding of history. Indeed, Jews' understanding of their own history as victims of Europeans is an important wellspring of Jewish identity and Jewish activism against European-Americans. As Paul Johnson said in describing the philosophy of Walter Benjamin, a Jewish cultural Marxist: "Politics [is] not merely a fierce physical struggle to control the present, and so the future, but an intellectual battle to control the record of the past."

Even worse, it prevents these organizations from making explicit attempts to oppose the very real power that the organized Jewish community and other strongly identified Jews continue to exert in a wide range of areas in opposition to the interests of European-Americans. Again, the best role for Jews in these movements is to be vocal critics of the Jewish community and its role in the dispossession of European-Americans. But the unfortunate reality is that, just like mainstream politicians forced to never mention the power of the Israel Lobby, these pro-European-American groups end up ignoring the 800-lb gorilla in their midst—a wonderful comment on Jewish power in America.

In guarded optimism, we might look to the future and hope that some influential Jews will be able to look at this history without their ethnic blinders and come to see their own best interests lie with a renewed European America.

Counter-Currents, September 13, 2016

TRUMP, THE ALT RIGHT, &
THE REVOLT AGAINST POLITICAL
CORRECTNESS

AEDON CASSIEL

On June 6, 2015, dark clouds swirled over Trump Tower in New York City. Wolves howled. Lightning flashed. And The Words that Changed It All were spoken:

> When Mexico sends its people, they're not sending the best. They're not sending you; they're sending people that have lots of problems, and they're bringing those problems. They're bringing drugs; they're bringing crime. They're rapists, and some, I assume, are good people. But I speak to border guards, and they're telling us what we're getting.

The world was thus divided between two groups of people. One group believed that the world is divided between *racists* and *all other good and decent people*. The second group was sick and tired of the first group dominating the conversation.

It is interesting to note that in 2013, Ted Cruz was already pushing legislation to militarize the US border[1] — while Donald Trump had recently called Mitt Romney's self-deportation policy "maniacal" and "mean-spirited," complaining that Republicans "didn't have anything going for them with respect to Latinos," whereas the Democrats, Trump said, "were kind."[2]

If this was, at its core, about immigration, then why did the

---

[1] http://trailblazersblog.dallasnews.com/2013/05/sen-ted-cruzs-border-security-amendment-to-immigration-legislation-voted-down.html/

[2] http://www.politico.com/story/2012/11/trump-romneys-crazy-policy-of-self-deportation-cost-votes-084238

Alternative Right end up associated with Donald Trump instead of Ted Cruz? For the same reason you know about Trump's comments but not Ted Cruz's: the media turned on the moral outrage machine in response to Trump but not Cruz.

And that's the central clue to this whole thing.

If the critics think they can write the Alternative Right off with the typical tactics of moralistic outrage, they're in for a rude awakening. What the critics have missed is that the growth of the Alt Right isn't due to some sudden increase in "racist" or "sexist" views that just happen to be politically incorrect. It's a reaction to political correctness itself.

Although there is no clean overlap between support for Donald Trump and the growth of the Alternative Right, the same basic phenomenon underlies both. Well-seasoned observers of the 2016 Presidential race repeatedly predicted that Donald Trump's insensitivity would soon result in his downfall. Instead, every single media controversy that condemned Trump only caused his ratings to soar. Leftists were outraged that it seemed to be precisely Trump's "racist" and "sexist" viewpoints that so endeared him to voters.

Whether he goes on to win the national election or not, what happened for Donald Trump's campaign for the Republican nomination is exactly what will happen for the Alternative Right: its pending downfall will be predicted by critics every step of the way towards its rise. And this will happen because the critics are missing something *big*: *They* are what is fueling its rise.

When Trump's popularity surged after the media's attacks over his statement, it was about immigration, yes. But even more fundamentally than that, it was a statement of protest against the Left's attempts to condemn Trump as "racist" *in order to silence him* for even daring to discuss how our immigration policies effect native-born Americans. Never mind that Trump describes illegal immigration as something by which "black Americans have been particularly harmed"[3]—and is right to do so,

---

[3] http://www.thecrimson.com/article/2005/1/14/summers-comments-on-women-and-science/

according to a US Commission on Civil Rights report which found that "even those experts who viewed the effects [of illegal immigration on black wages and employment] as modest overall found significant effects in [some] occupations."

We understood perfectly well that Trump was not "stereotyping all Mexicans as rapists." Nor was he stereotyping all immigrants as rapists. And for that matter, he wasn't even stereotyping all *illegal* immigrants as rapists (some "are good people"). But if *per capita* rates of crime are *higher* amongst some immigrant groups than others, then most ordinary Americans have the audacity to want to talk about that and formulate immigration policies accordingly.

But the Left was trying to silence the whole conversation by distorting Trump's comments into a crude and simplistic "All Mexicans are rapists!" caricature.

By this time, we'd been watching this happen for a long time.

In 2005, for instance, then-President of Harvard Larry Summers addressed a private economics conference concerning the causes of the under-representation of female scientists at elite universities. *After* acknowledging that women with young children are often unwilling or unable to put in the demanding hours needed to succeed in those fields, which Summers recognized "raised a whole set of questions about how job expectations were defined and how family responsibilities were defined," he moved on to discuss other possibilities.

One of them involved the hypothesis that there is more biological variability between men than there is between women — that the average woman has an IQ closer to the average female IQ than the average man has to the average male IQ, because there are both more "geniuses" and more "idiots" in the population of men, compared to women. This was, to be clear, a perfectly scientific suggestion with tremendous empirical backing in support of it.[4] After discussing this, Summers moved on to address gender-based discrimination, and agreed that it should be reduced. But he expressed the conviction that discrimination

---

[4] http://qz.com/441905/men-are-both-dumber-and-smarter-than-women/

explains less of the under-representation of women than the combination of the first two factors.

In the minds of Leftists, Summers' talk was boiled down to the extremely crude, oversimplified notion that "Women are not as clever as men,"[5] even though nothing about the hypothesis Summers referred to implied anything about the intelligence of any given woman compared to any given man (while there appear to be more male "geniuses," there also appear to be more male "idiots" too, because the fundamental point here appears to be not that men are "smarter" than women, but that they are more *variable* towards *all* extremes).

Summers stated his conclusion in a remarkably calm and measured way:

> So my best guess, to provoke you, of what's behind all of this is that the largest phenomenon, by far, is the general clash between people's legitimate family desires and employers' current desire for high power and high intensity, that in the special case of science and engineering, there are issues of intrinsic aptitude, and particularly of the variability of aptitude, and that those considerations are reinforced by what are in fact lesser factors involving socialization and continuing discrimination. I would like nothing better than to be proved wrong, because I would like nothing better than for these problems to be addressable simply by everybody understanding what they are, and working very hard to address them."[6]

Many, and perhaps even most, women were reasonable enough to understand that Summers was exploring a real possibility. Claudia Goldin, a Professor of Economics whose own research has addressed women's issues,[7] believed Summers' speech was "utter brilliance." Sheryl Sandberg, his research as-

---

[5] http://www.theguardian.com/comment/story/ 0,,1724446,00.html

[6] https://web.archive.org/web/20080130023006/http:// www.president.harvard.edu/speeches/2005/nber.html

[7] http://www.econlib.org/library/Enc1/GenderGap.html

sistant, remarked that "What few seem to note is that it is re-markable that he was giving the speech in the first place—that he cared enough about women's careers and their trajectory in the fields of math and science to proactively analyze the issues and talk about what was going wrong."[8]

But MIT biologist Nancy Summers claimed she had to leave the room because, if she hadn't, she "would've either blacked out or thrown up"[9]; the National Organization for Women said that "Apologies are not enough; Summers must go."[10] And a national controversy ensued which helped ensure Summers' resignation from Harvard a year later.[11]

Episodes like these made it become clearer as time went on that "political correctness" wasn't just an unreasonable series of hoops we were required to jump through, retarding dialogue on certain sensitive topics. It was a weapon for destroying those who attempt to open such conversations altogether. And it worked by turning valid hypotheses into crude caricatures of what was actually said—"There is more overall genetic variability between men than between women" becomes "Women are not as clever as men"—and then slandering its victims to render them incapable of defending themselves long enough to even clarify the truth about what was said ("You really want to let Larry Summers mansplain his misogyny?!") And even apologies *"are not enough"*—you must *pay*.

Leftists are absolutely right to fear that a process of radicalization is taking place, both across the Right as well as across society at large. But Leftists, themselves, are directly and solely to blame for it—and they're to blame for it because these are the tactics they chose. Even liberals are increasingly noticing just how blatant and counterproductive these double standards are:

[8] http://www.huffingtonpost.com/sheryl-sandberg/what-larry-summers-has-do_b_142126.html

[9] https://www.princeton.edu/~deaton/downloads/letterfromamerica_oct2005.pdf

[10] http://www.engr.psu.edu/fff/misc/summers-v-XX_press_050209.pdf

[11] https://web.archive.org/web/20080130023006/http://www.president.harvard.edu/speeches/2005/nber.html

for example, Matt Bruenig notices that when black communities oppose gay marriage in greater numbers than any other demographic, liberals' response is to blame themselves for not engaging black communities enough—but when poor whites oppose gay marriage, liberals' response is to simply condemn them as a bigoted outgroup.[12]

And amusingly enough, even as I write this, Matt Bruenig has just been fired from his employer for criticizing Neera Tanden, an Indian woman, for what he perceived as her tacit complicity in the Clinton Administration's welfare reform. The conversation started with Joan Walsh rejecting "the moral superiority of a [Bernie Sanders] coalition led by white men vs. the will of black, brown and female voters [for Hillary Clinton]," to which Bruenig responded that a majority of *young* minority voters actually prefer Sanders, to which Walsh told Bruenig to "go to Hell." Tanden then entered the conversation on Walsh's behalf, which occasioned the response Bruenig was fired for[1314]—yet Bruenig's criticisms of white men Ezra Klein, Nicholas Kristof, and David Brooks in equally uncivil terms, calling them "fuckups," "irresponsible morons," and "moral degenerates" in years prior hadn't been enough to cause his ousting.[15]

Hmm.

Bruenig seems particularly tenacious about fighting to retain social membership in the group treating him with such hypocrisy. But inevitably, many others will respond to this kind of treatment by coming to see that they have more to gain from simply abandoning that membership outright than they do from fighting to keep it.

And the Alt Right's critics have failed to realize just how diverse the groups coming together thanks to the fallout from Leftist behavior have actually become. As Keith Preston wrote in

---

[12] http://mattbruenig.com/2016/05/17/demonizing-not-engaging/

[13] http://www.mediaite.com/online/think-tank-demos-fires-blogger-over-personal-attacks-on-twitter/

[14] https://twitter.com/CarlBeijer/status/733753173274439681?ref_src=twsrc%5Etfw

[15] http://mattbruenig.com/2014/01/17/on-civility/

2010, speaking of the webzine *Alternative Right*,

> *Alternative Right* is not a party, but a collection of writers and thinkers. . . . [it] include[s] a Catholic traditionalist (Jim Kalb), a Russian nationalist (Nina Kouprianova), a racialist anarcho-capitalist (Richard Hoste), a gay-masculinist ex-Satanist (Jack Donovan), a neo-pagan white nationalist (Alex Kurtagic), a curmudgeonly Old Rightist (Paul Gottfried), and a Nietzschean-Bakuninist old anarchist (yours truly). Richard Spencer himself seems to lean towards paleolibertarianism. As a hat tip to one of the conventional pieties of our time, we might call this "diversity."[16]

It becomes rather difficult to maintain the facade that this is about, say, "homophobia" when this same movement includes both a Catholic traditionalist who rejects the morality of homosexuality on principle[17] *and* a gay ex-Satanist who published a book whose blurb describes it as "call(ing) into question stereotypes . . . about homosexuals . . . crafted by . . . Christian fundamentalists."[18] What is it that unites such disparate people?

The answer, again, is fallout from Leftist tactics that we've come to no longer perceive as merely irritating, or even odious, but as *a weapon* designed to silence *all* of us—*regardless* of what we actually want to say. The Left has defined us and created our alliance *by defining all of us as its enemies* and therefore *giving us* a common goal.[19] Why is this so hard for Leftists to understand?

Aren't they the ones criticizing the prison system on the grounds that putting people in jail for small crimes and *treating them* as criminals can actually *turn them* into criminals by alienating them from mainstream society and giving them new criminal associates? How could it be so hard for them to see that

---

[16] https://attackthesystem.com/2010/06/26/almost-doest-thou-persuadist/

[17] http://www.amnation.com/vfr/archives/001421.html

[18] http://www.amazon.com/Androphilia-Jack-Donovan/dp/0985452315

[19] https://www.youtube.com/watch?v=Ojlj8KOJkwI

they've helped create the growth of the Alternative Right through exactly the same kind of process?

When the Left makes a great show about "racism" because a village emblem supposedly displays a white man strangling a Native American, and it turns out that it actually depicts a voluntary wrestling match in which a white man *earned the local Natives' respect*,[20] or because of the use of the word "Redskins" for a sports team when it turns out that 9 out of 10 Native Americans don't really care,[21] the Left is crying wolf. They're desensitizing us to the very sound of the word "racist," and showing us that people who most loudly condemn it are, more likely than not, simply wasting our time with non-issues.

But then we notice that non-issues like these are given great publicity whereas on the very week I'm writing this, Google can "honor" the birthday of a so-called "anti-racist" who claimed that the US is "the main enemy of the world's people" while praising Osama bin Laden as "one of the people that [she] admire[s]" — a "strong leader who brought consciousness to [his] people . . . [and] felt the US government [was] racist . . ."[22] And nothing is done.

And then we watch the progression of the "Black Lives Matter" movement. And we're told that "All Lives Matter" is *a racist slur*, because black people are "literally being gunned down in the street" — even though both the national data and the best experimental studies show that any given white person who interacts with police is actually *twice* as likely to be shot than any given black person who interacts with police; whites only have to commit half as many crimes as blacks do—and therefore have about half as many interactions with police—before one white person will end up being shot.[23]

[20] http://www.villagevoice.com/news/mayor-of-whitesboro-ny-insists-this-village-seal-is-not-racist-7341880

[21] http://espn.go.com/nfl/story/_/id/15608840/native-americans-say-unbothered-redskins-team-name-washington-post-poll

[22] http://freebeacon.com/issues/google-honors-activist-deemed-u-s-government-worlds-main-terrorist/

[23] http://www.washingtontimes.com/news/2016/feb/25/

And then we watch white people who criticize "Black Lives Matter" because of those statistics end up slurred and censored[24]—never mind that the very case studies that spurred that "movement" into action were more often than not cases where white people *were assaulted* by black people and merely *defended themselves*,[25] only for the Left to attempt to ruin the rest of their lives, ending their careers, allowing bounties to be publically placed on their heads,[26] and even requiring *their parents* to go into hiding as a result of the death threats.[27] And yet, although about half of the suspects shot by police are white, most people can't even remember the name of a single white victim—even though a *black* cop was let off for shooting an unarmed, non-violent white suspect just two days after the events of Ferguson, Missouri.[28]

Then we realize how many people are willing to defend someone for trying to pin a white person in a hallway corner to call him racist and threaten him with a forced haircut just for wearing his hair in a certain style. And we see that these people hold this attitude despite the fact that the Rastafarians actually "appropriated" dreadlocks from the same place they took the Sanskrit word *"ganja"*—from Indians,[29] whose gurus matted their hair and treated *"ganja"* as a spiritual sacrament much earlier; and we see how few of these people care that dreadlocks are

---

marissa-johnson-black-lives-matter-leader-explains

[24] http://www.washingtontimes.com/news/2016/feb/25/marissa-johnson-black-lives-matter-leader-explains/

[25] https://zombiemeditations.com/2015/07/12/is-dylann-roof-white-like-me-pt-2/

[26] http://www.npr.org/sections/thetwo-way/2012/03/26/149399082/new-black-panther-party-offers-10k-bounty-for-george-zimmerman

[27] http://abcnews.go.com/US/zimmermans-parents-hiding-enormous-amount-death-threats-abc/story?id=19670456

[28] http://www.copblock.org/128554/full-body-cam-video-released-utah-police-killing-dillon-taylor/

[29] http://www.thesouthasiantimes.info/news-Film_finds_spiritual_links_between_Indian_sadhus_and_Jamaican_Rastafarians-69399-New%20York-112.html

in fact a part of "white" history, too.[30] Never mind that dreadlocks are simply what *anyone's* hair does after you stop washing it, which makes the claim that you can "culturally appropriate" dreadlocks about as asinine as claiming that you can "culturally appropriate" bad breath or body odor.

We've long crossed the line at which false claims of "racism" are just a matter of crying wolf; we've reached the point where it has transformed into a blatant attack against white people, plain and simple. And when we look to events in Europe, we see that "political correctness" is actually concretely ruining peoples' lives, and we realize how much we actually stand to lose if we don't stand up to it. Child sexual exploitation rings were actually allowed to continue abducting, raping, and torturing hundreds of children undisturbed for fifteen years — why? Because the police were afraid of being called "racist" if they prosecuted the Pakistanis responsible for it.[31] The lesson seems to be that if we don't act preemptively, we'll be headed for the same ultimate fate. And that is how the Left not only desensitized us to charges of "racism," it actually started to make some of us actively angered by them.

And that is how the Left created the "Alternative Right," as well as the rise of Donald Trump. First, not only did they desensitize us to charges of "racism," they taught us how easily it can be — and how often it is — used as a blatant weapon against perfectly innocent, decent people. Second, they forced all of these "unapproved" conversations underground. When people are told that they don't belong in the mainstream conversation anymore if they're worried about crime rates amongst illegal immigrants, or if they want to know how to make sure that a Rotherham child sexual exploitation scandal or that a mass sexual assault like what took place in Germany during New Year's Eve celebrations of 2016[32] don't happen here, neither their concerns

---

[30] https://en.wikipedia.org/wiki/Fairy-lock

[31] https://en.wikipedia.org/wiki/Rotherham_child_sexual_exploitation_scandal

[32] https://en.wikipedia.org/wiki/New_Year%27s_Eve_sexual_assaults_in_Germany

nor their opinions are thus eliminated.

And for that matter, neither are the conversations they're trying to have.

They're just being siphoned off someplace else. And if, thanks to the Left, the only places where that can happen now is the wilderness to which everyone else outside the Leftist fold has been banished, that's where they're going to be held. Perhaps some of those people will be critical of some of the details they've been taught about the Holocaust—with more or with less "noble" motivations behind their skepticism. Perhaps some of them actually *do* dislike other people for *no* other reason than their race, nationality, or religion. Most likely, these groups never would have had any reason to interact with each other at all—but now, it's *the Left's* fault that they've been pushed into one space and are therefore beginning to cross-fertilize into new *movements*. Out of what began as—and might have remained—disparate groups of isolated individuals each holding an unapproved interest or two, *the Left* is creating a *movement* by giving them all something in common: *the Left, its common enemy*.

And by 2010, these forces finally became powerful enough to unite groups as different as Catholic traditionalists and gay masculinist ex–Satanists into the same movement. No matter how deeply Jack Donovan and Jim Kalb might disagree with each other about the nature of homosexuality, what they hold in common is that they are both adult enough to hold a conversation about it that isn't dominated by attempts to gain status over each other by playing moral outrage games. And if they decide that their disagreements are intractable, they're adult enough to just walk away.

That's not to argue that the members of the Alt Right are paragons of the virtue of tolerance as liberals conceive it. Yes, nearly the whole of the Alt Right will admit to holding a commitment to some for or other of tribalism—and for many, this tribalistic instinct will become attached in some way to race. But is the Left any less "tribalistic?" Of course not. In fact, the entire point is precisely that the Left's double-handed tactics are *creating* white racial consciousness where in many cases *none at all* existed previously. Whites are beginning to consciously form their own tribes, in many cases because it's been repeatedly beaten into them that they *do not* belong to the tribe of the Left.

Research has found that while *all other extracurricular activities increase* a person's chance of being admitted to college, membership in ROTC, 4–H, and Future Farmers of America clubs actually decreases it.[33] What is this, if not blatant discrimination by the Leftist tribe against a culture that is overwhelmingly white, rural, and conservative? In turn, cultures that largely happen to be white, rural, and conservative are realizing that *they have no better choice* than to form tribes of their own — because after this many years reading headlines like "I Don't Know What To Do With Good White People" and "White Men Must be Stopped: The Very Future of Mankind Depends on It" — and after enough articles like "Dylann Roof is White Like Me" and "White America is Complicit [in Roof's crime]" contrasted with articles like "Stop asking Muslims to condemn terrorism. It's bigoted and Islamophobic" — it has become clear that compromise and negotiation are not actually being offered to us in the first place.

The Left isn't criticizing tribalism because it *actually* opposes tribalism on principle — it just opposes the interests of *our tribe*. As Christopher Robertson writes in *In Defense of Hatred*:

> John is a man who is "anti-gun." He claims that guns are immoral. Indeed, they are what's wrong with the world, and that if only we could get rid of them, we could get on with the joys and difficulties of living, without the unnecessary dangers of lethal violence breathing down our necks.
>
> John also carries a gun.
>
> When asked about this apparent hypocrisy, he vehemently declares that this does not in any way mean he likes guns, or *isn't* anti-gun. His gun is only to shoot other people with guns ("or people who support gun ownership," he adds as an afterthought). But that is why *everyone*

---

[33] https://web.archive.org/web/20110515165001/http://www.mindingthecampus.com/originals/2010/07/how_diversity_punishes_asians.html

else owns guns too, you point out. You're not an anti-gun advocate fighting fire with fire: in defending the legitimacy of your own gun carrying, you have become, to whatever small degree, *a gun-rights advocate.*

"Not at all," he says, "because unlike those guys, who just love to carry guns, I'm doing it because gun-owners deserve to be shot."

This caricature of an anti-gun-rights activist ceases to be a caricature when looked at metaphorically. "Hatred" is a kind of gun. It is a fundamentally coercive state designed to intimidate or to will oneself into violent action.

What is ridiculous is not John's articulated position. It is his characterization of himself as *anti-gun*. He's not against guns, but against guns being used by *the wrong people*, and *for the wrong reasons*.

The anti-hate activists, in all their forms, *ooze* with hatred. Like John, they attempt to square this circle by saying that they only hate "those who hate." Their intolerance is reserved for the intolerant. But this does not make them "anti-hatred" any more than John's justifications make him "anti-gun." More to the point, they never bother to explore why the targets of their own hatred hold the views that they do. Like John, they just assume that *those people* are just nasty, stupid bigots. Who cares if *they* also think they only hate others who are themselves hateful, or legitimate threats? Who cares if *they* only carry a gun because they know someone like *you* does too? *My* hatred is valid. *Your* hatred isn't.[34]

The same is true of the Left's pretenses of concern about "tribalism." What the rise of the Alternative Right—and, to a lesser extent, the popularity of Donald Trump amongst the American public in general—represents is a wising up to the dishonesty of these tactics. Having seen how the game works, we no longer see any reason to care to *try* to ingratiate ourselves to a Left that will attempt to destroy our reputations, destroy our

---

[34] http://cbrobertson.blogspot.com/2016/05/chapter-3-fearing-hate.html

lives, and destroy our careers if we should step out of line by even *asking* the wrong questions—a Left that exercises racist double standards and practices tribalism while *pretending* to be opposed to "racism" and "tribalism" merely in order to disarm us and advance their tribal interests. Watching the career-destroying and mass-rape producing machinations of political correctness has finally convinced us that a world *without* "racism" and "tribalism" simply isn't in the cards. It's convinced many of us that, for better or worse, the only question that is truly in the asking at all is, "*whose* tribalism?"

And, at the same time as it's done so, it's pushed us into halls of conversation where *everyone* who has been on the receiving end of those tactics for *any* reason has been forced to gather together. Now, *thanks to the Left*, when the person who (let's say) has been disaffected by the lies of the Black Lives Matter movement or the Cologne immigrant mass rapes looks over and sees a Holocaust denier, he may only *now* think to himself, "You know, both of us have been tarnished, labeled, and cast out of the mainstream conversation in just exactly the same way. I *used* to assume that the slanders of racism against him were valid, but *now* I can't assume that anymore, because I see clearly now that the process by which people are deemed worthy of that kind of censorship is illegitimate. What if what he's actually trying to say has been just as distorted by people trying to silence him as what I've been trying to say has? At the very least, I ought to reconsider the possibility, now that we've both been thrown into the same boat."

A process of radicalization *is* taking place; and the Left should be *terrified*. Because the more it tries to rely on the same tired tactics to try to silence this movement, the more they are *fueling its rise in the first place,* and the darker their future will continue to become.

Counter-Currents, August 12, 2016

CONSERVATISM & THE ALT RIGHT

GREGORY HOOD

Conservatism, said Russell Kirk, is "neither a religion nor an ideology." Today, its most stalwart defenders believe it is both. "True conservatism," we are told, is under attack from the Alt Right, a shadowy group which encompasses everyone from the CEO of Donald Trump's campaign to anonymous Twitter accounts who worship a cartoon frog. Because they do not agree with conservative "principles," the so-called "true conservatives" are already fantasizing about another Beltway Right "purge" of the unbelievers.

But what are these "true conservative principles?" The traditional Reagan tripod (free market economics and limited government, a strong national defense, and social conservatism) has always threatened to fall apart because of its internal tensions. Some of the most influential theorists now broadly accepted as part of the mainstream conservative movement, notably F. A. Hayek, explicitly disavowed the term "conservative." Meanwhile, loyal foot soldiers such as Pat Buchanan, who were well-grounded in conservative philosophy and who served in the Reagan White House, have long since been purged. Russell Kirk himself was probably only saved from being kicked out of the movement he named because of his death. A "strong national defense" doesn't permit criticism of the Israel-first tendencies of the neocons.

If you take a step back, this seemingly formidable "conservative movement" appears absurd. There's no philosophical reason for pro-life Christian Zionists from Middle America to be part of the same "movement" as pro-gay marriage financiers on Wall Street. A movement can't defend "limited government" while simultaneously promoting a "strong military" and an interventionist foreign policy, as war has always been the health of the state.

The Left's contradictory coalition of tribes, ranging from devout Muslims to militant homosexuals, is at least united by the common foe of traditional Western Civilization and its European ethnic core. The conservative movement's different ideological tribes don't even share a common interest or common enemy.

But that wasn't always the case. The conservative movement was, from the beginning, simply a coalition, a tactical creation. The unifying factor which held these disparate constituencies together was the threat from the Soviet Union. William F. Buckley famously said, "We have got to accept Big Government for the duration—for neither an offensive nor a defensive war can be waged . . . except through the instrumentality of a totalitarian bureaucracy within our shores." It was the John Birch Society's lack of support for the Vietnam War, not an attempt to purge the "crazies," which led to *National Review*'s war against the Birchers. Frank Meyer's "fusionism" was simply a plausible rationale to hold the whole rickety structure together.

Buckley was a former employee of the CIA—at the risk of devolving into conspiracy theory, perhaps he never stopped working for them. But regardless of whether he was on the payroll or not, Buckley's strategy for his anti-Soviet "conservatism" largely followed the activities of The Company.

The CIA backed anti-Stalinist Leftist movements not because it's the "far Right" organization so many conservatives secretly fantasize it is, but because they wanted to make sure the Soviets didn't own the Left. Similarly, Buckley ensured "conservatism" wasn't a critique of liberal democracy or the center-Left establishment, but a defense of it. Those conservatives who took critiques of liberalism too far, like L. Brent Bozell, ghostwriter of Goldwater's *The Conscience of a Conservative,* ended up fleeing the movement or even the United States for more reactionary locales.

As in most situations, a common enemy prevented the contradictions and tensions within the conservative movement from tearing itself apart. The vicious struggle between "paleoconservatives" and "neoconservatives" for control of the conservative movement didn't really explode until after the fall of the Berlin Wall.

Pat Buchanan, a Nixon loyalist and a man who served as Ronald Reagan's emissary to the conservative grassroots, challenged George H. W. Bush because he believed the end of the Cold War meant the American conservative movement needed to change with the times. Specifically, Buchanan identified moral collapse, the demographic threat of mass immigration, and the de-industrialization of the economy as critical threats American conservatives needed to attack.

Unfortunately, Buchanan was defeated. He was essentially purged from the movement to which he had given his life. Like so many other movements, conservatism had transformed from a cause to a business and finally a racket. The purpose of the conservative movement became to defend and define "conservatism" as a word. Championing a particular constituency or even the country was irrelevant.

Conservatism had become Conservatism Inc., and it had no stake in victory or in the well-being of its constituents. Instead, it was an interlocking series of institutions which could define the term in whatever way would best serve the Beltway Right's interests.

Yet despite the Beltway Right's essential irrelevance on the most critical issues of the today and its inability to halt the Cultural Marxists' Long March through the institutions, the long predicted "conservative crackup" never quite arrived. The movement held together through sheer inertia.

Conservatism has succeeded in creating a career path for mediocrities content to play the Washington Generals for the Left for a lifetime. And because the Beltway Right controls the access to the mass media and the legitimacy it conveys, conservative dissidents have been prevented from appealing to a mass constituency. Donald Trump was only able to break the *cordon sanitaire* created by Conservatism Inc.'s gatekeepers because of his unique background as a celebrity and his wealth. Conservatism Inc. won't lift a finger to build a wall on our southern border. But if Trump falters, we can expect the Beltway hacks to rebuild the wall around their compromised media citadels.

But Conservatism Inc. has a critical weakness. Ultimately,

the mass base conservatism depends on consists of European-Americans, especially those white Southerners who saw their cities and their public institutions destroyed because of desegregation. Opposition to "big government" is, in practice, opposition to forced diversity. Even if we grant the Left-wing argument that conservatives were cynically using racist "dog whistles" to whip up white voters, it's unquestionable that explicit appeals to white racial consciousness are career suicide within the Beltway Right.

It's not because it leads to bad press. It's because Identitarianism would blow apart the thin intellectual backing for American conservatism. The development of white racial consciousness would challenge too many of the premises of the movement, especially the pursuit of foreign wars ("strong national defense"), cheap labor and outsourcing ("free markets"), and dysgenic social policies ("social conservatism").

Thus, Conservatism Inc. has to constantly police itself, both for the Left's sake, and for its own. Like some barbarous savages who think killing their children will make the sun rise, the Beltway Right ritualistically sacrifices its members as if it's going to somehow change the Left's opinion of them. But the real unspoken purpose is to make sure Conservatism Inc. never leads to the kind of white racial consciousness which would allow the American Right to not just confront, but defeat its adversaries. Losing, for American conservatives, is part of their plan.

Unfortunately for the cucks, this can only go so far. Even the most cowardly conservatives need a certain amount of political relevance to keep the scam going. As the *Journal of American Greatness* contributor "Decius" put it in his widely circulated "The Flight 93 Election" piece, "Among the many things the 'Right' still doesn't understand is that the Left has concluded that this particular show need no longer go on." Though the supposed Hispanic electoral tidal wave is exaggerated by the lying press, eventually demographics are destiny, and there will be a permanent progressive majority.

Non-whites show no interest in any aspect of "conservative values." And absent at least a certain amount of power within the System, the plutocrats and influence peddlers who keep the Beltway Right scam rolling along will seek other places for their investments. The conservative movement simply cannot and will not continue as it has over the last half-century, regardless of whatever "principled" gibberish it comes up with to prolong its unworthy existence.

As many others have observed, the groundwork for the Alt Right was laid by many conservative dissidents, including Pat Buchanan, Sam Francis, Peter Brimelow, and many others. Of course, the Alt Right is *not* paleoconservatism, but is based in the take-no-prisoners chan culture built by /pol/ and other forums. Post-libertarianism, the culture wars sparked by Gamergate and other pushback against SJWs, and simply the tide of events are also important influences.

But none of this explains why the Alt Right is gaining a voice *within* the conservative movement itself, nor why movement conservatives are actually fearful they are being swept aside. As George Hawley, author of *Right-Wing Critics of American Conservatism*, accurately observes, the Alt Right isn't trying to *save* conservatism, like the paleos were trying to do. It's trying to *replace* conservatism.

The Alt Right, like the conservative movement, is a coalition, a tactical construction. It is defined by the crisis to which it is responding. For the conservative movement, the threat was international communism as represented by the geopolitical threat of the Soviet Union. For the Alt Right, the threat is the Death of the West.

The symptoms of our civilizational decline are many—the collapse of White identity, the war on politically incorrect history and symbols, the overtly anti-White hatred expressed by the heavily Jewish media and entertainment industries, and so many other plagues, each one of which justifies total rebellion. But the most obvious is "The Great Replacement"—the deliberate and overt dispossession of white populations throughout the West via mass Third World immigration. And mass immigration will break the conservative movement because the Beltway Right has no ability to cope with the electoral consequences.

It can cope with almost anything else. You can always change the goalposts on morality. Yesterday's ineffectual opposition to divorce becomes today's ineffectual opposition to gay marriage becomes tomorrow's ineffectual opposition to polygamy. The same rules apply to economic issues. You can still complain about "big government" year after year even when you never actually succeed in cutting the size of the state. Such failed opposition actually helps the Left by creating the illusion of a real choice.

But immigration is different. If current trends continue, it will be impossible for Republicans to compete on a national level. No amount of "outreach" or token minority Republicans will change the reality that non-whites, quite rationally, oppose limited government and favor redistribution of wealth along racial socialist lines. At best, Beltway Right hacks will be able to keep the scam going for a few more election cycles. No one can argue in good faith that Beltway-style conservatism has a future in a nonwhite America.

This existential crisis for the Republican Party, the conservative movement, the country, and our civilization provides the opening for the Alt Right. And the stakes are far higher than anything the conservative movement had to deal with. Enoch Powell once stated he would fight for his country even if it had a Communist government. A country can outlast a particular form of government—indeed, as we are learning from Eastern Europe, Soviet occupation may have been less destructive in the long run to national survival than being part of the "free world" during the Cold War.

But a country and a civilization cannot survive the loss of its core population. The nation is the people, not the institutions, the territory, or some kind of "culture" which mysteriously exists independently of the ethnic group.

The recognition that immigration is primarily a *racial* issue, not just a question of the "rule of law," is what defines the Alt Right. And once the reality and superlative importance of race is understood, other conclusions on economics, foreign policy, culture, feminism, and the influence of Jews necessarily follow.

Obviously, there is room to disagree on some of these issues. As with any movement or coalition, the Alt Right has different factions. But White racial identity and opposition to the dispossession of our people is core to the entire project and non-negotiable for anyone trying to be a part of it.

The Alt Right has an unquestionable imperative—the survival, self-determination, and upward development of our race in the nations our people created. Abstractions like "freedom" or "democracy" can mean whatever people in power want them to mean. But the survival of the white race is concrete, real, and existential.

The question is simple and cannot be avoided. White survival, yes or no? The Alt Right is for those who answer "yes."

"True conservatives" can't even comprehend the question. But they are being rendered irrelevant by the demographic crisis they refuse to notice. And in this time of civilizational crisis, they have nothing important to say.

Conservatism was never coherent. There is no "true conservative." And it's only natural now that the Soviet Union has vanished and a more existential threat has arisen, a new force on the Right will take its place.

Counter-Currents, September 26, 2016

THE END OF LIBERTARIANISM &
THE RISE OF THE ALT RIGHT

GREGORY HOOD

"We are, in a way, breaking a glass ceiling this year," said 2016 Libertarian Vice Presidential nominee William Weld. It's appropriate Weld uses a feminist metaphor. Like feminists and other Cultural Marxists, the Libertarians are masquerading as opposition to the System while functioning as an indispensable support. And though the Libertarian Party appears to be making the greatest electoral gains in its history this year, it has never been less relevant in terms of being a meaningful force for change.

As this is written, LP Presidential candidate Gary Johnson is polling near double digits, suggesting he may be included in the presidential debates. He also will likely secure federal funding for the party by polling above five percent. But just as the question "is the Pope Catholic?" is no longer rhetorical in the Current Year, it's a real question whether the Libertarian Party candidate is actually a libertarian.

In a way, some of the foolishness at this year's Libertarian Party convention, including an all but naked fat guy dancing on stage and Gary Johnson tossing an opponent's congratulatory gift in the trash, actually helped the party. It makes it look like more of a real alternative than it actually is.

Johnson is less Ron Paul come again than the John Anderson of 2016. He said he would have supported the Civil Rights Act, which means he already conceded the right of the federal government to control people's property for the purposes of social engineering. He does not support religious liberty, showing that whatever rhetoric he uses, he ultimately believes egalitarianism and nondiscrimination trump property rights. This is a key issue for some #NeverTrump social conservatives who would be otherwise inclined to support him, but Johnson has shown he doesn't want social conservative votes. He even mused on the idea of a carbon tax or fee to fight climate change.

Seeing as how Johnson is unlikely to win a single state, let alone the presidency, it's unclear why libertarians should bother with him even as a means for advancing their ideas. Trump is also promising to lower the federal debt, lower taxes, and cut government waste. Johnson's fiscal record is unimpressive, as he increased the debt while Governor of New Mexico. His defenders argue it wasn't really his fault because the legislature controls spending. Even if we accept this, how is the federal government any different?

Trump is also hammered daily by neoconservatives as a foreign policy novice who is insufficiently hostile to Russia. He also shocked the foreign policy establishment by championing America First. Can Johnson promise more to non-interventionists?

Johnson's Vice-Presidential nominee Weld is a living exemplar of WASP degeneracy and the collapse of the former American ruling class, much like Lincoln Chaffee. Put a Pilgrim hat on him and Weld's phenotype would fit in perfectly in an old painting of the arrival of the *Mayflower*. He supported both gun control and the Iraq War, positions which really shouldn't be tolerated among Libertarian Party members, let alone the Vice-Presidential nominee. Even *Reason* magazine, the flagship for left-libertarians, was mystified by the choice of Weld, saying he wasn't just a "softcore libertarian," but not a libertarian at all.

Jack Hunter, before covering himself in shame, used to mock the Beltway Right for defending "conservatism as a word" even though it had been stripped of all substance. Yet today's supposed liberty movement defends libertarianism as a word. What threat to the state does Johnson present? What personal freedoms can someone like Gary Johnson promise to regain for the American people, other than "lmao, weed"? In short, what does Johnson offer libertarians other than simple exposure?

The answer is a place at the trough. At a time when the Alternative Right is being identified by as nothing less than the biggest threat to hegemonic liberalism since communism, libertarianism (the capital L variety at least) is transforming into the loyal opposition for the System and the state. Johnson unhesitatingly accepts the premises of the Left when it comes to cultural questions. He also endorses using the power of government to force the Left's social program.

For example, Johnson said, explicitly, it's the federal government's job to prevent discrimination "in all cases." Of course, enforcing non-discrimination provides the rationale for unlimited government control, from mandating racial diversity in suburban neighborhoods to regulating social interaction at the office.

Johnson continued: "I mean under the guise of religious freedom, anybody can do anything . . . Why shouldn't somebody be able to shoot somebody else because their freedom of religion says that God has spoken to them and that they can shoot somebody dead?"

Aside from the obvious answer of "laws against murder," I'm tempted to say "because it would be Islamophobic to say they can't." But Johnson actually said this in reference to *Mormons*, even though his best chance to do well is in Western states. It was also mere moments after Johnson bemoaned the potential for anti-Muslim discrimination.

Johnson's swift suggestion that some cake shop refusing to serve homosexuals is equivalent to murder is revealing. Indeed, Johnson does the usual Leftist tactic of conflating any opposition to Leftist cultural policies to racist tyranny.

On immigration, a divisive issue among libertarians, Johnson appears blithely unaware that there are even arguments against it. He looked on the brink of tears when he said Trump is "racist, just racist." Instead, taking Rand Paul's "Detroit Republicans" angle to the next level, Johnson is now "lowriding" to show how much he loves the Hispanics who are replacing the gross European-Americans who once populated the Southwest.

On Black Lives Matter, Johnson now says he supports the movement because it opened his eyes to "discrimination." Whether he is even aware of BLM's demands for massive transfers of wealth and government programs to benefit their race is unknown.

Would-be Vice President Weld, again, a *Libertarian* candidate, explicitly stated the federal government would be justified in taking massive action to appease these activists.

"I think we have a national emergency in the number of male black youth who are unemployed without prospects," Weld said, according to *Politico*. "They're four times as likely to be incarcerated if they have intersection with law enforcement as white people are. Their educational opportunities are not there. We have to get them in to education and just concentrate the power of the government, trying to make sure that there are jobs available for them. It's a national emergency and when there's a national emergency, the government has to respond. Libertarian or no libertarian."

If blacks being arrested at higher rates, having higher unemployment, or having lower rates of education constitutes a "national emergency" forcing drastic government action, then we will always have a permanent emergency and practically unlimited government.

But we know this. And this is what is so frustrating about the Libertarian Party's recent direction and so triggering for the Alt Right. In the past, Libertarianism has attracted many intelligent young Rightists because it's less obviously foolish than the hoary bromides and self-interested rhetoric coming from the Beltway Right. For those who didn't start out as nationalists, Identitarians, racial realists, or National Socialists, it usually begins with Ayn Rand. But it doesn't end there unless, like conservatives, you retreat into protective stupidity to guard your ideology from reality.

Much of the history of the libertarian movement in the latter part of the century is about dedicated champions of limited government trying to grapple with inconvenient facts like human biodiversity and racial realism, the inherent inability of a democracy to protect liberty, the drawbacks of universal suffrage, and the self-destructive implications of open borders or cultural degeneracy. If you don't address these issues, even if *arguendo* we ignore race and demographics, libertarians can at best make a destructive System function more efficiently.

Consider the case of Milton Friedman, the author of *Capital-*

ism and Freedom and one of the more influential libertarians of the last century. He was also one of those who created income tax withholding, which, because it removes the burden from wage earners for writing a check for their taxes and creates the impression of a "gift" when you get a return, makes it far more difficult for supporters of limited government to get tax cuts. Though he wasn't the only person responsible for this idea, the negative impact of income tax withholding far outweighs whatever Friedman contributed to his cause with books and videos about how to make a pencil.

Thinkers such as Hans-Herman Hoppe, Murray Rothbard, Joseph Sobran, and others who we could call paleolibertarians didn't just say "freedom works!" Whatever their failings from the viewpoint of those of us who put race first, these men and those like them at least honestly approached the question of how one can achieve and maintain a libertarian society. And their work made an important contribution to Neo-Reaction, which also helped lead to the emergence of the Alternative Right. You can't talk about the Alt Right without acknowledging how so many libertarians and former libertarians understand there should be a government helicopter program.

With Johnson and much of the mainstream libertarian movement, the objective is not to limit the state or even think critically about how to approach the problem. Instead, literally decades of arguments and research are ignored as self-declared enemies of the state flock to Washington DC to lobby and labor in the government they are supposed to fight. By openly adopting Leftist and egalitarian premises, they ensure they never face any real opposition. The most degraded College Republican has more courage.

Thus, the figures toying with the idea of endorsing Gary Johnson reportedly include Mitt Romney, Susan Collins, and even Jeb Bush. Weld calls the campaign a "six-lane highway going right up the middle between the two parties." If this is true, why bother calling it Libertarian? Why not resurrect Sam Waterston's Unity08 proposal for a moderate third party? Or why not just hand the country over to Michael Bloomberg and call it a day? At least then we wouldn't be kidding ourselves that this is some kind of a real opposition to Washington DC.

The Alt Right wants an alternative to the current political, and more important, cultural system. Libertarians want a place inside that system where they can goof off about regulatory reforms which will never happen and make fun of Middle Americans who think "liberty" means something other than degeneracy. Just as the conservative movement became Conservatism Inc., the opposition to the state has transformed into Libertarianism Inc., a racket for mediocrities to eke out a living in the capital of the Hollow Empire.

This is a danger the Alt Right may face as well if it continues to grow in prominence. Already, we see attempts at co-option and a push to deny the role of race as central to the Alt Right.

As the movement grows, we have to remember what the Libertarian Party has forgotten. We don't want to giggle and offer polite suggestions to our enemies about how to do things better. Our role is not to serve as the loyal opposition to Leviathan, but to ensure our people can escape its poisonous grasp.

The Alt Right is not just an alternative to the mainstream conservative movement. It's an alternative to the regime and its rulers which govern us, hate us, and mandate our destruction. And the Libertarian Party, and much of the libertarian movement, is now just another part of the System we need to displace.

Counter-Currents, August 29, 2016

THE ALT RIGHT &
NATIONAL GREATNESS

AEDON CASSIEL

What would you say if I asked you what your vision of an ideal society is? What are the values that your society would be centered on and organized toward achieving?

A libertarian may have values he wants to achieve, and he may even think that a libertarian order would be the most effective means for achieving them, but he doesn't think *society* should be organized towards achieving *anything*. At least, not anything other than giving people an economy that makes it easier for them to buy *whatever* goods or services they'd like to buy.

Most libertarians focus on the ways in which value is subjective: if I want to spend my life masturbating and eating Cheetos, then the *value* of that activity is subjective to me. If you want to spend your life raising well-adjusted children, then the value of that activity is subjective to you. And if I'm willing to spend more money to be able to masturbate and eat Cheetos than you are on raising healthy families, then, well . . . it follows that in the libertarian framework, masturbating and eating Cheetos is *more valuable* than raising families in the only sense of the word "value" that means anything to the libertarian.

Most readers will be familiar by now with the research of Jonathan Haidt, the social psychologist at New York University. We could summarize the research of Jonathan Haidt by saying that according to liberals, the supreme value around which society should be organized is *everyone being nice to everyone*. In his academic research on moral foundations, Haidt identifies five primary dimensions by which morality can be measured. Liberals don't care about what he calls "authority," "loyalty," or "purity," but they do care about "fairness" and "care." Thus, the two most important things to ask are, was everyone treated according to the same rules, and did anyone get hurt?

Haidt has infamously established that conservatives actually understand the way liberals think far better than liberals understand conservatives. Because of research like this, Haidt has distanced himself from the liberal label. But Haidt's framing of these issues still reflects the fact that he is, in his heart of hearts, a liberal. He still doesn't *intuitively get* the impulses that a Rightist naturally feels. I believe Haidt is best understood as a reformer—that his inner hopes are on reforming liberalism so that he could feel comfortable calling himself a liberal once again.

This is an extremely important point: those of us on the Right side of the political spectrum don't care about "authority" and "loyalty" just because we think those things are important in and of themselves. With these terms in place, the questions still remain: loyalty *to whom*? Who do you recognize *as* an authority? Hillary Clinton? The SPLC? CNN?

And when I think of the process by which Social Justice Warriors have infiltrated institutions and done things like watering down the standards for becoming a firefighter in order to allow in greater numbers of people from groups that perform *worse* on the entry tests, it occurs to me that those kinds of rules will necessarily be put in place and enforced by . . . "*authorities.*" Yet, no matter how high the New Right, or the Right more generally, might score on "authoritarianism," I can't bring myself to imagine a world where defending these kinds of rules just because *authorities* implemented them is the central point of the Right's moral compass. Indeed, I could very well imagine conservatives actively working to subvert those rules, and the kinds of authorities that would uphold them. So claiming the Right puts greater value on "authority" than the Left really seems to miss the point.

I'd like to propose that when Donald Trump made "Make America Great Again" his campaign slogan, as trite as it may seem, this actually struck a much deeper chord than it appears at first glance, even to those of us who were taken in by his campaign. Those of us in the Alt Right will be more explicit

about this, but I think it struck the same chord with a significant portion of the "normie" public as well: the value we want
our ideal society to be organized towards achieving is *greatness.*
And this really is just as significant and central to our political
philosophy as the individual's *natural rights* are for the libertarian or *care* and *fairness* are for the liberal. We may have different views of what it would take to achieve greatness, or of
what greatness would look like, but the fact that we share this
core value in common when we envision an ideal society is an
extremely significant aspect of what unites us despite these differences.

Thus, the reason I can't picture Right-wingers defending the
kinds of "authorities" who do things like lower standards for
entry into firefighting departments for the sake of so-called
"equality" is this: these kinds of rules directly undermine the
greatness of that firefighting department's performance. The
rationale for attributing an intrinsic valuing of "authority" to
the Right is only because "authorities" are *usually* people who
are leading institutions towards *greatness.* But as in the case of
firefighting departments lowering their entry standards, we
can clearly see that when "authority" and "greatness" come
into conflict with one another, the Right would choose greatness, and thus, greatness is the essential value.

To his credit, Richard Spencer may be the only person I've
yet heard who explicitly picked up on this when, in his 2016
appearance at Texas A&M, he said:

> I agree with liberals who say, "Oh, Donald Trump, he's
> vulgar, he's ridiculous." Look, I agree. But just the fact
> that Donald Trump said that word, "great"—that he had
> a sense of height, of upward movement, of greatness, that
> striving towards infinity—however vulgar he might be,
> at least he had a *sense* of it. And that's what inspired the
> Alt Right . . .

This, I'd suggest, is why atheistic Nietzscheans and Randi-
ans find a natural home in the New Right alongside *Deus Vult*
Catholics: the ideal of the *Übermensch* is about nothing other

than placing *greatness* at the center of the reason for why society exists.

Quoting from Nietzsche's *Thus Spake Zarathustra*: "The overman is the meaning of the earth. . . . Man is a rope, tied between beast and overman . . . What is great in man is that he is a bridge and not an end . . ."[1]

Quoting from the *Internet Encyclopedia of Philosophy*'s exposition of Nietzsche:

> In modernity, the emergence of such figures seems possible only as an isolated event, as a flash of lightning from the dark cloud of humanity. Was there ever a culture, in contrast to modernity, which saw these sorts of higher types emerge in congress as a matter of expectation and design? Nietzsche's early philological studies on the Greeks, such as *Philosophy in the Tragic Age of the Greeks, The Pre-Platonic Philosophers*, "Homer on Competition," and "The Greek State," concur that, indeed, the ancient world before Plato produced many exemplary human beings, coming forth independently of each other but "hewn from the same stone," made possible by the fertile cultural milieu, the social expectation of greatness, and opportunities to prove individual merit in various competitive arenas. Indeed, Greek athletic contests, festivals of music and tragedy, and political life reflected, in Nietzsche's view, a general appreciation for competition, rank, ingenuity, and the dynamic variation of formal structures of all sorts. Such institutions thereby promoted the elevation of human exemplars.[2]

We can see here that it is central to the Nietzschean worldview that society is organized towards achieving greatness—that the value of greatness be reflected in the *structures* underpinning society.

---

[1] Walter Kaufmann, ed., *The Portable Nietzsche* (New York: Viking Penguin, 1982), pp. 125–27.

[2] http://www.iep.utm.edu/nietzsch/

Commentators often note that while the Right side of the political spectrum is united by its *rejection* of egalitarianism, it has no equivalent uniting principle of its own. This perspective defines Right-wing philosophy in the negative: it is *anti-egalitarian*, it is about *opposition* to the value the Left-wing places on egalitarianism. But why do we oppose egalitarianism? Is it not obvious that it's not only because it is a fact that people are unequal, but because they are unequal in *achieving greatness*? And is the reason we care about this not because *greatness* needs to be differentiated from inferiority *because we want to see, and be a part of, a society that works to elevate, promote, and encourage the former?*

I would suggest, too, that this is why Ayn Rand's fiction has always been more popular than her non-fiction in her so-called "philosophy." While my view of the latter is mostly negative (I think she was a nearly incoherent philosopher in many ways), I also think the underlying spirit of her fiction is one of fixation on greatness. In a letter to Ayn Rand dated January 1958, Ludwig von Mises made this observation in a particularly biting way:

> *Atlas Shrugged* is not merely a novel. It is also—or may I say: first of all—a cogent analysis of the evils that plague our society . . . You have the courage to tell the masses what no politician told them: "You are inferior and all the improvements in your conditions which you simply take for granted you owe to the effort of men who are better than you."[3]

There is obviously harsh emotion behind this statement, but I would suggest that the disdain he displays is not merely a reaction to the masses' inferiority; it is a reaction to their *lack of appreciation* for greatness. Were the masses to remain just as "inferior" as they already are, but *appreciate* the greatness represented by those of their betters who improve the human con-

---

[3] Jörg Guido Hülsmann, *Mises: The Last Knight of Liberalism* (Auburn, Al.: Ludwig von Mises Institute, 2007), p. 996.

dition, I see no reason to think Rand would have held the same contempt towards them. She loathed the masses not merely for being what they *were*, but for *their lack of appreciation* for the achievements of greatness.

Quoting from a dialogue between Cherryl Taggart and James Taggart in *Atlas Shrugged*:

> All of you welfare preachers — it's not unearned money that you're after. You want handouts, but of a different kind. I'm a gold-digger of the spirit, you said, because I look for value. Then you, the welfare preachers . . . it's the spirit that you want to loot. I never thought and nobody ever told us how it could be thought of and what it would mean — the unearned in spirit. But that is what you want. You want unearned love. You want unearned admiration. You want unearned greatness.[4]

Counter-Currents, April 13, 2017

---

[4] Ayn Rand, *Atlas Shrugged* (New York: Signet, 1996), p. 821.

MEMES, IMAGE BOARDS, & TROLL CULTURE

ADAM WALLACE

DEFINING THE ALTERNATIVE RIGHT

The "Alternative Right" is an umbrella-term used to group-together a mass of Right-wing spheres — "Right-wing" meaning antiliberal, anti-egalitarian, and anti-Whig as an ultimate out-look (though with plenty of room for intercommunity disa-greement). These spheres all differ and consist of think-tanks, small communities, blogs, websites, street movements, groups within colleges or universities, *et cetera*. It is a culmination of intellectual-types emerging from all stripes of life in joined dis-satisfaction with contemporary Western civilization. Different spheres within the Alternative Right as well as its influences have existed for varied amounts of time — the Manosphere and MGTOW movements have only existed (in articulated, self-aware form) for a few years, where something like European ethnonationalism has existed for centuries.

The Alternative Right is not a hivemind with one specific goal in mind to accomplish in one specific way. Various once separate entities have now, in this modern era, found them-selves a common enemy — modern, progressive, globalist liber-alism — though different individuals and communities will have different justifications for their suspicion of this enemy. The Alternative Right is not as unified and monolithic as some would want to believe. There is constant debate, discussion, and disagreement over ideology and methods between people in the community.

What is key to this inter-Alternative Right diversity is that the core of it pre-existed the internet and the information age, and is an outgrowth of academic sensibilities at home in jour-nals, universities, and governments. However, the Alternative Right is not a political party. It has no manifesto. Any major sociocultural shift is marked prior by psychological and spiritual undercurrents which later culminate at moments of strategic importance. Europe's Identitarian movement (*à la* Generation Identity) is one such undercurrent, the Alternative Right (*à la* Counter-Currents Publishing) itself is another, as is Neo-Reaction (*à la* the work of Mencius Moldbug), as are all of the various think-tanks, groups and organizations online and offline which follow a similar trajectory which is (generally) pro-identity, pro-tradition, and thus anti-establishment.

DEFINING IMAGEBOARD CULTURE

Emerging almost as soon as the internet became a public phenomenon wherein there was a free market for entertainment and instant communication between like-minded but far-apart people, the internet became the site of its own unique culture. People using the internet, on the internet alone, developed a separate grammar, moral code and way of conducting oneself than that which exists in physical face-to-face interaction.[1] Anonymity is a huge part of developing this alternative behavior, which in-turn creates an alternative culture which only subsists on the internet. A culture free from the social restraints of the physical world, where a new social code is developed; the internet provides a clean slate where social norms which exist outside of it are easily disregarded. And that is exactly what has happened, not only within various imageboards, but generally on the web on forums, online videogames and chatrooms. Take the stereotypical example of a hyper-introverted computer geek who spends all of his time on the internet; this is his world, not the world of the ordinary person.

What people refer to as "chan" is in reference to—mostly, but not wholly—the imageboard forum created in 2003 by Christopher "moot" Poole, 4chan. To be specific, the /pol/ board on 4chan, titled "Politically Incorrect" (previously /new/ for "News"), where there exists a style drawing from the old-internet culture of anonymity and the escape of social

---

[1] http://www.huffingtonpost.com/2012/10/11/facebook-psychology-7-reasons_n_1951856.html

norms, and the directing of that into the realm of politics. Of course, the most politically incorrect politicking involves sentiments of an antiliberal, antidemocratic, anti-egalitarian, anti-masses bent. One does not have to venture far or for long on such a corner of the net before you are bombarded with anti-semitism, various -phobias, -isms, and other assorted fun and games. That is not to say a place like 4chan's /pol/ is utterly contrarian for its own sake, but it is free from the taboos and social expectations which would stifle such opinions and expressions in the physical world, therefore thoughtcrime flourishes as it has no other avenues though which to filter into mainstream society. Again, the internet has its own culture — which may be confusing for those non-tech-savvy weirdos out there — that is distinct from the physical world, and it is certainly manifest in a place like 4chan's /pol/.

REGARDING /POL/

The actual make-up of /pol/, as far as opinions are concerned, is rather synthetic. There is a body of National Socialists, a body of fascists, nationalists, traditionalists, libertarians, anarchists, reactionaries, conservatives, etc. There are posters of nearly every stripe — which might confuse those who have not spent a massive amount of time on /pol/ — but the only group which is not present (at least not noticeably) is that of a kindly, liberal, socially progressive persuasion. The overarching culture is a kind of tongue-in-cheek Hitlerism which rants as much as it delicately articulates, and, furthermore, professes unending hatred and malice, and at the same time, a huge capacity for loving concern and a nearly obsessive craving for justice and the righting of wrongs. There is, to such a passionate style, a kind of sensible schizophrenia: massive amounts of energy swirling in every direction, every channel, and for every purpose — even if two directions are counter-propositional. You will find threads on /pol/ endorsing the legalization of slavery or prostitution; at the same time you will notice threads calling for others to convert to Christianity; or to get into healthy physical and mental shape; or threads on how to find a good wife, and so on. You can find threads decrying the Holocaust and Nazi terror outright, and simultaneously find threads of a much more tempered nature on the same topic. There are threads claiming that Europe must return to its pagan roots, and at the same time threads claiming the exact opposite; sometimes from a Christian perspective or even a Nietzschean perspective. For a rabble of assumed "bigots," there is great diversity in this place. "/pol/ is not one person," as the saying goes in reply to people who assert that those who browse these places are of one type and one type only.

THE CHAN *ZEITGEIST*

The hostile and anti-outsider *Zeitgeist* chans tend to envelop themselves with is a survival mechanism so that the site maintains a stable foundational identity. Newcomers are discouraged from posting, from using names, or from breaking the specific unwritten rules which preceded their arrival. You submit, and become another nameless ideologue where the only thing which matters is facts, humor, and brotherhood-in-anonymity. Occasionally, posters (typically someone answering questions) will use a name and differentiate themselves from the mass. Such a thing is looked down upon when it is abused, however, and used as a tool to attract attention and form an ego. The distaste for "namefagging" as it is called is not that the individual is different, but that the individual is basing their differentiation upon an arbitrary label instead of their mental healthiness. It can be a helpful tool for people who have a presence elsewhere to maintain that presence on an imageboard so they are then recognized, but most of the time, unless the person is already known and liked within the culture, it is strongly abhorred.

Imageboards such as 4chan and 8chan are unique within internet culture due to the popularity of their political spaces. Some other paces on the net where political discussion is an energetic force are Reddit, Tumblr, and YouTube. The former two are liberal in flavor, and due to the ego-centric essences of each site (having "Like" systems, for example) they maintain an acceptable, as far as "real life" standards are concerned, etiquette. They are liberal hubs, and Tumblr itself is notorious for its far-Left mobbiness.[2] YouTube is an interesting beast as though on the surface it might appear "normal" (i.e., liberal), there is actually a noticeable presence of illiberal comments, channels, and personalities. The fact that individuals involved in the Alternative Right can maintain an income off of such a site by making videos says enough about its friendliness to out-of-the-box thinking. But, nevertheless, YouTube will never be totally antinormal in the way in which 8chan is, for instance.

The energy, the swirling vortex of creativity, which exists on 8chan (and other chans) is not capable of being realized any-where else due to both the make-up of the site in its member-ship, as well as how the website is organized and constructed. There are, as already mentioned, no "Like" functions; unlike Reddit, posts are by default ordered chronologically instead of by popularity; forming a distinct ego is looked down upon to the point where distinguishing yourself with a name can cause other users to filter your posts so anything sent by your I.P. is not seen; and threads are not normally saved or archived be-fore they are pruned (deleted), which forces users to both re-peat and reaffirm themselves as well as—and this is of utmost importance—re-evaluate themselves and their views constant-ly; daily; hourly; by the minute (hence "/pol/ is always right," as another saying goes).

DARK HUMOR

As for some of the more famous accretions of this communi-ty, memes and trolling, we can offer brief explanations of these phenomena.

A "meme" is defined as "a unit of cultural information, such as a cultural practice or idea, that is transmitted verbally or by repeated action from one mind to another."[3] One type of meme adored by imageboards is the "image macro," often an expres-sive picture of a person or animal overlayed with an amusing

---

[2] http://www.breitbart.com/tech/2015/11/02/sjws-bullied-a-young-artist-into-a-suicide-attempt-and-didnt-stop/

[3] *The American Heritage Dictionary of the English Language*, 4th Edi-tion

caption. Such pictures can be found all over the internet nowa-days, but it was the imageboard which birthed them proper. Famous examples include the "Doge," "Pepe," "Good Guy Greg," and other variants. Other "picture-memes" include "re-action images" which are often posted on imageboards instead of text to convey a particular emotion in visual, rather than de-scriptive, format. For every sarcasm-, mockery-, or sadness-inducing post, there is an appropriate reaction image some-where (often in the form of anime girls, as noted commentator Rick Wilson famously misunderstood).[4] The reason why imag-es are often used in place of words is simply due to their direct, no-nonsense message. One does not need to provide argu-ments as to why someone is wrong in debate, an image of a smug-looking cartoon woman signals simply-enough that "You're wrong, so shut-up and LURK MOAR" (as yet another saying goes).

As for the well-known art of "trolling," of irritating and cyber-harassing people, such nastiness, best exemplified *via* the case of Jessi Slaughter,[5] stems largely not from the /pol/ sub-culture, but the /b/ — "Random" — subculture, a realm notori-ous for all sorts of things, including various "raids" on particu-lar websites and the like, wherein, as is sometimes the case with the avatar-based social media platform Habbo Hotel, im-ageboard-goers band-together in an effort to disrupt or shock another online community. Humor and ridicule are integral parts of chan culture, and this is the primary basis for trolling people and communities — doing it for "the lulz."[6]

Such activities, however, can carry over onto /pol/ in the form of mockery and ridicule of Jews, nonwhites, feminists, progressives, liberals, Muslims, and various other minority or so-called "oppressed" groups. The one thing /pol/ respects is power, and those without it are fair game for ridicule by virtue

---

[4] http://www.breitbart.com/video/2016/01/20/gop-consultant-rick-wilson-to-msnbc-trump-supporters-childless-single-men-who-masturbate-to-anime/

[5] http://knowyourmeme.com/memes/events/jessi-slaughter

[6] https://encyclopediadramatica.se/I_did_it_for_the_lulz

of it being not only hilarious, but morally justified in the spit-
ting-upon of one's enemies. If one has ideological reasons to
dislike someone else and to see them as a threat to society, it
does help in the justification of their torment. The "Alt-Right
Twitter Army," as it has been called, joyously delights in the
humiliation and mockery of apparent liberals and assorted
ninnies ripe for the trolling—all in under one hundred and forty characters a piece. And while all this does stem from humor
and mockery, it is not always as simple as that.

Humor and comedy are a very powerful tool which can disarm people in debate instantly. Similar to the oft-spewed liberal buzzword "racist" (a word so brazenly overused nowadays
that it has lost all meaning in many circles), humor can shut-
down a discussion in a moment of cultural microdomination.
Call someone a racist, and all is evident: they are amoral, wicked, violent, ignorant, and on the wrong side of history. Call
someone a "cuck" and all is evident: they are weak, feeble, pathetic, incompetent, and will likely die off in the coming race
war. Words amid /pol/-friendly Alt-Righters have immense
power, and are deployed like tactical missiles to shame weak-
lings and those who are facilitating the destruction of Western
civilization and all that is right and proper.

Conclusion

I hope I have given those who are not familiar with the culture of imageboards a somewhat serviceable overview. The
brief analysis above really is not enough, and the only way to
actually see what I am babbling about is to actually experience
it for yourself. Be warned, however, simply because there is a
good deal of overlap between /pol/ and the Alternative Right
does not guarantee safe-passage between the two for everyone.
The Alternative Right is borne of academia, where /pol/ is
borne of an entirely fresh slate where intellect is important, but
humor and a sense of belonging are more so. Of course, the
overlap between the two areas is rather prominent. The emergence of *The Right Stuff,* a blog which was originally formulat-
ed on 4chan's /pol/, has introduced into the blogosphere the
humor of imageboards. We owe the circulation of terms such

as "dindu," "LARPing," "cuckservative," and many more to this website and its memetic influence. The fact that these two areas have overlapped and merged to a certain degree should not be surprising. Where there is academic space, there is room for humor, and where there is humor, there is room for academic sensibility. The key feature of imageboard culture is energy, raw energy which only needs directing. The intellectual structure of the Alternative Right has provided a directing framework for the more playful energies existent within individuals in the sphere who have not previously been introduced to imageboard culture where the emergence, the rearing of the head, of imageboard culture has ignited the spark. It is a circle.

There are dangers with such a scenario, however. It is fair to point-out that much of the energy existing within the /pol/ substratum of imageboard culture exists as a reaction against the insanity of progressive liberalism and the like (and rightly so), where the Alternative Right proper has its bedrock in various pre-existent ideologies and traditions such as European conservatism and nationalism; it is part of a larger chain which encompasses the European New Right, the German Conservative Revolution, and so forth, where imageboard culture is essentially "square one" with few proper ties to anything prior to it due to its place on the internet, and it not being in the form of anything more than a strange kind of social club where nothing and everything is discussed. Where the Alternative Right would critique liberalism from a fixed ideological reference point such as ethnonationalism, /pol/ simply deconstructs it and declares "It doesn't work, so let's try something else." That "something else" could, depending on who you ask on /pol/ be a form of fascism, nationalism, libertarianism, etc.—but who do you ask? Everyone is Anonymous! Hence there cannot be total overlap between the two; any overlap thus far has existed dialectically, synthetically, *à la* threads on /pol/ about Neo-Reactionary philosophy, or jokes about "muh six million" and other memes in Alternative Right podcasts. Thus, it is erroneous to say that this is a "chan generation" which is involved with the Alternative Right, or that the Reactosphere is full of people who visit 4chan or 8chan.[7] There are of course those who are involved simultaneously in the two—there is overlap, as already said—but chan-goers are not the ideological bedrock of the Alternative Right proper; they make up a large portion of the audience, not the intellectual or creative vanguard.

There are distinctions which must be drawn, and the importance of both spaces must be understood. The Alternative Right is immensely threatening towards its victims, even if the victims are thus far unaware of the threat approaching them, as it presents (or exposes, brings back to us) doctrines which are perfectly opposed logically, spiritually, and emotionally to the present epoch in complete intellectual, academic serenity. The culture of imageboards, "chan culture," is a massive threat to its potential victims as it is purely anarchistic in a frighteningly antilogical and sadistic way—or at least the potential exists for it to be so.

Counter-Currents, December 23, 2016

---

[7] http://www.vox.com/2016/4/18/11434098/alt-right-explained

THE ALT SOUTH

HUNTER WALLACE

The crisis began around late 2014 when a year and a half of public rallies by the League of the South had begun to take its toll. We had spent the previous two years building up an amazing real-world network of activists across the South. There was nothing else like it on the American Far Right. We were holding monthly rallies, annual national conferences, state conferences, private events, etc.

Believe me, it was *fun* taking it into the real world after spending a decade or more camped out in the anonymity of cyberspace. We learned that our enemies in Dixie were not as organized as we had imagined them to be. We learned that doxing is not as problematic here as it is elsewhere. We learned that various issues like opposition to immigration and refugee resettlement were broadly popular in our region. In hindsight, I think you could say that we saw the Trump movement coming.

Somewhere along the way, we began attracting women to our movement. It is striking how most of us are married and have young children now. We can't do the public activism like we used to anymore because our responsibilities have multiplied. If you look at the Far Right as a whole, it is not a problem we should complain about. Whereas White Nationalists have argued about the lack of women in the movement, our wives spend enormous amounts of time talking and networking on Facebook. Women seem to really enjoy the social aspect of our movement that you can't get by interacting exclusively with anonymous people online. We don't go to immigration rallies now so much as weddings and baby showers.

Anyway, I look back fondly on 2013 and 2014. I got married, had a son, and met lots of great people who share my views all across the South. That was *fun*. That was *valuable*. That was a *good investment*. We needed an institution that would enable us to propagate our views, coordinate our energies, build real world networks, challenge the *status quo* in public space and overcome the well-known weaknesses (i.e., the autism and extremism) of a purely online movement.

At the same time, we eventually came to see the limitations of this approach. It was easy for the opposition to violate our civil rights and knock down billboards which were very expensive to put up. It was impossible to keep up the pace of the rallies—too expensive, too much traveling, we hit a ceiling, etc. More than anything else though, the constant bickering on Facebook over small points of disagreement and the willingness of some to tread into violent territory which made others uncomfortable began to fracture the movement. What's the point of spending so much time recruiting ordinary people at public rallies only to squander it by alienating them with extremism on social media?

During the first half of 2015, the pace of our public rallies began to slow down. Several leaders including Michael Cushman dropped out of the League of the South. That was the case until the Dylann Roof mass shooting in Charleston ignited a campaign of cultural genocide across the South. We lost the Confederate Battle Flag at the South Carolina Statehouse. The Southern Heritage movement and the League were briefly reenergized. We held more rallies than ever before, but eventually the news cycle rolled on, the enemy was repulsed, enthusiasm faded, and burn out returned as a major problem.

In the midst of the reaction to Charleston, Donald Trump announced he was running for president on June 16, 2015. Everything was about to change. The inconceivable started to happen.

DONALD TRUMP CHANGES AMERICA

Southern Nationalists weren't prepared for Donald Trump.

We are so accustomed to thinking *regionally*, but the anger and alienation that we saw at our protests in the South was *national* in scope. It was even *global*. No one was even trying to summon all that anger and alienation and channel it against the liberal establishment.

How should we feel about this? We have been too narrowly

focused on the Confederacy. We never entertained the possibility of a successful nationalist and populist revolt in our lifetimes, another Andrew Jackson, put into the White House by a MARS coalition led by the South. The Populists had mounted a fierce challenge in the 1890s and even briefly captured the Democratic Party, but they were beaten back. We have just witnessed the most improbable election since Jackson's victory in 1828.

In light of our own history, we shouldn't be surprised. It actually makes sense. Radical Reconstruction changed the nature of our people. Previously, the South had been much less coherent, which was one the major reasons we lost the War Between the States. But living under the boot of radicalism changed America. The differences between the lowland and upland South faded into the Solid South of the Jim Crow era. White Northerners lost interest in pushing Radical Reconstruction. The Yankee mind of the late 19th and early 20th centuries turned instead to imperialism and commercial progress.

As hard as it is to believe, eight years of living under President Barack Hussein Obama may have had a similar effect. The experiment seems to have cooled the enthusiasm of non-Southerners for "social justice." Maybe it was all the Black Lives Matter rioting in the streets? Whatever the cause, a critical mass of White Northerners in rural areas started voting a lot more like rural White Southerners and changed the world. The racial and cultural gap between coastal urbanites and interior ruralites has widened to such a degree that it has become the primary polarity of American politics.

I've occasionally written about this over the years. We have seen Upper South states like Arkansas, Missouri, Kentucky, and West Virginia become much more Republican. The same process has now moved across the Mason-Dixon line and into the Rust Belt and Midwest. The Left has demonized and written off the White working class. President Donald Trump is the result.

LIVING THROUGH HISTORY

When Donald Trump began to steamroll over his Republican rivals during the "Summer of Trump," I dropped everything else I was doing and started blogging about it. I sensed that something historic was unfolding in this country. I wanted to capture it and be a part of it.

This was not because I had changed my convictions. As always, I remain a proud Southern Nationalist, but there were a lot of exciting developments going on outside the movement. Suddenly, the Alt Right was rising like a sleeping giant that had awakened after a long slumber. I found this extremely fascinating because I had come to Southern Nationalism *from* the world of the Alt Right in 2011. The Alt Right's focus on identity raised awareness of my Southern ethnic and cultural identity.

Unlike other Southern Nationalists, I backed Trump to the end, voted for Trump in the primary and general election, and preferred a Trump victory. I was delighted when he won the presidency. In my view, Trump was weakening mainstream conservatism, undermining taboos, polarizing the electorate, and mainstreaming a diluted form of populism and nationalism. He was having an impact like Pat Buchanan or Ron Paul, but on a vastly greater scale. Just from experience alone, I knew it would redound to our benefit. I saw Trumpism as a necessary stepping stone on a much longer journey.

The Tea Party was another stepping stone. It looks like nothing more than silly mainstream conservatism in hindsight, but it too was part of a long-term process. The populist wing of the Tea Party moved to *Breitbart* and eventually pushed the Right in a more nationalist direction. We need to be more historically conscious because one day President Trump will be gone, we will still be here, and something else probably even more radical will emerge as the successor of Trumpism.

As with Jacksonian America, this moment too will pass sooner than we think. It is an episode, not the season finale. We've got to remain historically aware and take a longer view.

THE RISE OF THE ALT RIGHT

2015 and 2016 were breakout years for the Alt Right.

Southern Nationalists have a lot to learn from why and how this happened. The Alt Right aggressively pushed itself into the national conversation and by doing so reaped a windfall of publicity and converts. Southern Nationalists were consumed by bickering on Facebook. The Alt Right was pragmatic, worked within the system to promote its own ends, and rallied behind President Donald Trump. Southern Nationalists, who are convinced the system is hopelessly beyond reform and that they should have nothing do with it, were ideologically inflexible and sat on the sidelines.

The Alt Right through its links to Gamergate and the Manosphere grasped the importance of memes, swarming social media, particularly Twitter, to discourse poison or push a Narrative. The Alt Right moved and planted its flag on Twitter and learned how to roll with the news cycle. In contrast, Southern Nationalists retreated further into their own bubble and away from their audience. Southern Nationalists were becoming more militant, more open to violence, more alienated and thus more divided during this same period. The Alt Right understood the appeal of being edgy, having fun, and smashing taboos to a younger audience. Southern Nationalists were becoming more dour, pessimistic, and angry. Overall, they were in a really sour mood, and that had a negative impact on the movement.

For the Alt Right, the most striking development of 2016 was the rise of the Alt-Lite brands. I've been extremely critical of these brands many of whom I believe are financially motivated hucksters, but they are not without their virtues. We can still learn a lot from their success. First and foremost, there is *Breitbart* which transformed the Right and the entire American political spectrum. There are also brands like PJW and Cernovich who amassed huge followings by skillfully exploiting social media to reach new audiences. There is a lot here we ought to study and adapt for our own purposes.

THE ALT-SOUTH

Southern Nationalism has become a bit unglued.

We haven't adapted to the Trump era. The movement is being pulled in different directions: some want to move closer to our people, as they have moved toward us under Trump, while others want to move further away. I'm here today to share with you a vision which I have named the Alternative South. This is actually a project which I have talked about with Michael Cushman many times over the years which never came to fruition. Strangely enough, we unconsciously began working on it years ago.

The Alt-South isn't a membership organization. It is inspired by the relationship of White Nationalism to the Alt Right. Basically, the Alt-South would be a space for everyone in Dixie who isn't some kind of Leftist or mainstream conservative (i.e., nationalists, populists, reactionaries) to come together to discuss our past, present, and common future. Southern Nationalists would be at the core of the Alt-South. The Atlanta Forum could become our annual gathering similar to the role the NPI conference plays with the Alt Right. Instead of narrowing our influence and alienating people who are somewhat sympathetic, the idea here would be to reach out to all kinds of different rightwing tendencies as well as average Trump supporters and imbue them with a renewed sense of Southern national consciousness.

The Alt-South would be a *ton* of work:

❖ From our experience with the League of the South, we would love to continue the real-world meetups, networking, and conferences. There is no reason why these meetups or conferences have to be public. We don't have to host public demonstrations to take our movement offline. In fact, it would probably make more sense to host several private gatherings in major Southern metro areas to get the movement started. We've already tested a model of this at the Augusta meetup.

❖ There's no reason why we couldn't host public events like the AmRen conference. James Edwards has suggested to me organizing another conference like the one in Memphis in 2014. I'm sure there are plenty of people who would love for us to do that who would volunteer to provide the security.

❖ Many of us have already gone public with our beliefs. There is no reason why we couldn't continue
the demonstrations at a far slower pace. They were a
useful entry point into Southern Nationalism. We
have to learn from our mistakes though and avoid
burnout. We're also living in a different era with the
Trump administration in Washington being broadly
sympathetic to many of our issues. Instead of holding our own protests, maybe we could engage in
some counter-protesting for a change?

❖ There is no reason why we can't continue to publish
deconstructionist e-books. I have in mind here Michael Cushman's *Our Southern Nation* and Paul Ker-
sey's *The Truth About Selma*. We need more books in
this vein about a variety of subjects. I highly recommend both of these books. You can find and pur-
chase them through the *Occidental Dissent* sidebar.
We need to build our own canon and make it available to newcomers.

This probably sounds familiar to you. It is what we have
been doing for a number of years now. How would the Alt-
South be any different from Southern Nationalism?

❖ Specifically, we need to borrow the meme warfare
and swarming from the Alt Right. I was shocked by
the efficacy of trolling in 2016. Sadly, the golden age
of Twitter trolling is over, but we can still manage
without the aggression, the targeting, and the hard
edge racial language that gets our social media accounts banned. The #DraftOurDaughters campaign
is one example that was very effective.

❖ From the Alt-Lite brands, there are many lessons to
be learned. We need to look at *Breitbart* as a model of
what we should be doing. We need to pool our resources, organize as our own company, generate
enormous amounts of content, and roll with the
news cycle on Twitter. We need elbow our way into

the national conversation. That's what we are attempting to do right now with *AltRight.com*.

❖ We need to get into punditry, build platforms, and
learn how to monetize our content. We need to build
more attractive websites to propagate a discourse
about Southern ethnic and cultural identity.

❖ Perhaps the most important thing we need to be doing is mastering and building up our presence on social media platforms: Twitter, Facebook, YouTube,
and Periscope. The *Rebel Yell* podcast is a great example of the content we ought to be producing. Ideally, we would have the means to distribute our content (blogs, podcasts, e-books) to large receptive audiences. The Alt-Lite brands now have the power to
do this with a few tweets. That's worth thinking
about.

❖ We need to be far more ambitious and serious about
our writing and podcasting. The success of BREXIT
and President Trump should inspire us to believe
that the future we want to achieve is possible.

❖ We need to be looking for nationalist and populist
candidates in state and local races — the Southern
equivalents of Paul Nehlen — that we can rally behind and support.

In such a way, we will blend the Alt Right and Southern Nationalism into the Alt-South. We will take the strengths from
both and try to minimize the weaknesses.

OCCIDENTAL DISSENT WILL BE A MODEL

Just watch what I am doing at *Occidental Dissent*.

I'm already in the process of implementing everything I
have said here and more. I haven't spelled it out, but many of
you have no doubt noticed the recent changes. I'm confident
that *Occidental Dissent* as a platform of the Alt-South will explode and reach never before seen heights.

Southern Nationalism will thrive during the Trump years as
we organize and build bridges with Dixie's Deplorables.

Things are not nearly as bad as so many believe. Southerners aren't going back to sleep. They're edged much closer to our way of thinking. The polarization is going to reach never before seen heights as The Resistance begins in earnest. We will live through this, prosper, and come out on the other side like our Southern Nationalist forebears in Jackson and Polk's America.

This is not yet our time, but we are closer to it than ever before. Thank you! Deo Vindice!

Note: Let there be no confusion on the matter of security. The recent events by the so-called antifa in Washington, DC and Atlanta continue to illustrate why a security force is necessary. The Left's open embrace of political violence also makes me wonder if this will all end in bloodshed after all. They are the ones initiating violence and systematically attempting to violate the rights of their political opponents. We're not the ones doing this, and the Trump administration needs to come down hard on them.

Also, I'm extremely happy with what I have seen from the Trump administration so far. I think President Trump has the potential to be another Andrew Jackson. I think he is doing a lot of good things, but like Presidents Jackson and Polk, I am not sure what that will lead to 20 years from now. As with Jackson and Polk, the Northeast has never been known for supporting American Greatness.

Occidental Dissent, January 30, 2017

SAFE EAST EUROPEAN HOME

RUUBEN KAALEP

The ancestral continent of all white people, Europe, can still be roughly divided in two according to the results of World War II. The East, which remained under Communist occupation for half a century, is still different in many aspects from the West. Most importantly, this difference is manifested in values and philosophical outlooks on the world. As compared to the West, Eastern Europe looks like more of a nationalist stronghold with each passing year.

Nationalism in Soviet-occupied countries survived the Communist period and was even able to be the main catalyst for the fall of Communism. It survived because the Communists relied on hard power in order to extinguish dissent. Unlike the West, where the soft power of liberalism has effectively made nationalism a pariah in the political scene, Communist propaganda, being merely a cover for a violent regime of terror, was never truly taken seriously.

World War II, however, resulted in seriously limiting the political choices of individual Western nations. As any nationalist geopolitical bloc was seemingly impossible, the people desiring freedom from Communism were left with but one option: dreamily looking up to whatever liberalism had to offer. They were fooled by the promises of economic prosperity and countless freedoms, rarely noticing that the freedom *to remain who you are* was not on the table.

From the liberal perspective, the nationalist revolutions in Eastern Europe evoked dangerous ideas, but ultimately led to a desired outcome. For the nationalists, it was different: these national awakenings were the greatest things to have happened for a very long time. But as the memories of the Singing Revolution, the Velvet Revolution, the fall of the Berlin Wall, and other similar events slowly faded into history, the feeling began to take shape that the dangers to the ethnic identities formerly posed by the Soviet Union had not disappeared.

After many of these countries became members of the European Union, an identity crisis followed. What do we strive for now? Is this really what we wanted? The fact that so-called "Western values" were simply incompatible with constitutional ethnostates was confirmed when the liberal agenda of multicultural globalism became part of the day-to-day life of the Eastern European political scene. How much talk of "shared values" can there really be between a country dedicated to "life, liberty, and the pursuit of happiness"[1] and a country with a sacred mission to preserve its "ethnicity, language, and culture throughout the ages"?[2]

This realization brought a specific moment of disappointment, following a peak point of liberalism, in the late 2000s or 2010s for different countries. Disappointed in the West, nationalists realized that their countries had to go through yet another awakening, a final awakening that would bring truly nationalist regimes to power. It had to be, at the same time, a restoration of something old and a foundation of something completely new, that would be able to last in the 21st century. A nationalist movement with similar perspectives emerged in almost all of these countries.

With nationalism increasingly taking hold in the public mindset of Eastern European countries, their ruling classes have been left with two options. The great immigration crisis of 2015 brought a moment of reckoning. In some countries of the East, the rulers have wisely steered toward nationalism. In others, they still cling to pro-Western liberalism but are unable to contain the growing unrest, and as a result, they will be replaced with nationalist regimes sooner or later.

For example, in Hungary, where the nationalist Jobbik party is the second largest political party, the ruling Fidesz party has begun to adopt most of their nationalist platform, ranging from opposing the centralization of the European Union to famously stopping the migrant wave on the country's borders in 2015,

---

[1] United States Declaration of Independence.
[2] Constitution of Estonia, preamble.

explicitly doing so to protect Western civilization. In Poland, the Law and Justice party, allied in the European Parliament with the British Conservatives whom one can hardly call nationalist, has implemented strong nationalist policies clearly inspired by Hungary, even though Polish nationalist parties are relatively small and scattered.

This Right-wing drift does not affect only nominally Right-wing parties. The Social Democrats who rule Slovakia have similarly adapted a nationalist immigration policy and as a result, joined the struggle against the globalist agenda of Brussels. In addition, Slovakia has two strong nationalist parties, effectively paving the way towards a nationalist hegemony: no matter who you vote for on the political spectrum, your national interests will be secure. This will most likely be the future of all Eastern European countries, as ever more politicians realize that heralding anti-white multiculturalism is akin to political suicide.

Even in countries such as Estonia or Romania, where the old-fashioned political class is still resisting the seeds of nationalism and attempting to build a *cordon sanitaire* around nationalist parties, they are unable to limit the growth of nationalism by all practical means. Every attack seems to only make the nationalists stronger. The rulers have to start making concessions in order to preserve their grip over a nationalist society, or be overthrown.

One concession would be lifting the *cordon sanitaire* and allowing nationalist parties to enter the government while keeping the majority liberal. This has happened in Latvia and Finland. But this concession has meant that nationalist ideas have been allowed to enter mainstream discussion. They can no longer be disregarded as fringe, "extremist" ideas that should be kept under wraps in order to be a good European country. In fact, the liberals who have accepted nationalists as their coalition partners are forced to defend them even in Brussels, because they have made their own power dependent on nationalist support.

This can be partly explained by the fact that being exposed to Communism made the peoples of the Eastern Europe immune to all kinds of Leftist, universalist, anti-national ideas. When a fundamentally similar agenda began flowing in from the West, it sparked a nationalist reaction, a Right-wing drift either with or without the ruling class. Where the ruling class failed to adapt, it only has pushed the nationalists even further to the Right, causing a remarkable difference in the Overton windows of the Western and Eastern Europe. In the East, you simply have to accept at least *some* amount of nationalism.

So what is Eastern Europe? In short, it is the last refuge of a living European tradition. It is the place where the unbroken, centuries-long line of a healthy national development has been able to survive in the consciousness of the people. If there is a place in Europe where all the golden eras of our civilization still can be felt, even merging with the current technological age and giving ground for a hope that new achievements — new *European* achievements — can be made, untainted by destructive impulses of Leftist liberalism, it is Eastern Europe, having survived the Communist years and showing promise of surviving even more vicious strains of the same ideology.

The greatest asset of nationalism in Eastern Europe is its people's extant connection with their soil. While in the West, large scale urbanization — which simply means the globalization of the homeland — has cut many people off from a personal, private relationship with their homeland. This creates the perfect foundation for a multiculturalism of rootless individuals from every corner of the globe. But this process has been much slower and less catastrophic in Eastern Europe. In the cultural, economic, and psychological sphere, Eastern Europe keeps celebrating the local.

Accordingly, nationalists in Eastern Europe usually place a great emphasis on the preservation and expansion of local economies as opposed to globalization, traditional villages as opposed to urban conglomerates, natural wilderness as opposed to industrial landscapes. The failure of the West to preserve this traditional environment, which frankly is a precondition for the continuation of a nation and its culture, is seen as both a cause and a consequence of the triumph of liberalism, that has led to whole nations being cut off from their roots.

Nationalists in these countries understand that a nation and its culture are born out of its surroundings. Our landscape and climate have shaped us for generations into what we are. There can be no Estonian culture without the untouched solitude of vast forests, wetlands, and the long Baltic coastline, as there can be no Romanian culture without the purity and magnificence of the Carpathian Mountains. An unbroken link to the ancestors of the living is preserved in nature. Thus, the necessity of its protection amounts to the urgency of securing the survival of the whole nation.

Eastern Europe, therefore, has maintained all the cultural and ecological means for a successful national reawakening at its disposal. It has become something of a vault for the West and all European peoples around the world, taking the deeper components of European culture under its protection and keeping them safe for a future restoration of all European ethnostates while the West temporarily continues its downfall. It is a responsibility that many Eastern European nationalists increasingly realize and accept.

By far the greatest immediate problem for the survival of Europeans in both the East and the West lies in demographics. Almost every white ethnic group in the world has a birth rate below replacement. In the West, the only solution offered by liberal politicians is immigration from non-European countries. Obviously if we are talking about the survival of *Europeans,* this is no solution at all and indeed worsens the situation. In the East that luckily lacks immigration, the demographic problem is often more visible but not necessarily greater compared to the West.

Low birth rates can be tackled and ultimately reversed by nationalist demographic policies. For example, there are the policies proposed by the Conservative People's Party of Estonia (EKRE) that I helped to draft. First, parents would be rewarded with exemptions from income tax and extra retirement pay, which would increase with every child they raise. Second, if a young family is stuck in debt buying a home, the state would pay off one fourth of their mortgage for each child born. Third, the state must guarantee a place in kindergarten and school for each child, partly covering the educational costs. If young European children start to be valued on the governmental level, the continuation of our people will no longer be under a question mark.

The emergence of the youthful, energetic, and intellectual Alt Right in the West spells hope for the Eastern European nationalists too. It is a great sign that we are not alone protecting the last bastions of Western civilization. While our frontline against non-European invasion and liberal brainwashing runs across the border of Hungary, for us the Alt Right are like guerrillas fighting in enemy-occupied territories. We are fighting for the survival of all Europeans, and no part of the white world can hope to survive on its own.

Thus the crucial connection developing between the Alt Right and nationalists in Eastern Europe has to flow in both directions. The part of Europe where integral nationalism survives can profit from the very existence of the Alt Right. Its experience, insight, and strategies in fighting the destructive globalist ideology will sooner or later prove useful, as all European nationalists are more or less waging the same cultural struggle. In this struggle, the Alt Right has stood up for European nationalism, and European nationalists will have to return the favor.

The fact that similar nationalist ideas are widespread throughout the West and poised to enter mainstream discussion and political power, provides an argument against the pro-Western politicians who argue that nationalism is an impediment to winning favors in the international scene. With nationalism rising all over the globe, their own logic dictates that it is a force to be taken into account. And finally, the Alt Right will be the best ally one can hope for in the coming metapolitical Reconquista, in which Eastern Europe has to show the West the way back to its roots.

In a similar way, European nationalists of the globalist-free countries can help the Alt Right. Our insight into traditionalism and ethnonationalism can prove a valuable asset in the ongoing media war. But we can also build a safe hub for Alt Right ideas to be freely exchanged, polished, and mirrored back to the

West. Currently, the Alt Right enjoys positive publicity only in the Western media outlets of the geopolitically anti-Western countries such as Russia and Iran. In Eastern Europe, we look favorably on the Alt Right not because we regard it as a tool to weaken the West, but because we are fighting the same struggle.

European nationalism is built on the ethnonationalist principle of preserving every nation, the multitude of cultures endangered by globalist ideology. Europe already has rich cultural diversity, true diversity that has to be protected. In this sense, Eastern Europe is about to assume the role of a beacon of the light of Western civilization and national freedom, something that America never was. And if all fails and the West falls before the invaders, sparking civil wars in Europe, nationalists from the East are ready to come and help their brothers in the physical struggle.

Ethnonationalism does not mean revisiting the historical conflicts between different European nations. On the contrary, facing a civilizational threat from outside Europe, nationalists can unite under their common European identity and find peaceful ways to solve those conflicts of the past. If there is a place in the world where this is possible, it must be Eastern Europe. There are already signs of relaxation between historical enemies such as Hungarian and Romanian, Polish and Lithuanian nationalists.

While this has not been possible in the Ukrainian conflict, it must be noted that the Ukrainian nationalists are facing another civilizational threat from the East. Russian imperialism—as with all imperialisms—posits an antithesis to the ethnonationalist principle. If the nationalists in the West get similarly stuck in the post-World War II forced (and false) choice between only two geopolitical options, they will sooner or later experience a similar moment of disappointment as the Eastern European nationalists had after the fall of Communism.

In fact, Ukrainian nationalism has been a great energizer for all Eastern European nationalists. Although Ukraine has not yet had a nationalist government, the ongoing conflict and continuing corruption of their rulers is contributing to the steady rise of nationalism within the country. It is encouraged by strong connections between Ukrainian and other Eastern European nationalists, the strongest connections of which come in the form of many volunteers from the Baltic countries, Sweden, Croatia, and other places who have risked their lives for the freedom of a fellow European nation. Among them, even, is a number of true Russian nationalists.

Ethnonationalism emphasizes saving every nation, including those that have no independent countries. Who are the most traditional peoples in the most traditional part of Europe? Perhaps the Finno-Ugric nations who live in Russia, who lack any political power for self-expression but have preserved their connection with the soil to the fullest, often still professing their ancient religion, similar to that of the ancestors of all Europeans. With them, an invaluable part of the European heritage still survives. If they are able to survive in spite of Russian imperialism, they can provide a connection to ancient European roots and therefore to a reawakening.

A reawakened Europe must be built in its most fundamental level on nationalism and nothing else. Even in the religious sphere, nationalism implies a most basic form of religion, the cult of ancestors. This has to be a 21st-century nationalism, and therefore different from the nationalisms of the previous centuries, but in its basis still the same. The nationalism of the 21st century is exactly what the Alt Right has to offer, with its futuristic occult meme magic, overcoming all liberal predispositions since the French Revolution and even riding the tiger of Europe's seeming downfall.

In this new Europe, the cultural centers of the West might move East, to Budapest, Warsaw, and Tallinn, rather than New York, Hollywood, or Jerusalem. Mastering its demographic processes rather than leaving them in the hands of liberals, the new Europe will actually be able to economically and culturally compete with the rest of the world. Only then can we realize our destiny, exploring the galaxy and penetrating the secrets of subatomic reality. In the end, a prerequisite for European greatness is the physical and cultural survival of its nations.

Similarly, an affection for the local and care for nature must prevail in the new Europe. With the comforts provided by technological advancement, there is less and less need for urbanization. Accordingly, the Hungarian government's recent program of building a network of narrow-gauge railways that emphasize life in the countryside—and from which no multinational corporation has anything to gain—is actually one of the most Alt-Right tasks ever developed by a country in the 21st century.

Having survived Communism and showing strong resistance to liberalism, Eastern Europe is the greatest hope for a reawakening in the white world. It needs the Alt Right to uphold the idea of nationalism in the West and can provide it with a safe space more or less free from globalist ideology. What survives in Eastern Europe and has to be resparked in the West is the principle of ethnonationalism: protection of the true diversity of mankind in both the biological and cultural sense. This principle can be used to bring forth a new Europe after the fall of the current liberal system, a new Europe that can last at least as long as the old one did.

Counter-Currents, September 8, 2016

WHAT THE ALT RIGHT ISN'T

PATRICK LE BRUN

In the early days of GRECE, the think tank of the *Nouvelle Droite* (New Right), which included such luminaries as Alain de Benoist and Pierre Vial, it was considered necessary to make a clean break with the failures of the past, totems that many on the Right still clung to. This new generation of writers, mostly in their 20s during the cultural revolution of '68, felt that nostalgia for a lost cause—and there were several—stood in the way of their values finding political and cultural support from the majority of their countryman. This left a void which the Left exploited without hesitation or limit.

Moving on is so hard, when the memories are so sublime.

In essays and pamphlets, the writers of GRECE systematically wrote *what they were not,* in order to clarify what they were still in the process of becoming. They were *not* seeking a return to monarchy, Vichy, pre-Vatican II Ultramontanism, classical liberalism, etc. At first glance, many Rightists asked themselves, "Then what is left?" The fact that this was such a clean break and a fresh start, many were left to realize that they had lost touch with the essence of what their revered ancestors were fighting for.

The Alt Right exists as a clean break in the American Right as well. At its intellectual heights it borrows heavily from the *Nouvelle Droite*, but familiarity with that school of thought is not necessary for productive action in the American struggle. However, this fresh start is well overdue. Today is a time to act, not simply for a set of values, but for our very survival as a people. Our genocide has been programmed into the system, and the political dead-ends of the far Right and the kosher poltergeists that attract truth seekers have been laid out before our path like so many trap doors. It is time to innovate or die.

Now at this late hour, the Alt Right has emerged. The time has come to clarify what the Alt Right is *not* in the American context. Many have rallied to this banner after reaching one of the following dead ends, and some do not realize yet to what extent they must transcend that earlier concern in order to "secure the existence of our people and a future for white children." This article seeks to create an understanding as to how these other schools of thought understand better than the mainstream narrative what is wrong with our society, but they fall short of providing a holistic view or a manageable solution.

1. NOT FIGHTING FOR THE ONE TRUE FAITH

The *Ecclesia Dei*, the *Ummah*, and the "Universal Lodge" of the Mason have this one thing in common, the fatherhood of God and the Brotherhood of Man. This is a chimera. A healthy, racially conscious nation needs spiritual values, but this works at cross purposes if that spirituality is universalist or if sectarianism dissolves national unity.

Some have tried to reshape the universalism in Christianity by taking three verses out of context in the hopes of making racial nationalism excusable. This approach to Biblical exegesis is not so different from the young earth creationist approach to geology . . . and its conclusions are just as convincing.

There are some writers and activists who apply the "One True Faith" approach to Roman Catholicism and Orthodoxy. Men like E. Michael Jones and Father M. Raphael Johnson can be called fellow travelers, to adopt the Communist terminology, but the primacy of their religious commitments diverts them from the primary goals of the Alt Right.

In the end, those fighting to impose the "One True Faith" do not care if we survive as a people. Ask any true believers and they will tell you that they have more in common with their co-religionist from the Congo than with a professor at MIT. The saddest thing is, sometimes it's true.

2. NOT LOBBYING FOR THE INTERESTS OF THE BOURGEOISIE

Gavin McInnes thinks that "revering the entrepreneur," not masturbating, and wearing a suit three times a week will stop the destruction of our civilization. Race-mixing and Jewish media-political-financial dominance are not the problem.

Take a copy of *Forbes* magazine to your nearest welfare office and look over the list of richest individuals and highest paid CEOs. You will notice a lighter tone of skin on *makers* than on *takers*. This leads many well-meaning white people to conclude that defending the policies that make the efforts of those people in *Forbes* magazine easier (lowering trade barriers, eliminating regulatory oversight, and weakening unions, etc.) will unleash the greatness of our race. It is "Us or Them," and we look a lot more like the CEOs than the welfare queens.

Some are even so foolish enough to believe that the handful of darker faces found at the top of corporate America are evidence that excellence is open to everyone. It is only a matter of culture and free will, rather than innate genetic differences, that keeps the country club white and the ghetto black.

The fact is more white people today are getting shafted by globalization than are reaping benefits. The pressures of the "free market" are preying upon the white family. As Pierre Vial says, "the liberty promised by the American Free Marketers is nothing but the liberty of the fox to roam the henhouse." This beast is eating our children.[1]

3. NOT WISHING FOR THE STATE TO DISAPPEAR

Contrary to popular myth, there is no correlation between wishing for the fall and the ability to impose Order after the fall.

A close cousin of the previous dead end is the hope for the end of the state. There are two camps when it comes to how this will be accomplished: the libertarians believe that voting can make the state disappear; the self-proclaimed "patriots" believe that the entire global system will collapse, usually due to a lack of gold. Whether they expect a popular mood swing or an apocalyptic reckoning, the problems that are at the root of their attitudes are evident to every white person in the US.

The front-line employees of the state are most often underqualified black women. The military, once a testing ground for

---

[1] Alain de Benoist has referred to immigrants as "the reserve army of capitalism" which have been unleashed upon the native working class.

cutting edge weaponry, is now a testing ground for Cultural Marxist social theories. The stability of the global economy seems to be based on Americans consuming things and the rest of the world making things, an obviously unsustainable system. The federally subsidized universities, apart from propagating insanity, leave most of their students with less promising futures than a welding apprenticeship would.

It is only natural that so many white men would conclude that *"The state is the problem."* It speaks volumes about the US government's pathetic performance that so many of its citizens cannot even conceive of a state that enables its citizens to have a better future than can be scraped out of the hidden valleys of northern Idaho. The US government is so bad in their eyes, they cannot even conjure an imaginary state capable of worthwhile contributions to the society it serves.

However, when we coldly examine these libertarians, especially the patriot survivalists, we realize that they are making a virtue of white flight. They take white flight almost to its logical conclusion, beyond the suburbs but just before the final white family is run down by Soros-funded colored mobs.

Our enemies can only be exiled and brought to heel by a strong state. Our future as a people, a collective future that still gives enough leeway to the individual to allow genius to flourish, can only be guaranteed by a White Nationalist state. And of course, it is only a white state, not a soulless corporation or a mixed-race state, which will colonize space.

4. NOT RESTORING THE CONSTITUTION

Patriots and libertarians, as well as quite a few middle-class whites employed in the private sector, have concluded that a strict reading of the US constitution is all that is needed to set things right. The excesses of the Cultural Marxists are only possible through a loose reading of the constitution. The constitution did help a liberty-loving white nation's rise to be the world's greatest superpower. The constitution allowed whites with a diversity of faiths, political convictions, and professions, that could not be contained in a single European country, to work together to maintain the defense necessary for independence and the commercial system necessary for prosperity. The Bill of Rights gave individuals protections from tyranny not seen since antiquity, and perhaps unsurpassed in all history. This unprecedented liberty unleashed the ambitions of white men to conquer an entire continent in a single century. America still stands out as a land of opportunity to denizens of developing countries. When these people sneak into Europe it is to get welfare; when they sneak into America it is to work hard and make their fortune.

It is not hard to understand why so many white Americans believe that if the same recipe is used, the meal will taste the same. Unfortunately, ingredients matter. The constitution, as some of the Founders pointed out in the Federalist Papers, assumed a common culture and common morality. This cannot be willed back into existence. Furthermore, the constitution and the high trust, virtuous society that made it possible were manifestations of white cultural traits. Restoring the constitution can be considered after a nice white country is reestablished (hopefully incorporating the lessons of America's failed racial experiments). But it cannot be the first step towards restoring the liberty, prosperity, and order appreciated by the white founding stock of the US.

5. NOT PRETENDING "THE SOUTH WILL RISE AGAIN"

The American southeast, despite large rivers and some small mountain ranges, is a land without natural borders.

North is a direction; the South is a place, a culture, and a source of pride. It is no surprise that many descendants of the heroic soldiers of the South cherish the memory of their ancestors. This strain of Albion's seed, the traditionalists, are far less culpable than their Northern cousins, the moralists, in allowing the United States to be subverted by the eternal enemy of our people. The culture distorters who control the media of the US have done all they could to discredit the Southerner, both the aristocratic and down-and-out archetypes. When these proud and demonized Southerners observe the recent evils of the Federal government noted above, the same Federal government that made war upon their ancestors, it is no surprise that many would dream of a renewed separatist struggle.

The Romantic in each of us can conclude that the South has everything it needs for such a struggle; the classicists, however, realize there is more to be desired. The South has the bulk of US mainland and retrievable deep-sea oil. Most American refinery capacity and infrastructure are in the South. The South also has an incredibly long border with the rest of the US that does not benefit from serious geographical impediments to invasion. There is no "rump South" with defensible borders that can be retreated to, but there are plenty of mountain refuges where Southerners could make another last stand. There is not a single planner in the Pentagon who would look at this and accept a peaceful separation that would result in such a sovereign country to be placed in a newly created soft underbelly. National liberation struggles with imperial powers only succeed when there is an asymmetrical interest[2] in changing the *status quo* between the colonizer and the colonized.

Though the South is the most economically dynamic and is the fastest growing region, this is thanks to internal migration of highly educated whites and Asians who do not share a desire for Southern separatism. Furthermore, about 1 in 4 Southerners are Black. In the age of guerilla warfare and highly propagated small arms, this large a population will not accept leaving the US, which will make even a peaceful separation of the South impossible.

The struggle to preserve a future for our people will be an all or nothing struggle. The empire cannot allow for a separate peace, and it certainly won't be based on reverence for a political economy that was dysgenic and anti-nationalist.

---

[2] Asymmetric Interest Theory developed out of Game Theory experiments. When one party views a point of negotiation as a priority and the other party views it as contingent on more important priorities being met, there is an asymmetry of interest. As a result, when the first party makes the second party's highest priorities impossible to achieve without surrendering on first party's priority, the first party is at an advantage.

6. NOT REPEATING THE LIE OF "JUDEO-CHRISTIAN" CIVILIZATION

After the attacks of September 11th, as Americans looked for allies who could help make sense of radical Islam, the organized Jewish community stepped forward. If jihadists were attacking both of us, we must have something in common. The *Shabbos goy*, Victor Davis Hanson, explained to us that the foundations of Western civilization were Athens, Rome, and Jerusalem. More recently, Gavin McInnes is attempting to redefine the Alt Right as "Western Cultural Chauvinism." Under normal circumstances, an alignment of interests is the best foundation for an alliance. Unfortunately, there is nothing normal about Jewish cultural norms. When any element of the organized Jewish community is the counterparty in an agreement, like the fable of the frog and the scorpion, the compulsion towards betrayal, even against allies, is irresistible for the Jew.

Unless they live in a handful of major cities, most Americans only know two Jews intimately, Moses and Seinfeld. In school, American history books start with the Pilgrims. In Church, Sunday school history lessons end in first-century Palestine. Most Americans lack the opportunity to be red-pilled through personal interactions with Jews and lack the historical/cultural formation to understand the long history of this indissoluble node and its parasitic relationship with Europe's Third Estate.[3]

---

[3] The relationship between Jews and their European host populations varied by estate/caste, falling into essentially four categories of bilateral economic relationships. There was no economic, ideological, or governmental relationship between Jews and the clergy, with a handful of exceptional debates or investigations carried out with the Second Estate into Jews masquerading as Christians. The Second Estate had a largely positive relationship with Jews because they were guaranteed friendly rates to borrow money (a necessity in the long cycles between harvests, then as now), access to an international trade network, a source of intelligence, and the Medieval form of diplomatic back channels. The fixed, guaranteed interest rate was a loss leader, allowing access to black market lending to the Christian peasants, merchants, and artisans of the Third Estate. The fourth and worst bilateral relations began in the Polish-Lithuanian Commonwealth

Leaving the history lessons aside, simply looking at the "Judeo-Christian" alliance of the last 15 years should make it abundantly clear that such an alliance is a non-starter and that our allegedly common civilization is not enough to ensure mutual concern. It requires just a small amount of political maturity to understand the one-two punch of the Jewish Left, which oversees our invasion and cultural demoralization, and the Jewish Right, which has created an environment of Christian genocide in the Levant, emboldened a brand of jihadism more focused on attacking the West rather than Israel, and created the push factors of the so-called "refugee crisis." If Jews are white, as a ruling elite that arose from within white civilization, why are there no brakes on their material greed? The need for order and sustainability, which would be compelling to any organic elite that is linked to its subjects through bonds of race and civilization, was definitely not guiding the criminal banksters who knowingly crashed the global economy. While a handful of egregious crimes committed by Jews have been prosecuted, the Jewish parasitic elites who created the systemic bribery, theft, and destruction of that defines the European and American economies have not been brought to justice.

George Lincoln Rockwell, when describing the principles of civilization, stated: "Civilization is built because I am willing to give up something for my family, and the family is willing to give up something in order to have the town succeed, and the town is willing to give up something so that the state can be in business, and the state is willing to give up something so that the nation can succeed. Self-sacrifice is the first principle of civilization." Whether we are looking at the degenerate popular media and culture, the rolls of soldiers lost in Iraq and Afghanistan, or the nearly nonexistent prosecutorial response to criminal Jewish banksters following the economic crisis, it is clear that the overwhelming contribution of the Jewish community to Western civilization is not as a foundational component but as a parasitic squatter that threatens catastrophic collapse.

---

where the nobles hired the Jews to act as tax farmers and mid-level government administrators over the Third Estate.

This "not" may be the most important to enumerate. The most likely subversion of the Alt Right will come in the form of well-funded, well-organized philo-Semitic media outlets and 501(c)(4) advocacy organizations. The kosher media will be a partner in defining the Alt Right in the mind of the masses. Remember that the Tea Party was a genuine grass roots movement that largely grew as a continuation of the Ron Paul campaign. FreedomWorks was created by the Koch Brothers and funded by their fellow oligarchs to rein in this movement. They made very generous grants to local Tea Party groups as long as they agreed not to criticize neocon war-mongering, mass immigration, or the Federal Reserve. Within a year they were successful. Glenn Beck and the Zionist-bankrolled Pastor Hagee started national networks and put on large spectacles to divert energy of Tea Party sympathizers toward the neocon agenda. The 2010 midterm election was the last time Tea Party has had an impact on government. If we are not aware of this risk, our brief moment in the sun will be followed by a decade in the darkness.

7. NOT STARTING WITH REVISIONISM

Since we are not shying away from criticizing the role of Jews in destroying Western civilization, why not snap people out of their slumber by enumerating all the lies of kosher historiography and Jewish criminality? Creating a nice, white country is a 21st-century political challenge, not a 20th-century historical debate. For some readers, exposure to historical revisionism was a major moment in their political awakening. Discovering a lie so big fills one with a missionary zeal to spread the truth. Attacking a metapolitical foundation for the current order seems like the linchpin that, once pulled, will destroy the entire psychological control mechanism put in place by the political and media elite.

Understand that in the life cycle of revolutionary movements, different types of people join at different stages. Far fewer people will have the ears to hear something that contradicts their beliefs, but they are concerned about the "kitchen table issues" that the kosher multicultural regime fails to address. For many new arrivals, revisionism may be a metaphorical advanced degree that they can shoot for once their prerequisites are finished, but an encounter with a wild-eyed revisionist trying to "wake them up" at their first real world meeting with Alt Rightists would send them packing. At the same time, it is clear that the sensibilities of Millennials, on both sides of this issue, are different than that of their predecessors.

Many of our last-minute supporters who will take us over the top may never have the interest or capacity to understand the complexities of Revisionism. But rest assured, after the revolution, there will be a "Mark Weber Chair of Modern History" at Harvard, and Eric Hunt will be an executive producer at the History Channel.

8. NOT DIVERTED BY THE BATTLE OF THE SEXES

Our people are failing to reproduce at replacement levels in most historically white countries; divorce and degeneracy are commonplace and celebrated, respectively. In school underqualified teachers prefer to force parents to drug young boys into submission rather than deal with the aggressive, energetic nature of these boys.[4] Young men fall prey to nonmarket strategies in the workplace, often blindsided by female and homosexual colleagues who outclass them in EQ when productivity and meritocracy is sandbagged by egalitarian Federal regulations and social sanctions that stigmatize the "privileged" heterosexual white males. Shockingly, 15% of men in their early 20s have not had a single sexual partner since turning 18, mostly "InCels" (Involuntary Celibates).[5] For other young men first dates have become easier than ever thanks to dating apps, but meaningful relationships are like a sip of water to Tantalus. College campuses are in the grip of a new post-Christian puritanism that decries "rape culture" and claims that *all men* are potential rapists who must be reined in, a rather Calvinist view of the masculine soul.

---

[4] According to the CDC's National Center for Health Statistics, 14.1% of boys and 6.2% of girls aged 5–17 were diagnosed with ADHD between 2012–2014.

[5] Archives of Sexual Behavior, August 2016: "Sexual Inactivity During Young Adulthood Is More Common Among U.S. Millennials and iGen: Age, Period, and Cohort Effects on Having No Sexual Partners After Age 18."

While many of the previously mentioned problems affect on-ly a few, there is a universal character to these problems as all of us came from a union of a man and woman, and all of us have a need for emotional companionship. These basics have been chal-lenged in the past when societies have been decimated by fam-ine or pandemic, or when peoples have been brutalized by war and oppression, but never have these basic needs been so threat-ened by a decadence that affects not just the idle rich, as in times past, but the entire society.

There are many in the Manosphere, who stay strictly within their own expertise (divorce lawyers, counselors, economists, fitness trainers, nutritionists, martial artists, etc.) and who make valuable contributions. There are many positive testimonies of well-meaning men who were told to "give [women] what [they say] they want and they'll be happy" but through a pro-social application of lessons from the Manosphere have created health-ier marriages, such as *Daily Shoah* contributor Hateful Heretic.[6]

There are essentially three groups which seek to reach "the logical conclusion" in their response to these social pathologies. Two of them are nihilists, Pick Up Artists (PUA) and Men Going Their Own Way (MGTOW). The third, self-proclaimed tradi-tionalists, seeks to adopt Satmar-style social norms and fertility levels in order to resolve the demographic crisis.

PUAs pumping and dumping women will never help us rec-reate a nice white country. Instead they have embraced the Brazilification of sexual norms and identity as a kind of protec-tive shell against the coming pain of the Brazilification of our racial demographics. There have been quite a few MGTOW in history deserving of respect. The Hindu Sadhus, Buddha and his Arhats, and the Desert Fathers come to mind. Unfortunately, the internet subculture of MGTOW lack the many of their qualities. Like the PUAs, they are emotionally devastated by the social pathologies related to gender and sexuality that are so common in this age, but their risk aversion and poor social skills lead them to sequester themselves from any attempt at creating a lov-ing family . . . sadly, for many of them, there is no model to fol-

---

[6] Fash the Nation, Week 51; 1h06m.

low from their personal lives, and, if there was, they lack the finesse to understand the interpersonal dynamics that led to success.

The final group is the most sympathetic as they have not given up on the white race and/or Western civilization. However, there are three errors in their approach. Most importantly, when they reject the positive aspects of the contribution of white women to public life in Europe and America, they are abandoning a distinguishing characteristic of the white race. Also, every successful revolution and national liberation movement of the modern era so greatly benefitted from the active participation of women in every aspect of struggle (propaganda, logistics, political organizing, espionage, armed struggle, etc.) that they were indispensable. Finally, it assumes a zero-sum game between including women whose greatest ambition and aptitude is to raise a large family and including those women whose ambitions, aptitudes, age, and fertility guide them toward every other field known to man.

The American experience has led many in our movement to believe that the feminine soul is essentially anti-nationalist and anti-traditionalist. Restricting this rebuttal to a single counter-example, in France women's suffrage did not come until 1945. It was actively opposed by the socialists and radicals of the Third Republic who feared that women would listen to the political advice of their priests and would support patriarchal leaders. In the Fifth Republic, when women started voting at the same rate as men, there was not a Left-wing government until 1981 (which was elected with only 39% of the female vote). Today, the National Front enjoys proportionally more support from women than from men. So, if there is a problem, it is not women or feminism but rather the American cultural expectations of women and American expressions of feminism.

If the problem is cultural and not biological, then perhaps we should look to the media for a culprit. The media is not notable for being in the hands of women; the media is notable for being 90% in the hands of six Jewish families plus Rupert Murdoch. Someone is standing in the way of our nice white country but it is not women . . . it is the organized Jewish community.

CONCLUSION

While articles like this have a certain impact on the thinking of a small number of people within the movement, ultimately, it is those who speak in poetry rather than prose who have the broadest impact. As RamzPaul stated, following the Bastille Day attack in Nice, "White Nationalism is about our need for a home, a home of our own." All of these movements that the Alt Right is *not*—whether they are centuries old or are simply YouTube channels that have been around a couple years—diagnose some of the problems of our civilizational and racial decline, but none of them have the whole story or the proper prognosis.

White people need living spaces separate from the other races to survive and thrive. Jews of all political stripes are a parasitic element that will stand in the way of that goal. Achieving these goals requires a broad movement that seeks total victory, and the resulting peace and order will only be maintained by a strong state. Our historic religious commitments, enlightenment ideals, and family values will be reinterpreted through the lens of racial survival . . . we are free to keep what works and discard what doesn't work well with this goal.

We are also free to maintain our commitments to these Dead Ends that lie outside the Alt Right, but we do so at the peril of securing the existence of our people and a future for white children. What could be more important than that?

Counter-Currents, October 7, 2016

THE CASTE SYSTEM OF
THE ALT RIGHT

MICHAEL BELL

Over the last few months there has been quite a bit of hubbub within the Alt Right movement over who exactly can be counted among our ranks and who can credibly be representing us to the public. This discussion has become particularly prominent in our circles since Hillary gave her lackluster speech on our movement and warned everyone about the dangers of our cartoon frog. It has also been understandably alarming to some that the media seems to be painting the gay Jew Milo Yiannopoulos as one of our spokesmen.

Greg Johnson of *Counter-Currents* has asserted that the Alt Right is "a broad umbrella term for ideological tendencies that reject mainstream American conservatism." He contends, however, that White Nationalists need to give it a more concrete identity by making it *our* movement: "the Alternative Right means White Nationalism — or it means nothing at all . . . go forth into battle and make this concept of the Alternative Right the dominant one."

Andrew Anglin of *The Daily Stormer* fame agrees in his article "A Normie's Guide to the Alt Right": "The short story is that although the term could refer to a lot of different people saying a lot of different things, the people that it is being used to refer to by the media — Trump-supporting white racial advocates who engage in trolling and other activism on the internet — are the core of the movement, with any other groups and figures being peripheral." As far as fulfilling Greg Johnson's objective, Anglin argues that we are already on the verge of reaching that consensus.

Even from a non-White Nationalist corner of the Alt Right, it is agreed that the Alt Right is a broad ideological gathering but that the core is white Identity. Vox Day stated in an interview with Stefan Molyneux that ". . . what the Alt Right is at its core is we are the descendants of those who were read out of the conservative movement . . . mostly due to an unwillingness to defer to the conservative movement's attempt to ingratiate itself with the industrial mil complex, and the neoconservatives, and the Bush administration." He states that our ideological ancestors are "the John Birch Society, of Sam Francis, of Pat Buchanan . . . of everyone from John Derbyshire to Ann Coulter." He leaves out some very important thinkers, but still ultimately concludes that "The Alt Right takes an Identity approach to the world . . . which 95% of the world takes. . . . White Americans are beginning to learn that they have to play the game (of identity politics) just like everybody else." Vox is not even white, yet he understands our plight and appears to sympathize with our cause while he himself focuses on combating Social Justice Warrior agendas.

Taking these viewpoints into consideration, my own view is this:

❖ The Alt Right is a movement consisting of many different viewpoints, all of which agree that the mainstream conservative doctrines of free trade, open-door immigration, multiculturalism, and interventionist wars in the Middle East are net negatives.

❖ The Alt Right traces its ideological origins back to the more nationalistic conservative ideologues who were purged from the mainstream conservative movement by Bill Buckley, as well as to men like Kevin MacDonald, William Pierce, George Lincoln Rockwell, Jared Taylor, and other old-school White Nationalists. I would even argue that Adolf Hitler deserves to be on this list, which I'm sure will make some of the "Alt Lite" folks cringe. One also cannot discount philosophers like Julius Evola, Oswald Spengler, and Francis Parker Yockey.

❖ The Alt Right needs to be turned 100% into a vehicle for *our* message. Lawrence Murray did a good job of outlining this message in his article "The Fight for the

Alt Right: The Rising Tide of Ideological Autism Against Big Tent-Supremacy" (below). To summarize: Human equality is a myth; our world is tribal; the white tribe is being suppressed in its own nations; men and women are different; freedom is a responsibility and not a right; democracy ought to be of limited form or replaced entirely; and the Jews exercise a negative influence on our societies, which they do out of some biological impulse. To this I would add Andrew Anglin's "Cultural Normalization, Common-Sense Economics, and White Countries for White People."

❖ While we pursue our goal of fully occupying the helm of the Alt Right, we must recognize that those who are not fully on board with *all* of our principles can nonetheless be considered a part of the Alt Right provided they aid us in our efforts and do not work to contradict us. Many of these types can eventually be turned into full White Nationalists anyway, as their views are only a few inches away from ours. To quote Lawrence Murray, "The big tent is worth preserving to persevere against our common enemies, for our struggle is revolutionary."

The fourth point leads us into the main purpose of my article. To quote Anglin again: "The Alt Right is a 'mass movement' in the truest possible sense of the term, a type of mass-movement that could only exist on the internet, where everyone's voice is as loud as they are able to make it. In the world of the internet, top-down hierarchy can only be based on the value, or perceived value, of someone's ideas."

I have taken it upon myself to delineate this hierarchy, as I have always had a predisposition toward putting things into categories since I was barely able to speak. I shall call it . . . the Caste System of Alt Righteousness. Our race has a history of creating caste-based societies, after all (though on a much grander scale).

This caste system is based on the idea that full-on White Nationalists who embrace all of Murray's and Anglin's principles represent the highest peak, which descends downward into castes of people who embrace less radical narratives. However, like an initiatic society, the system is meritocratic; one can ascend to the heights as they begin to embrace more principles of our worldview.

STRUCTURE

White Nationalists must occupy the helm of this pyramid, as we deal in the ultimate truths when it comes to race, politics, economics, and culture. We tackle the "meta" stuff, whereas the lesser Alt Rightists go after the more immediate things. In the same light, the higher priestly castes of ancient societies tackled the *meta*-physical questions while the other castes dealt primarily with the physical.

The very existence of Western civilization, which most of the Alt Right purports to champion, hinges on the biologically-distinct white race that created it as a natural consequence of its unique mental and spiritual impulses. The deep, dark level of decadence the West has descended to is largely because of the influence of Jews, who have created their various movements and causes to undermine our foundations as a result of their own unique mental and spiritual characteristics. Since the Alt Right wishes to remedy the modern-day symptoms of the Jewish disease within white societies to save them, it only follows that those groups who promote white advocacy and discuss the Jewish question are fit to lead the movement.

THE TOP TIER

In this top-tier, Brahmin level of Alt Righteousness, I would include the following groups, websites, and individuals. Forgive me if I have left any big players out:

Counter-Currents, The Right Stuff, The Daily Stormer, David Duke (who probably uses the word "Jews" more than he uses the word "the"), Kevin MacDonald, weev, Millennial Woes, Red Ice Radio, Evalion (who focused more on naming the Jew than White Nationalism, and who is apparently part Amerindian), Murdoch Murdoch, the *Occidental Observer,* Uncuck the Right (now known as Walt Bismarck), and older-school websites like

National Vanguard and *Stormfront*. All of them—whether in the form of print, videos, or even music—argue that whites are a distinct socio-biological entity that has a right to its own exclusive set of homelands and cultures, and that Jews are a distinctly different group that works to undermine our very existence.

SECOND TIER

Below this rank of ultimate bro-tier, I would place all of those groups and individuals who address racial realism and promote white advocacy, but who for whatever reason choose not to cover the Jews or who adopt a soft position on them. These are the guys who you respect and love (at least I do), but to whom you say "Bro . . . c'mon . . . are you serious?" It's like when your brother is a good-looking dude but chooses to date an ugly chick way below his league. You simply don't understand it, and you feel disdainful towards him, but you still love and respect him because he *is* your brother, and you've shared so much of your life together. In this rank I would include the following: Jared Taylor and *American Renaissance*, Richard Spencer and *Radix Journal*, and *VDare*.

Guys, c'mon now. The anti-white narrative comes from Cultural Marxism, which comes from the schools of Critical Theory and Cultural Anthropology; the former comes from the Jewish intellectuals Marcuse, Adorno, Horkheimer, etc., and the latter comes from the Jew Franz Boas. Their theories and books were disseminated by other Jews in academia, and their educational programs were funded by Jewish money. The Jewish intellectuals of Critical Theory were influenced by the coked-out pervert Jew Sigmund Freud and the out-of-touch-with-reality Jew Karl Marx. Karl Marx was largely influenced by the teachings of the Jew Moses Hess. The Jews at large have developed an evolutionary mechanism wherein they seek to undermine the cohesion of other ethnicities and societies for their own benefit, and many times they do this without even realizing what they are doing. I know that *post hoc ergo proctor hoc* is a logical fallacy . . . but guys . . . c'mon now. To quote a scene from *Family Guy* where Lois attends a skinhead meeting: "No but seriously, the Jews are bad."

THIRD TIER

Third from the top, I would place those Alt Righters who acknowledge the greatness of Western Civilization and address the dangers of non-white immigration without being overtly pro-white. These are the ones who will openly condemn non-Western cultures as being backward or deficient, or who stress the impracticality of Third-World immigration into the West, but who don't walk the next five inches into discussing race. Of course, they will on occasion acknowledge that whites built Western Civilization and America and that "white privilege" is a false concept. They are the civic nationalists, paleocons, and even libertarians. I feel that they aren't totally outside the spectrum of the Alt Right because they argue against many of the Left's most sacred cows and earn its revulsion as a result. They also serve as a possible entry point into the Alt Right. A member of my own family has stepped through the gateway of places like *TakiMag* only to end up at the beautiful floating city of White Nationalism. He now listens to Red Ice Radio and *The Daily Shoah* and reads *VDare*, and mind you, this was a man who used to tell me to calm down at age 14 because my views were too "virulent."

While it may seem counterintuitive to place the God Emperor in a spot underneath the apex caste, Donald Trump must go here. Let's be honest guys, he's a civic nationalist who means well, and who has been instrumental in the ascension of our movement to mainstream recognition, but he is no White Nationalist. Alongside him would be his priestess Ann Coulter, the former libertarian Stefan Molyneux, Pat Buchanan, *TakiMag*, Gavin McInnes, and RamzPaul.

RamzPaul has explicitly stated that he is not a White Nationalist, and he often mocks us for the amount of time we spend discussing the Jews and derides us as "1488ers." I suspect this is just because of some chip he has on his shoulder, or some desire to set himself apart from the larger group to feel cool. I cannot be sure. What I do know however, is that his videos are incredibly pro-white and anti-multiculturalism, he loves Europe, he argues that every people has a right to a homeland, he mocks Jews on occasion ("Let's call them *Finns*"), and he looks like British comedian Stephen Merchant (irrelevant, but I felt someone needed to bring it up). I love his videos, but because of his attitude, he gets the third caste.

Black Pidgeon Speaks is another excellent YouTuber who belongs in this caste, though he is borderline White Nationalist. His videos are very well-produced and accessible, covering topics such as gender differences, race, IQ, immigration, George Soros, globalism, and economics from a pro-Western perspective. I suspect that in his heart he actually belongs at the top, but for now he goes here. He has not overtly labeled himself as a White Nationalist or said anything against the Jews as a group.

FOURTH TIER

Beneath this caste I would place the people who work to combat the professional and intellectual thuggery of the Social Justice Warriors and very particular Leftist narratives, but who don't have any kind of overarching pro-white, pro-Western, or anti-Semitic ideology driving it.

Author and video-game designer Vox Day goes here. In fact, I would elect him the leader of this caste if such a thing existed. He was an outspoken supporter of Gamergate and organized the Rabid Puppies movement, which at its core sought to diminish the influence of Left-minded authors like George R. R. Martin over the science-fiction Hugo Awards. Rather than giving awards to books about transsexual vampires fighting against homophobic dragons, Day and his followers felt that the science fiction community should once again seek to emulate luminaries like J. R. R. Tolkien and Frank Herbert, who were essentially pro-Western and Right-wing in their thought. His book *SJWs Always Lie* is a must read for every member of the Alt Right. Of course, he is only part-white and does not explicitly push a pro-white or pro-Western agenda (though he comes close.)

This caste is also home to the Manosphere crowd. While many of them are outright degenerates who encourage nihilistic bed-hopping among white men who should be focusing their energies elsewhere, they still do a good job of dismantling the feminist narrative with their discussions of female psychology and other related topics. Encouraging men to take greater control over their lives and improving their minds and bodies is also commendable. I'm sure that some among them are actual White Nationalists, but the overarching Manosphere as a whole is not. It does become a problem though when some of them promote genocidal lifestyles like miscegenation on the one hand and completely disengaging from relationships with all women on the other. They should be accepted on a case-by-case basis.

It is within this caste that I would also place the Gamergate movement, for which I happen to have a lot of respect and appreciation. In my opinion, Gamergate was to the Alt Right what the Spanish Civil War was to World War II. It was the rehearsal for the much larger war to come. During the conflict between the Axis-backed Francoists and the Soviet-backed Republicans, the armies of Germany and the Soviet Union tested out their new arsenals and military capabilities to see how well they would fare in the coming conflict. The forces of the Right under Francisco Franco, with support from the Axis powers, managed to crush the Leftists and shield Spain from Leftist corruption for many years. Unlike the Axis Powers though, I believe Kek has ordained that we will win the coming war.

Gamergate began in 2013 when it became evident to members of the video gaming community that certain types of video games—that is, games that pushed forth some kind of social justice narrative—were being promoted by gaming journalists, largely as a result of sexual favors and other forms of nepotism between certain developers and journalists. What ensued was a mostly online struggle between the gaming community and its allies: Vox Day, Milo Yiannopoulos, some YouTube personalities like Internet Aristocrat (now known as Mister Metokur) and Thunderfoot, Adam Baldwin from *Firefly*, some non-Leftist game developers, Christina Hoff Sommers, the porn star Mercedes Carrera, and a legion of angry chaners; and the Leftist game journalists and their allies: the cucky white knight NFL player Chris Kluwe, Anita Sarkeesian of *Feminist Frequency* and her cucky boyfriend Jon McIntosh, the feminist tranny Brianna Wu, the treacherous Moot of 4chan, and the writers of *Law and Order: SVU*. Thousands of tweets were unleashed by both sides, several doxings occurred, threatening phone calls were issued, a bomb threat was made against a SXSW convention, and most

importantly, some of the earliest precursors of meme magic issued forth from the keyboards of righteous Gamergaters.

By the time it was all over the forces of the Left had a few
black eyes. The journalists were revealed to be nepotistic, corrupt liars who put ideology and personal connections above the
community they were supposed to represent. One could argue
that the same thing is happening to the mainstream media right
now thanks to Donald Trump and the Alt Right's memes. In the
grander scheme of things, the Left itself was revealed to be an
authoritarian enemy of fun, which up until then had been the
average gamer's view of the Right.

In summation, Gamergate was not a Right-wing Identitarian
movement by any stretch, though many future Alt Righters
probably took part in it. It was, however, a major victory of a
hitherto apolitical subculture against a Left-wing attempt at
subverting it. These tactics would later prove useful in the memetic war against cuckservatives, liberal and Jewish journalists,
and others who work to undermine white collective interests.

I would staff this caste further with anti-SJW YouTube personalities, a shining example of which is Mister Metokur. He has
made a number of hilarious podcasts and videos where he
mocks the hell out of black supremacists, Otherkin, feminists,
social networking websites, and other generic SJWs. His more
serious work has covered the Michelle Fields hoax, San Bernar-
dino, and Gamergate. He is not explicitly pro-white, though he
has appeared on Millennial Woes and, as I see it, deserves a
place under the Alt Right tent. For Alt Rightists who happen to
also be into the gaming subculture, I highly recommend his video "InternetAristocrat's #gamergate series."

To be sure, there are other similar YouTube figures that I've
probably left out . . . and no, I'm not including the "classic liberal" partial-Negro Sargon of Akkad, who feels entirely too cool to
accept any ideology that espouses racial collectivism. To his
credit though, he has given White Nationalists platforms on
which to speak and has also appeared on Millennial Woes a few
times.

Alex Jones's associate Paul Joseph Watson also belongs in this
caste. I strongly abhor him for arguing that Jews have nothing to

do with the decline of the West, and that people who argue such never provide any evidence to support their claims. This was an outright lie, and he had to know it was. However, his other YouTube videos are explicitly pro-Western, anti-SJW, anti-Left, anti-BLM, and anti-Hillary Clinton, among other good things. Apart from being informative, his videos are often funny as well.

This is probably a good place to stick the historical revisionists. They are not openly White Nationalist or pro-Western *per se*, but the information they disseminate helps to debunk the narrative about the Jews and their perpetual victimhood. Some individual revisionists are, of course, White Nationalists.

Million Dollar Extreme (MDE) belongs here as well. Much of their comedy is absurd and surreal, but a lot of it also mocks the main pillars of the establishment. On their Cartoon Network show *World Peace* and in some of Sam Hyde's stand-up routines, ridicule and mockery are heaped upon the idea of white privilege, the myth of systemic racism, anti-bullying programs, the Jews, and race-mixing, among various other tropes. Unless I am totally missing the mark, I'd say MDE even gives some nods to the Alt Right movement on their show:

> **SAM HYDE:** "Your new nickname is Moonman . . . Your secret name, which neither myself nor Nitrodubs will call you, will be . . . David Duke. (Sam then smirks at the screen.)

The whiny Jew Joe Bernstein of *Buzzfeed* sure seems to think that Sam is guilty of wrong-think.

To summarize:

1) The Helm—Anti-Semitic White Nationalists
2) Non-anti-Semitic White Nationalists
3) Western Chauvinists and Civic Nationalists
4) Anti-SJWs and opponents of the Leftist narrative

Some may argue that I spend entirely too much time discussing lower-caste phenomena. This is because I feel that most of my readers already know what they need to about the players in the upper castes.

TRIBUTARIES

There are some who vocally oppose White Nationalism and anti-Semitism and support liberal democracy, but who nonetheless manage to do some good works that inadvertently red-pill people into our Cause. They cannot be considered part of the Alt Right because their efforts would likely cause us harm in the long run. However, their roles as entry-points into more radical ways of thinking makes them worthy of note. Among them are Alex Jones, Steven Crowder, and Sargon of Akkad.

How could I leave out the man whom the media alleges to be our leader?

Milo Yiannopoulos is an open race-mixing homosexual and self-avowed Jew. He has tried to argue that our movement is not serious in its racialism or anti-Semitism, and that all we seek to do is troll people for the LOLz. He may have stolen money from a college fund he organized to help young white males. He is also pro-Israel. On the other hand, he has done quite a bit of good. His appearances on college campuses and televised interviews are legendary, often leaving his SJW opponents apoplectic with rage and incoherence; in one instance he even said that white people "invented all the good shit." During the Gamergate controversy he supplied the pro-gamers with evidence that the Leftist gaming journalists were conspiring as a whole to promote a certain narrative. The troll barrage that he incited against the allegedly-funny Leslie Jones will not be forgotten. On the *Dave Rubin Show* he unflinchingly admitted that Jews control Hollywood and the media. Many red pills have likely been issued upon white youth from Milo's hands. However, his personal identity, his attempt to distort what the Alt Right is about, and his overall aura of untrustworthiness relegate him to the outside of our movement. It honestly stings me a little to do this, as I find him immensely entertaining and appreciate the good things he has done. But I must consider the greater good, and he is entirely too risky of a figure to be representing us.

Radical Traditionalism as a school of thought needs to be addressed. One cannot delve into a hierarchy of Right-wing thinking without giving some coverage to this philosophy. To summarize, Radical Traditionalism holds the following views:

1. History is cyclical, and civilizations progress from a Golden Age of development and prosperity into a Dark Age of decadence and collapse.
2. Western Civilization is currently nearing the end of the Dark Age.
3. There is an ultimate metaphysical Reality which supersedes and makes possible the physical universe.
4. All major world religions offer a path to experiencing the ultimate Reality.
5. Ancient civilizations centered their cultures around metaphysical Truths and principles. As they strayed from their original doctrines, they began to slowly decay until finally collapsing.
6. Race is a tripartite concept: it is physical, mental, and spiritual.
7. Different kinds of races create different kinds of civilizations. If a civilization has a multiplicity of physical, mental, and spiritual types, it suffers an inner tension until one type prevails, or the collapse is hastened.
8. Individual races and civilizations are internally hierarchical: some individuals are meant to be priests and thinkers, others to be leaders and warriors, others to be merchants and tradesmen, and others to be laborers. This is organized via caste systems.
9. Men and women are physical manifestations of different cosmic principles that complement one another.

The philosophy is anti-democratic and anti-egalitarian, it argues that racial pluralism causes internal strife, and it holds that Indo-European religions offer an excellent pathway to higher enlightenment and overall balance in life. But the philosophy is not exclusively pro-white, pro-Western, or anti-Semitic, because people from every race can essentially follow it. You can be a Radical Traditionalist if you are a Germanic neo-pagan, an Italian Catholic monk, an Arab Sufi Muslim, a Lebanese Druze, a Tibetan Buddhist, an Indian Hindu, or even a Jew who studies Kabbalah.

As such, I opted not to include Radical Traditionalism in the Caste System of Alt Righteousness, even though I would say that I myself essentially subscribe to it as do many White Nationalists. It functions more like a world-historical outlook that can be complementary to the Alt Right while at the same time syncing up with the agendas of entirely different movements. There can be Radical Traditionalists who are ardent White Nationalists, just as there can be Muslim Radical Traditionalists who seek to destroy Western Civilization for the supremacy of their civilization. A member of the Sons of Odin who practices Asatru rituals and is willing to charge into a fray of Muslim rapists is a Radical Traditionalist, as is a devout member of Hezbollah who is willing to blow himself up to force Israeli soldiers into a retreat.

I would encourage Alt Rightists to read *Revolt Against the Modern World* by Julius Evola. Some notable Radical Traditionalist figures with a pro-white and pro-Western bent are Varg Vikernes and Troy Southgate; an excellent source of Radical Traditionalist literature is Arktos Media.

FINAL WORDS

My caste system is mostly intended as food for thought. I leave it to you to decide upon its usefulness. My main argument can be summarized thusly: the Alt Right should be made into a vehicle for White Nationalism, but should include those Right-wing and anti-Left thinkers and agitators who help us in combating our enemies and spreading the core concepts of our worldview, provided they do not work to undermine us. The caste system illustrates who is closest to fully promoting this worldview. When and if we all reach a consensus, there will no longer be a need for this system.

Counter-Currents, September 22, 2016

ALT RIGHT VS. NEW RIGHT

JOHN B. MORGAN IV

When I wrote this essay in February of 2017, I thought the Alt Right had potential. That potential was squandered, so today this should be read simply as a historical document born of a brief, unique moment in American history.

Today I want to talk about two schools of political thought that on the surface seem similar, but that are in fact quite different in a number of fundamental ways: namely the Alt Right and the European New Right. Although I've titled this talk "Alt Right versus New Right," I don't want to make it sound like I am suggesting that there is an inherent conflict between the two, as obviously there are many points of overlap and potential for cooperation. However, I do believe that they are two distinct, if interrelated, phenomena, and I hold that it is important to understand that the Alt Right is a uniquely American creation that can't be exported wholesale into other cultural contexts, just as the European New Right is something very particular to Western Europe. I understand that, given all the media attention it's been receiving lately, there's a temptation to adopt the term "Alt Right" universally. I, however, insist on viewing the Alt Right as something exclusively American, and the New Right as something particularly European.

One thing that the two movements certainly share is a difficulty in determining what exactly they are. Especially in the hands of the mainstream media, "New Right" and "Alt Right" are two terms that have been used to refer to everything ranging from Tea Party-style populism to outright neo-Nazism, and everything in between, a problem that was inevitable given that neither group has a central authority that can pronounce who is and who isn't orthodox, we might say, nor even what exactly that orthodoxy is. For my own purposes today, by New Right I mean the current of thought centered upon Alain de Benoist's

GRECE movement in France and its various offshoots since 1968, which represents a towering edifice of thought unparalleled anywhere else on the Right since the Conservative Revolution in Germany of the Weimar era.

The Alt Right is a much trickier animal to pin down. The New Right has produced literally hundreds of books outlining its premises, beliefs, and positions over the past half-century. The Alt Right, on the other hand, is a culture primarily of blogs, memes, podcasts, and videos. It has yet to produce a single book or other statement of principles that everyone involved would agree is the quintessence of the Alt Right's worldview. This is a natural outgrowth of the anti-intellectualism inherent in Anglo-American political and cultural discourse, as opposed to the more innovative and livelier—dare I say superior—Rightist political tradition on the Continent. In attempting to think of a book that could in any way lay claim to being the Alt Right manifesto, the only thing I could come up with is Greg Johnson's *New Right versus Old Right*. Otherwise, the shelves of the Alt Right library remain pretty bare, although hopefully that will soon be changing. So for the Alt Right, I will draw on some ideas from that book, as well as from a meme that was circulating online last summer called "What Does the Alt Right Want?," which presents nine theses of the Alt Right.[1]

The main thing that the Alt Right and the New Right share is, first of all, a recognition that the legacy of fascism and the Second World War was a fiasco for the "true Right," and that it is something that must be transcended. Groups and individuals who want to refight the Second World War, or who insist on reusing the iconography and rhetoric of that era, are soundly rejected by both. In no way can neo-Nazis be regarded as Alt Right or New Right. At the same time, however, both the Alt Right and the New Right must not allow themselves to become caught up in apologizing for or addressing the crimes and mistakes of the past. As Jonathan Bowden once called for us to do, when our opponents keep throwing them in our path, we should simply

---

[1] Online at www.counter-currents.com/2017/02/alt-right-versus-new-right/

step over them. And as Markus Willinger says in his book *Generation Identity*, to those who constantly try to trip us up by bringing up the legacy of the Second World War, we simply have to respond that we no longer see it as relevant to what is happening in the world today. We are only interested in addressing the problems of our time.

Simultaneously, however, we should not allow our opponents to decide what we can and cannot talk about. The mere fact that an individual or a group is Jewish, for instance, as with our old friend George Soros, does not mean that they are therefore above criticism and that we are Nazis if we do criticize them. Kevin MacDonald has done brilliant work in showing how we can discuss the role of Jewish power in our societies without resorting to theories about the Elders of Zion or otherwise dehumanizing Jews, but rather understanding them from a realistic rather than a supernatural perspective, as a group with specific interests and desires that occasionally conflict with our own. To reduce all of our problems to a question of Jewish influence, however, is just as absurd as those who ignore the question altogether.

The other crucial insight that the Alt Right and the New Right share is the understanding that, since the 1960s, the liberal Left rapidly assumed control over the cultural institutions of Western Europe and North America, which soon led to them securing dominance over our political institutions as well. This is why the conservative Right in our countries gradually came to adapt itself to this new reality, continually ceding ground until it became "cuckservatism," to use the parlance of our times. This is something which the mainstream still seems to struggle with at times; namely, that we regard the liberal Left and liberal conservatism merely as two heads of the same monster. The Alt Right and the New Right are in lockstep in recognizing that the struggle to defeat this monster is as much cultural as political, in fact more so, and that creating the groundwork for the revival of a healthy culture is the necessary soil out of which a genuine illiberal political movement will eventually grow. Hence why the intellectual and cultural work that we are doing is so important, and why even now, when we see some signs of stirring in the world of politics, we shouldn't limit ourselves to political activism alone. Things are getting better, but we still have a long way to go. Seeing Donald Trump get into office and then reducing ourselves to a cheerleading squad for him is not the end for us. To paraphrase Churchill, his victory is not the end, nor even the beginning of the end, but it may perhaps mark the end of the beginning.

But while the Alt Right and the New Right are coming at the problem of liberalism from similar angles, they do remain divided by several fundamental issues. First and foremost is race. The American Right (just as the American Left, albeit in different ways) is absolutely obsessed with race: evolutionary theories, comparative IQ scores, crime statistics, and the like. In America, this has led to the development of the term "white" to refer to anyone of European descent. This makes sense in America, where people whose ancestors came from Europe generations ago, regardless of whether they came from Sweden or Sicily, in most cases have become virtually indistinguishable in a cultural and ethnic sense, and all have come to be defined in terms of their alleged "privilege" over those of non-European races and ethnicities. And "White Nationalism," in the American context, is a sensible attempt to make everyone of European descent in America realize that they have common interests at stake. However, I do believe that the attempt of some to import this idea of "White Nationalism" into Europe, and who in some cases have even called for political unification between America, Europe, and Russia, is a severe disservice to the diversity inherent in European civilization. The issue for Europe, as the New Right has always understood, is as much based in ethnicity, language, and culture as it is on race. We can't pretend that an Irishman and a Russian are interchangeable, or that they would be well served by being contained within a single sociopolitical system. This is not to suggest that there is no basis for Europeans and those of the European diaspora around the world to work together towards common ends, but I believe this can only be rooted in the specificity of particular nations, regions, and traditions, otherwise we will simply be exchanging the cosmopolitan homogenization of global multiculturalism for a "white" form of homogenization. The various European peoples and their offshoots have specific needs and identities, and these must all be respected and nourished under separate and unique institutions. So while I would never suggest that studies of or concern with race are without value, I believe that ethnicity has to take first priority over race as we consider what we are fighting for.

A related issue to this is a belief in ethnopluralism. The New Right has always advocated for the right of all peoples, and not just those of European descent, to stand for and fight, if necessary, for their particular identity and political autonomy in the face of globalization and foreign aggression. In the aforementioned nine theses of the Alt Right, we find "protection of cultural diversity" and "protection from international corporate oppression: we support nationalist economies with a focus on local industry and small businesses." This is the Alt Right at its best, when it understands that the struggle of the European peoples is the same as the fight of all peoples around the world in the face of Coca-Colonialism.

However, there are certainly elements associated with the Alt Right who have an unfortunate tendency to glorify colonialism and its attendant exploitations, such as slavery, and in some cases call for a return to those times. Besides the fact that globalization essentially represents a continuation of colonialism through other means, I believe that both the New Right and the Alt Right must resolutely reject this sort of colonialist nostalgia. This is not to say that we should hang our heads in shame, as the liberals would have us do, at its legacy, or deny that there was a great deal of positive achievement in it that went along with its negatives, as one can see in the development of social institutions and infrastructure in India, for instance. (It is no less true, of course, that colonialism also had a detrimental effect on the colonizers, as anyone who has walked the streets of London, and seen the legacy of the Commonwealth of Nations firsthand, can surely attest.) Nevertheless, we are entering a new age, and calling for the imposition of rule by one people over another against their will is not just wrong, but it's anachronistic. Therefore, we should afford no tolerance towards neo-colonialists in today's Right. Empire can be a noble form, but empires should only consist of ethnically and culturally compatible peoples, and not be built purely on economic expediency, as were the great European transcontinental empires of the 19th century. The Alt Right and the New Right are united in recognizing the right of all the peoples of the world to maintain their own beliefs, cultures, and traditions—in their own lands, of course. This is why we reject mass immigration, since the importation of large numbers of people from fundamentally different cultures into a single system can only lead to a sense of alienation, dissatisfaction, and natural hostility, both on the part of the native population as well as among the immigrants themselves.

And speaking of cultural alienation, another reason why I warn Europeans against embracing the Alt Right label is that the Alt Right was born out of the very specific American context. America was founded on liberalism; this is an undeniable fact. "All men are created equal" is among the first words in our founding document. It's not too difficult to see how the history of America since then, and most especially over the last half-century, has been the consequence of that principle, even if it's taken two centuries to see its full implications play out. In Europe, nations have histories which stretch back into primordial, mythic times, and traditions of political organization and hierarchies that go back just as far. Europeans know who they are. They have thousands of years of historical and cultural heritage to inform them about who they are. Even today, they have political institutions that predate the coming of liberal democracy and the attendant notion that "all men are created equal" that they imported from us.

To be an American, on the other hand, simply means to be an individual invested with vague notions of "rights," and anyone from anywhere who shows up in America today only needs to pass a basic civics test in order to become just as much an American as someone whose forefathers fought in the American Revolution. When the Alt Right is at its best, it draws on the pre-liberal European legacy of political and cultural thought, in particular European notions of natural hierarchies and identity. I don't mean to disparage the so-called "Alt Lite" too harshly, but one can see in much of the Alt Lite's rhetoric an inability to think beyond the liberal principles upon which America is presently founded. To be frank, American constitutionalism and excep-tionalism are not going to be the vehicles that rescue European-Americans from multiculturalism and their ultimate displace-ment as the architects of our country. We need to get back to the ideas that our ancestors left behind in Europe. Like the French revolutionaries and the Soviet Communists, the fathers of the American Revolution thought they could rebel against nature and establish something new — but we can see now that this dream was just as ill-conceived as the utopian dreams of those others. To save ourselves, we Americans have to reconnect with our European roots and with European ideas. In short: white Americans need Europeans a lot more than Europeans need them. Of course, it would be good for everyone, and Europe in particular, to get America to a point where it stops harming the rest of the world with its endless geopolitical machinations. But we're going to need help in order to get there.

Which brings me to two more deficiencies of the Alt-Right project, at least as it has played out so far: it lacks any solid eco-nomic or geopolitical viewpoint. It's too focused on problems at home and on identity politics to be worried about the larger pic-ture, but it will eventually need to engage with these matters if it is to really tackle the problems it has set out to address. Again, this is an area where the New Right has excelled. The Alt Right seems very hesitant to be critical of capitalism, which I think stems from the fact that globalist capitalism and the American Right became very closely intertwined during the Cold War, in opposition to Communism, and remain so today, which is why all mainstream political arguments in the US can usually be boiled down to differing views concerning how best to grow the economy. The simple fact is that we will never be able to achieve the changes we want to see while retaining economic growth as the sole measuring stick of political success or failure.

Alain de Benoist has been quite vocal in insisting that we must seek changes in our economic system if we want to restore our nations as places for our own people to grow and thrive, something that we hear a faint, if inadequate, echo of in Donald Trump's own protectionist proposals, or in the Alt Right's sup-

port for tariffs to protect domestic goods. As Benoist famously
said in his essay "Immigration: The Reserve Army of Capital,"
"Whoever criticizes capitalism, while approving immigration,
whose working class is its first victim, had better shut up. Whoever criticizes immigration, while remaining silent about capitalism, should do the same."

There is one positive point of convergence here, though: the
New Right recognizes that, as Rightists, it is our duty to be stew-
ards of the Earth and its environment (which, as Roger Scruton
has written, has always been something more natural to the
Right than to the humanistic Left); this is paralleled in the nine
theses of the Alt Right, which state, "We support regulations designed to preserve our natural heritage."

Again, however, the Alt Right falters when it comes to geo-
politics. The mere isolationism proposed by the Alt Right in international relations, while certainly an improvement over
America's destructive legacy of interventionism, will be insuffi-
cient to deal with the problems that lie ahead. The true Right
must be able to forge new alliances and perhaps name new enemies if it is to undo the damage that globalism has already
wrought across the globe.

I may have sounded very critical of the Alt Right, and indeed,
I think it still has a long way to go before it can be taken seriously as a political movement worthy of contending for actual power, as opposed to the vague influence it exerts today. But I don't
intend to censure it entirely. In it, we do see the first glimmer-
ings of a revolution against liberalism; they just need to be
fanned until they burst into real flame. To do that, it will have to
attain a much greater degree of inner discipline and intellectual
maturity. That's where we need help from Europe. In short, we
need Europe to help us to grow up. The European New Right is
not something that can be exactly replicated in America, I con-
cede, given our different cultural contexts, but I believe that the
two have more commonalities than differences, and in fact the
communitarianism that has been suggested by GRECE as a solution to the problems of mass immigration is perhaps even better
suited to the American context than to the European, given that
America has been communitarian in nature since its inception:

groups of different peoples living side by side, but according to different traditions and customs, and in their own spaces.

But the one area where the Alt Right has already proven its mastery is in the metapolitical arena. If you had told me a year ago that Pepe the Frog and triple parentheses were going to become flashpoints in the 2016 presidential race—a race that our guy won, a fact which still amazes me—I would have suggested that you put your drink down. But the forces of the Alt Right mobilized a youthful vigor and a wicked, creative sense of humor, and tapped into the American collective unconscious in a way that was unparalleled in modern times. I wouldn't say that the Alt Right won the election, as many forces were in play, but it was certainly a factor. And this is the one way in which Europeans can perhaps take lessons from us Americans. The European New Right has built an elegant intellectual edifice over decades that is unmatched; the problem is that its call for metapolitical battle has never truly left the pages of books and articles and been manifested in the real world. The Alt Right needs to learn from Europe, that much is clear. But what we also need now is for Europeans, with the strength of their ideas and traditions, to link up with the guerrilla prankster spirit that drives the Alt Right. I already see signs of this coming into being, but it needs to be taken much further, and done so in a matter tailored to specifically European tastes rather than merely copied from America. So I will leave you with one, final warning. The Alt Right's relationship to the Trump administration is not the first time in recent decades that the true Right has flirted with genuine political power. In the mid-1980s, many veterans of GRECE ended up going to work for the Front National, but unfortunately it was more of a divorce than an example of influence, as the activists, such as Guillaume Faye, grew frustrated with the thinkers' lack of action, and the thinkers grew contemptuous of the lack of intellectual seriousness and rigor on the part of the activists. I think it's possible we may see a similar split in the Alt Right before long, as the harsh realities of politics become apparent. Greg Johnson has a brief essay called "Theory and Practice" in *New Right vs. Old Right* on what happened in France:

[Faye] claims that the New Right never engaged the Front National, because its members fundamentally misunderstood Gramsci, whose cultural battle was organically connected with the economic and political struggle of the Italian Communist Party. The New Right, however, treated the battle as entirely cultural and intellectual. Thus they were not really Gramscians. They were actually followers of Augustin Cochin's theory of the role of intellectual salons in paving the way for the French Revolution. Unlike the men of the old regime, however, we do not enjoy the luxury of ignoring party and electoral politics. . . . [W]e must influence people who have power, or who can attain it. That means we must engage organized political parties and movements. No, in the end, white people are not going to vote ourselves out of the present mess. But we are not in the endgame yet, and it may still be possible to influence policy through the existing system. Moreover, parties do not exist merely for the sake of elections. They provide a nucleus for the new order they advocate. Finally, there are other ways to attain power besides elections. (pp. 36–37)

Greg is right about this, and it's a difficult balance we will have to strike: between influencing politics with our ideas on the one hand, while not turning our noses up at everyday politics — which, admittedly, is a dirty and unpleasant business — and eschewing it out of a desire to remain pure to our ideals. Yes, we will have to compromise at times, but a tremendous amount can still be achieved. The current wave of populism across the Western world is an indication of that, and it's a wave we must ride. In this, I think a marriage between the ideas of the New Right and the techniques of the Alt Right can be a very happy and fruitful one. We have two very different battles to fight, but if we learn from each other's strengths, eventually we will meet and clasp hands as victorious brothers on the battlefield of history.

Counter-Currents, February 28, 2017

WHITE NATIONALISM, THE ALT RIGHT, & THE ALT LITE

GREG JOHNSON

There is a lot of confusion about the relationship of White Nationalism, the Alt Right, and the so-called Alt Lite.

The "Alt Right" is a vague category that encompasses different tendencies of thought united by their rejection of mainstream conservatism. White Nationalism is one such tendency, and the Alt Lite is another.

The Alt Lite is defined by civic nationalism as opposed to racial nationalism. Whereas White Nationalists believe that true nationhood is defined by race and ethnicity, civic nationalists believe that a nation can be multiracial and multicultural but unified on the basis of common laws and values. It is, in short, a version of the "proposition nation."

The Alt Lite differs from the mainstream of proposition nation conservatives by opposing economic globalization and open borders in favor of nationalism, upholding the superiority of "Western" culture and values, and opposing feminism and political correctness.

It is easy to understand why the various Alt-Lite figures adopt these positions. Gavin McInnes, for example, is married to an American Indian woman, so obviously he cannot embrace White Nationalism. Milo Yiannopoulos is partly Jewish, so clearly he can't get behind White Nationalism. Mike Cernovich has both affirmed and denied being Jewish, and he is married to a Persian woman, so he is not a good fit for White Nationalism, either. Paul Joseph Watson is allegedly married to an Asian woman; Stefan Molyneux is part Jewish; and so on. (Vox Day is of mixed race, but he has no problem with racial nationalism.)

So instead of arguing for White Nationalism, these figures argue against economic globalization, open borders, feminism, and political correctness, and for Trumpian populist ideas. I agree with all these positions, and I am glad to have allies supporting them. They are not in *full* agreement with me, of course, but the Alt Lite is really as close as these people can come to White Nationalism while remaining authentic to who they are. Of course, the Alt Lite decries identity politics, but for these figures, it is at bottom no different from any other kind of multiculturalism, i.e.: it is just the identity politics of diaspora Jews and white miscegenators.

The vast bulk of the Alt Lite audience, however, consists of whites without such entanglements, and I look upon them as potential converts to White Nationalism. Indeed, some of them already are White Nationalists, but they have chosen to stake out a position closer to the mainstream because they hope to better influence public discourse and the political process.

So how should White Nationalists relate to the Alt Lite? Naturally, there's a right way and a wrong way. I'll deal with the right way first.

I regard the Alt Lite, and the broader Alt Right, as an opportunity, not as a threat. Our movement can only grow by converting people who do not already agree with us. That requires that we talk to people who do not already agree with us. And those conversations require a safe space. The Alt Right provided that safe space.

This is why the Alt Right brand was so valuable to White Nationalists. It brought together people who rejected the conservative mainstream without requiring that they avow any specific ideology, especially those that might be outside their comfort zone, including White Nationalism and most especially National Socialism. Indeed, the original *Alternative Right* webzine was created as a tool of White Nationalist outreach and conversion, and the Alt Right continued to function that way long after it became simply a generic term for edgy alternatives to conservatism.

I think all of us can remember a time when we had to screw up our courage just to read dissident websites in the privacy of our own homes. Our movement is growing rapidly, which means that more people than ever before are in that very spot.

Which means that spaces like the Alt Right have never been more important.

That includes Alt Lite spaces as well. Thus we should welcome their growth. Let a thousand Deploraballs, webzines, YouTube channels, self-help books, and supplement lines bloom. Let them set up their tents, gather their crowds, and hawk their wares. A world in which there are fewer mainstream conservatives and more civic nationalists fighting against globalization, open borders, feminism, and political correctness, and upholding the superiority of Western civilization, is definitely moving in the right direction. Not all of these people will be White Nationalist material, but most will be, and if we can't convince them to come the rest of the way with this sort of setup, we are doing something wrong.

Does this mean that I don't believe in criticizing the Alt Lite and other non-White Nationalist currents in the Alt Right? Of course not. The "Don't criticize Milo, because he's a gateway drug" argument makes zero sense. The only way to make the big tent work for us is if we criticize other positions. For instance, we have to argue that racial and ethnic nationalism is better than civic nationalism if we are going to convert people to our way of thinking. And our criticisms should not just be on points of political philosophy. If Alt Right and Alt Lite figures engage in stupid, dishonest, or dishonorable behavior, we should criticize them as well.

Offering better arguments and upholding high standards of behavior is how we win the metapolitical struggle. We should not be restrained by silly taboos about not "punching Right." Instead, our only taboos should be against bad arguments, bad faith, and bad behavior.

If White Nationalists cultivate a collegial relationship with the Alt Lite, in which we affirm what we have in common, agree to differ in a civil manner, and keep open lines of communication, what is the worst that can happen? As far as I can see, the chief threat is that we will be deluged with more potential converts than we can assimilate and presented with more opportunities for cultural and political advancement than we can take advantage of. But those are good problems to have.

There's a lot of fearful talk about the Alt Lite "co-opting" or "subverting" the Alt Right, or preventing people from becoming further radicalized. Frankly, though, this would happen only if we fail at our mission. But we already know that failure is a theoretical possibility. The rewards, however, far outweigh the risks. So the solution is simply not to fail.

If this is the right way to relate to the Alt Lite, what is the wrong way? I would argue that the following behaviors are perverse and self-defeating:

1. **Trying to drive away people who are not fully on board with White Nationalist ideas.** We should be in the business of attracting rather than repelling converts. I have to ask the people who think that the movement will grow by repelling people: was there ever a time when you didn't hold your present positions? Was there ever a time when you held Alt Liteish views? If so, were you converted by encountering better ideas or by obnoxious trolling and bullying? If the former, then why are you not trying to bring new people along in the same way? If the latter, you probably have half-baked ideas and a weak character, and I doubt you are an asset to our cause.

2. **Trying to assert that the Alt Right is "nothing but" White Nationalism or National Socialism.** The only sense in which the Alt Right is "really" or "essentially" White Nationalist is that it was created as a tool of White Nationalist outreach and conversion. But it can perform that function only if it includes people who are not already White Nationalists. Indeed, they have to find it to be a safe and welcoming space, not a madhouse of trolling, bullying, and doxing.

Both of these self-defeating behaviors are versions of the failed Linderite strategy of "polarization," which seeks to destroy any positions between mainstream cuckservatism and White Nationalism by basically being an asshole, on the dubious assumption that if forced to choose between mainstream conservatism and Nazi assholes, people of quality will flock to the assholes. In fact, only weak people are attracted by bullying, and by creating a gulf between us and the mainstream, we only ensure our isolation and irrelevance. Besides, as the Alt Lite has proved, a third option is possible: namely, to build their own spaces.

Sadly, a productive relationship between White Nationalists and the Alt Lite may no longer be possible. A separate Alt Lite designation was necessary because civic nationalists felt they were being pushed out of the Alt Right camp by White Nationalists. And in the aftermath of Hailgate, many people have abandoned the Alt Right brand altogether. The Alt Lite is creating a *cordon sanitaire* to prevent Hailgate fiascos at events like the Deploraball.

So this article may be too little too late. But the principles here don't just apply to the Alt Lite. They are true of all relations between vanguardists like us and more mainstream groups. Even if the Alt Right is dead and White Nationalists and the Alt Lite are irreconcilably polarized, the forces that fuel both tendencies of thought are very much alive, so as new personalities and platforms emerge and others fall by the way, we will have an opportunity to get things right the next time.

Counter-Currents/*North American New Right*,
January 4, 2017

STAND YOUR GROUND:
MILO, THE ALT RIGHT, &
MAINSTREAM ATTENTION

DONALD THORESEN

It is hard not to like Milo Yiannopoulos. Watching him is like watching *Firing Line* if it were being hosted by Noël Coward. He is unquestionably a witty, bright-eyed, and charming individual. Politically, he inhabits the intellectual space in which White Nationalism and conservatism sometimes overlap. That is to say, he is a vocal opponent of feminism in its most flawed manifestations, opposes Muslim immigration, supports Donald Trump, and so on. And he does so fearlessly. Few reading this will not have taken some small delight in one of his particularly cutting phrases or his cool trouncing of some hysterical social justice warrior.

For whites, this is often all that it takes to be welcomed into the fold. As a largely politically voiceless group, whites tend to flock towards anyone who has the courage to speak publicly what they think in the privacy of their own minds or dare to say only to close associates.

The problem with Mr. Yiannopoulos is that he is not white. He is in fact half Jewish—a particularly thorny issue indeed. Despite all we know of history, many whites just cannot help themselves but to embrace anyone who is perceived as being supportive of white interests. At the same time, however, it is pure folly to reject the benefits of a sympathetic voice, especially one with such a large audience, just because he is a member of an out-group.

In the article "An Establishment Conservative's Guide To The Alt-Right" (*Breitbart*, March 29, 2016), co-written by Mr. Yiannopoulos and Allum Bokhari, the authors attempt to explain to Breitbart readers (mainstream conservatives who are slightly farther to the Right and more open-minded than the average

Republican) exactly what this "Alt Right" they have been hearing so much about actually stands for and why their Twitter timelines are filled with swastikas and "le happy merchant" memes.

The article, well-written and relatively informative, albeit highly selective in its subject matter, has reawakened a debate within our circles about a subject with which we are all familiar: what contributions, if any, can non-whites make to the Alt Right? Part of the problem is one of terminology. The controversy surrounding the concept of "allies of color" is, in part, that the term itself suggests a far more intimate working relationship between us and non-whites than White Nationalists feel comfortable having. An alternative phrase — "peripheral agents" — might provide a greater intellectual distance between sympathetic non-whites and White Nationalists while allowing us to more objectively and calmly analyze their impact on the movement and public perception.

If we answer the question of the role of peripheral agents simply by emphatically restating our foundational principle — *the creation of sovereign white nations* — and take all the ultimate restrictions that such a project will necessitate as a given, we are left to deal with three important issues: first, the question of whether sympathetic publicity is always good publicity, even if emanating from non-white voices; second, the question of how White Nationalists should make use of mainstream coverage; and third, who exactly is it that White Nationalists are seeking to attract (a question that is not quite as simple as one might guess).

It is not necessary to provide a complete synopsis of the article here but a short description of a couple of its elements is required. The authors define the Alt Right very broadly: they mention a number of well-known contemporary names, including Steve Sailer, Curtis Yarvin (the Jewish neoreactionary better known as Mencius Moldbug), Razib Khan, and Richard Spencer, as well as early luminaries such as Julius Evola, H. L. Mencken, and Oswald Spengler. Included in their genealogy of the Alt Right are various factions or fields of interest such as the human biodiversity movement, libertarianism, neoreaction, and the manosphere. Even a passing mention of the *Nouvelle*

Droite is made. It is an eclectic mix of ideas but each has in common a disdain for and a rejection of the oppressive and ill-informed world of politically correct pearl-clutchers on both the Left and the mainstream Right. Needless to say, most of those who are reading this will likely already have read the article but, if not, it is worth spending a few minutes perusing it because it *will* attract newcomers. For this reason, it can be seen as a benefit to the movement. But the fact that it will serve as an introduction for many people makes it that much more crucial for White Nationalists to assert our particular message clearly, loudly, and without compromise.

The head, heart, and muscle of the Alt Right is White Nationalism, a movement which is not mentioned once in the article. Considering the scope of the piece, this can hardly be construed as anything but deliberate. Without the tools of extra sensory perception, we cannot know for certain precisely why the authors have neglected White Nationalism but, with our understanding of Jewish intellectual movements to guide us, we can surmise that they chose to downplay the influence of radical White Nationalist intellectuals in favor of a more inclusive and socially acceptable collection of thinkers in an effort to secure for themselves a niche in the marketplace and a future for non-white writers. To do such a thing makes perfect sense. The authors cannot be faulted for this. It is not even out of the realm of possibility that they are genuinely sympathetic to White Nationalism in the same way some of us are sympathetic to Hindu Nationalism or various other anti- or postcolonial movements—i.e., as movements consistent with our ideology but within which we can play no part other than that of observers and commentators.

There can be no doubt, for example, that the Indologist Koenraad Elst has had a tremendously positive influence on Hindu Nationalism without pretending to be a Hindu Nationalist. His books are widely read and can certainly be seen as good publicity for that particular movement. Though the situation is not strictly analogous (especially considering the fact that he is not Jewish), in the context of Indian politics and demography, Dr. Elst is a "minority" who has devoted his career to a cause that is not, strictly speaking, his own. There are, of course, numerous other examples of this phenomenon, but the point is that it is certainly possible for members of an out-group to aid the cause of an in-group provided that the in-group is *firmly and explicitly committed to its own principles and that this is understood by both sides.*

If we approach the subject from this point of view, it seems clear that sympathetic publicity arising from anyone is good for the movement (with the above caveats). Good publicity is, of course, any publicity that attracts new people to one's project, whatever that may be. As Greg Paulson points out in his recent related piece at *Counter-Currents*, for many Millennials, involvement with the various factions of the Alt Right mentioned above provided their introduction to White Nationalism. He writes: ". . . they started out by simply finding our racial, anti-feminist, and un-PC memes funny (but not taking them seriously), and as time and engagement with our memes progressed, they started taking the legitimacy of our points and eventually embraced our ideas."[1]

The intellectual paths taken by individuals who end up becoming White Nationalists are probably as diverse as White Nationalists themselves. An in-depth study of this process will surely be undertaken someday, but anecdotal evidence abounds and would suggest that Mr. Paulson is correct. Thus it is important to cast as wide a net as possible. After all, we are attempting to undo many years of philosophical and political corruption, as well as — and most importantly — the suicidal psychological distortions inflicted upon a group of people that make up about 18% of the world's population. Some will, by nature, respond more slowly than others and to them we must show patience (a task that, admittedly, seems to grow more challenging the longer one has been in the movement). However, as long as we are honest about our goals and refuse to temper our basic message, providing a warm welcome to the curious will benefit us all tremendously.

---

[1] Greg Paulson, "Milo Yiannopoulos & 'Allies of Color,'" *Counter-Currents*, April 7, 2016.

One of the claims made by Mr. Yiannopoulos and Mr. Bokhari is that many in the Alt Right are simply being childishly rebellious and lack any real substance to their arguments. They write, for instance, that some are drawn to the movement because "it promises fun, transgression, and a challenge to social norms *they just don't understand* [italics mine]." And later: "Young people . . . are drawn to [the Alt Right] because it seems fresh, daring and funny, while the doctrines of their parents and grandparents seem unexciting, overly-controlling and overly-serious." This is doubtless true to some extent. But behind this jocularity is a deadly seriousness that risks getting lost in the "amorphous movement," as the authors term it, if it is not regularly checked and contextualized. It is the job of the older and/or more learned members of the community to ensure that the young do in fact understand the ideas behind the memes.

Though many have arrived on this side of the political spectrum from a variety of backgrounds and political philosophies, it must be remembered that the core ideas that propelled the Alt Right onto the pages of Breitbart in the first place were those of White Nationalists. We have gained strength and followers precisely because we do not compromise with our enemies. It should be obvious that there is no reason to start now. It is our honesty about *everything* that has made the movement a dynamic, cutting-edge, and ultimately unavoidable force in contemporary political discourse. One of our greatest powers is that we know we are right and we can prove it. And we do not back down under pressure. Simply put, White Nationalists are the alpha males of politics, and this is, without a doubt, partially what draws people towards us.

The question of who our audience actually is and which segments of the white population are most necessary to attract is one that also needs to be considered in the context of any conversation about publicity and mainstream attention. First and foremost, it must be stated that White Nationalism is neither a rebrand of conservatism nor is it a joke, despite sharing some positions with conservatives and having a uniquely talented number of true comedic talents in our ranks. It is now — and always has been — a radical political movement. We are not looking to restore the collapsing architecture of a system that brought us to this point in the first place. We are trying to create a new and healthy culture in which we freely and without sentimentality discard those ideas that have failed us and have helped to maintain the collective state of white psycho-social submission to Jewish elites. It is absolutely necessary to for us to begin to think exclusively as radicals, using the terms and ideas of radical politics, and to distance ourselves from conservatism with no compunction.

Radical political action is almost always the result of the dissemination of a particular ideology by a cadre of older intellectuals whose ideas, refined and crystallized by years of serious study, find traction with military-aged men, especially those on the younger side of this demographic. These people experience the effects of previous generations' bungles and missteps in ways that are often more immediate and pressing than they are for older, more secure, and less socially flexible individuals. The young tend not only to be more intellectually open but also more willing to undertake risk and to find delight in spiritually fulfilling thrill-seeking. A movement that is not seen as dangerous in some way is not going to attract these people and will always drift towards stagnation.

One of the fears often expressed at times like this is that of mainstreaming. We are all aware of both recent and historical examples of such behavior and rightly fear it. Who does mainstreaming attract? Primarily those with a heavy stake in the current system, people who believe that a few tweaks in the political climate will restore the stability of decades past, and those who long for a world that has either already passed or never actually existed, i.e., hopeless nostalgists. This is not the stuff of which radical political movements are made. Thus any attempt at mainstreaming our message will alienate the precise demographic that is most necessary for the success of any radical political movement. There must be a space for those entrenched in the system to find common ground with White Nationalists (they most certainly have as much to gain from us as we do from them), but at the same time those with youthful energy and a healthy sense of adventure must not be alienated. The "1488ers," despite occasionally being crudely over the top (those whom Greg Johnson has famously termed "vantards") should be corrected when appropriate and necessary but not to the point of demoralization. None of us need look too far to find sources of frustration and ennui. But this should not come from within our community if it can at all be helped. White Nationalists should be supportive and provide a safe haven for those who are pro-white and are not harming the movement either through stupid behavior or *fundamentally* misguided ideas.

In sum:

1. Any publicity that is not explicitly negative should be seen as a boon to the movement—even if it comes from a non-white.
2. In order to use such publicity most effectively, White Nationalists must be gracious and appreciative without *ever* straying from our fundamental beliefs or trying to downplay some particular aspect of our ideology in order to trick people into accepting us. This will guarantee that our ideas will be accepted by those ready to accept them and increases the likelihood that we will garner respect, however begrudgingly, from all whom we engage.
3. Replacing the term "allies of color" by the more neutral (and accurate) "peripheral agents" might go a surprisingly long way in reducing knee-jerk reactions to out-group attention in the future.

Finally, it is crucial to maintain a certain level of tolerance for the young and hot-headed so that they learn and progress as individuals and as activists rather than throwing their hands up into the air and gravitating towards unstable and marginal figures within the movement, thereby wasting their talents and energy pursuing chimeras.

Counter-Currents, April 12, 2016

THE FIGHT FOR THE ALT RIGHT:
THE RISING TIDE OF IDEOLOGICAL AUTISM AGAINST BIG TENT-SUPREMACY

LAWRENCE MURRAY

The growth of what is termed the Alt Right in recent months has led to a growth of criticism and some debate over its meaning and scope. (We're also on Wikipedia now). The "Alternative Right" is a 2010s political label with history I am sure most people reading this are familiar with, and if not it is beside the point. What I aim to discuss here is not so much Alt Right history or criticisms of it, but rather a survey of what basic tenets compose it now.

But before that, I would emphasize that by necessity the Alt Right is a "big tent" philosophy. Ideally this means that it functions as an intellectual alliance between *other* philosophies that embrace most or all of its core principles. Therefore, it is counter-productive for any of these philosophies attack one another *more* than they attack outside philosophies. Some people call this *no enemies on the Right* or *no enemies to the Right*, the latter being less inclusive, but what is most important ultimately is to not throw competent people who agree with you on major issues to the wolves. Having clear battle lines is crucial because it ensures we are our own moral authority rather than a third party that is opposed to most or all of our beliefs, which is a major problem if not *the* problem with the mainstream Right.

So what are the tenets of the big tent? I believe they are as follows:

1) People are different. Human inequality is a fact of life, and belief systems that deny this lead to distortion and oppression. Both individuals and populations vary in their characteristics in meaningful ways, such as intelligence and social behavior. One size does not fit all, not comfortably at least.

2) Our world is tribal. The struggle for survival which has produced all life on earth extends into biological human races, which both exist and matter to their members. Such conflict is neither immoral nor moral, but a condition we must engage with in order to develop any meaningful philosophy or ideology. It can be found on the streets, in the human resources department, at the ballot box, or in the trenches. Even something as trivial as the Oscars is fought over. Though it is currently politically incorrect to acknowledge that races and their national subdivisions exist and compete for resources, land, and influence over one another or over themselves, that does not mean the struggle has stopped. That one side has been cajoled into not struggling does not mean it is left alone.

3) Our tribe is being suppressed. The New Left doctrine of racial struggle in favor of non-whites only, a product of decolonization and the defeat of nationalists by egalitarians after WWII, must be repudiated, and whites must be allowed to take their own side in their affairs. A value system that says whites are not allowed to have collective interests and literally every other identity group can do so and ought to do so is unacceptable.

4) Men are not women and women are not men. Men and women have roles to fulfill for the species to persist in a stable and healthy way. Feminism and the sexual revolution, by destroying the conditions that promoted and sustained heterosexual monogamy, have had disastrous implications for the sexes and relationships between them. (I highly recommend F. Roger Devlin's *Sexual Utopia in Power* here for those interested in more.) No viable society can exist where the long-term union of one man and one woman producing a replacement level of offspring is not the norm. Some Western countries have obscured the impact of sexual degeneracy on birthrates by importing foreigners, but such measures only further the destruction of nations; they do not sustain a people but keep a state's balance sheets in order.

5) Freedom is a responsibility and not a right. The freedom of too many incompetent people to make too many bad decisions is harmful to society and constrains the freedom of virtuous and responsible people. There are externalities to most actions, and when these are harmful to non-actors it is a kind of injustice. These need to campaigned against, or suppressed by force or the threat of force—the basis of the rule of law. A virtuous society is an ordered one that provides *freedom* from anarcho-tyranny.

6) If we must be a democratic society, the franchise should be limited. Universal democracy is a bad system. It gives power to the worst and shackles the fittest. It is a degenerative institution in which the weak and unproductive collaborate against the strong and sustainable.

The final Alt-Right shit-test is whether or not someone agrees with the reality that *Jewish elites are opposed to our entire program.* It is the third rail for a reason. The hardest redpill to take is a suppository, the Jewish Question. (Here I highly recommend Dr. Kevin MacDonald's *Occidental Observer* if you don't have the time preference for an entire series of books on the subject.) The disproportionate influence of an elite Jewish minority in Western societies has been a net negative. Jews, who have a three-thousand-year history of regulating their communities to be as insular as possible among the nations whose territory they dwell in have a consistent pattern of promoting the interests of their own ethnoreligious minority at the expense of the majority nation. It is what they do, and when they do it here it is bad news for us. When given the power they have now it results in degeneracy, the losing of one's race. Even in Israel one will find Jews who are firmly dedicated to the destruction of their host's borders and hold in contempt the idea of loyalty to their national kin. Who shrieks loudest at anti-immigration nativism? Who praises their own ethnocentrism as a virtue and shames others for having the same feelings? It is a pattern that crosses time and borders, and there is a war against noticing it. The staunchest social egalitarians, anti-nationalists, and "anti-racists" are Jewish, inside and outside of Israel.

There are plenty of ideological directions one could go in from here, and as always there is no silver bullet solution to problems of the magnitude we deal with in Western societies. And people who claim to have the bullet tend to be the most zealous about it. Some proposals are modest, some are LARPy, and some won't be LARPy for long. But if they address our root issues, they are worth some consideration. And if after such consideration you find you only disagree about secondary or tertiary issues, there is definitely room to work together. The big tent is worth preserving to persevere against our common enemies, for our struggle is revolutionary. Stay fashy my friends.

Counter-Currents, March 7, 2016

THE ALT LITE & THE SPECTRUM AXIS

SPENCER J. QUINN

It is a very simple idea.

Remember that in the film *Moneyball*, the new Assistant General Manager, Peter Brand, said that "It's all about getting things down to one number." Like Spearman's g, but for baseball. A single number which could establish a player's objective worth. As the film showed, such a number becomes extremely useful for anyone with a limited budget attempting to build a championship ball club.

Distilling a multitude of secondary and tertiary concepts down to primary ones has similar utility in politics and political theory. If we can sift through the jumble of passions and ideologies of particular political movements and produce a single concept which differentiates them, that would be useful. For one, it would form a common ground upon which people of differing political stripes could agree to disagree. Secondly, it could be a starting point for discussion, forcing people to either bolster or challenge their own positions.

In the current American political climate, I estimate that there are four major concepts which act as the driving forces behind all relevant political movements: equality, freedom, tradition, and race. A political movement can be placed along a unified axis based on its regard for any two of these four concepts. Here is a visualization:

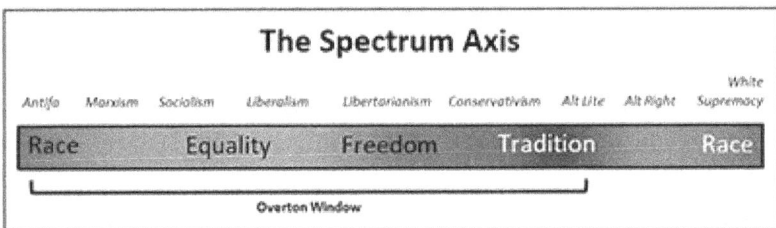

The Spectrum Axis

| Antifa | Marxism | Socialism | Liberalism | Libertarianism | Conservativism | Alt Lite | Alt Right | White Supremacy |

| Race | Equality | Freedom | Tradition | Race |

Overton Window

Note that tradition and equality never meet. They are opposites, and therefore a political movement which claims to adhere strongly and equally to both is either being dishonest or won't last very long. The same goes for freedom and race. A political movement can gravitate towards one of these, but not both. This is not to say that all race realists or ethnonationalists wish to do away with individual freedoms or that traditional societies never uphold equality in the eyes of the law. A political movement *can* pay homage to all four of these concepts at once. It's just that, according to the Spectrum Axis, it must somehow combine two of these as its *raison d'être*, and it doesn't really matter which of the remaining two concepts come in third and fourth place.

I'm sure there is much to quibble about here. For example, some might say that the Alt Lite has more in common with libertarians than conservatives, or that Marxism really isn't about equality at all. Also, where does eco-activism or the manosphere fit on this Spectrum Axis? All are interesting topics, but far beyond the scope of this essay. My main point is to systematize a vocabulary which can illustrate the political divisions which cause the greatest consternation on the Right these days in fundamental terms—that is, where conservatism ends and the Alt Lite begins, and where the Alt Lite ends and the Alt Right begins.

According to the Spectrum Axis, conservatism is a blend of freedom and tradition which cares less about race, whereas the Alt Right blends race and tradition and cares less about freedom. The Alt Lite, on the other hand, seems to want to get the best of both worlds by blending freedom, tradition, *and* race into one coherent ideology. Perhaps this is why the Alt Lite appears so silly from an Alt Right perspective. Sure, it is populated by a lot of smart, passionate, likeable guys. But essentially, what it proposes is unworkable *because* it stretches too far along the Spectrum Axis.

Observe: on the whole, the Alt Lite respects conservative, traditional values, with two examples being the acceptance of man's inveterate imperfectability as well as pre-feminist notions of sex differences. They also recognize race realism and the role race has played in forming the modern world. So far so good. But by being unwilling to relinquish the idea of freedom which is blended into the mix of traditional conservatism, they lack a mechanism to enforce the real-world implementation of their ideas.

I can think of two examples of this, one recent and one less so. The recent example I mentioned in my article, "On Gavin McInnes and the Alt Lite,"[1] in which I discussed McInnes' palpable distaste with the idea of rejecting an intelligent, honorable non-white into a white ethnostate. Such a rejection would violate the non-white's freedom, you see, and is therefore bad. The other example is one I remember from years ago (sorry, can't find the link), in which conservative pessimist and race realist John Derbyshire announced that he could think of no solution at all to the race question in America. In other words, he'd rather remain confined in the box of freedom than break out of it to find an answer.

So what good is accepting race realism or sticking up for the accomplishments of white people when our current hands-off, libertarian model of government disallows doing anything about it? If current trends continue, white people will become minorities in their own countries. What will we do when that happens? Hope that the non-whites who take charge will look beyond race and respect the freedom at the center of the Spectrum Axis (like they have *almost never* done before)? Hope that only the intelligent and honorable ones that Gavin McInnes would so generously allow into white nations will end up being the ones calling the shots?

This is what we call a rope of sand.

By trying to keep its white fingers in so many different pies, the Alt Lite is living in a dreamland, albeit an intellectually consistent and morally commendable dreamland. Furthermore, people on the Alt Lite don't realize that they can *afford* to do this *only as long as there is a white majority to protect them*. As soon as that evaporates (and it looks like in thirty or forty

---

[1] Spencer Quinn, "On Gavin McInnes & the Alt Lite," *Counter-Currents*, April 19, 2017.

years, it will) most on the Alt Lite will realize—too late, per-haps—that you can't have equally large quantities of freedom and race in the same pot without spoiling the soup.

Yes, today's conservatives may seem like dunderheads compared to the Alt Lite for ignoring race, but at least they have a historical precedent to fall back on. When the Alt-anything brings up the importance of race with a conservative, the conservative can always resort (with some justice) to what I would call the "But-but-but Reagan!" defense. Ronald Reagan didn't make race an issue, and yet look at all the prosperity he brought in. Why make race so important when America has *always* been a multi-racial nation of immigrants who just can't wait to dissolve into that old melting pot? A good example of this kind of thinking can be found in the later writing of Robert Putnam whenever he tries to explain away the inconvenient findings of his classic 2000 study, *Bowling Alone*. In 2017, Amer-ica indeed remains the planet's top superpower and can still boast of having the highest standard of living in the world de-spite being six parts white, two parts Hispanic, one part black, and one part Asian (or whatever it is these days). So why spoil the soup by adding race to the mix?

Of course, the conservatives are wrong, but at least they are *understandably* wrong, unlike the well-meaning intellectuals of the Alt Lite.

The Alt Right, on the other hand, is (mostly) willing to part with a good deal of freedom in order to establish and maintain the only possible solution to our current troubles: a white eth-nostate. There is no other way, and to suggest another way is to be either profoundly ignorant of history and human nature or, frankly, not serious. And if the Alt Right is anything, it is seri-ous.

Here is my stab at how a functioning white American eth-nostate might have to restrict the freedoms provided in the US Constitution in order to avert the troubles we're facing today and still resemble, as much as possible, what the Founding Fa-thers envisioned for our country. We would have to add strict and swiftly enforceable laws which would prohibit:

- ❖ all policies and practices which discriminate against white people
- ❖ all welfare and government services provided to non-whites
- ❖ equal political rights between whites and non-whites
- ❖ all immigration except by white individuals
- ❖ all illegal immigration, and the hiring or aiding and abetting of illegal immigrants
- ❖ white vs. non-white miscegenation
- ❖ all militant and subversive cults such as Islam

And this is just for starters. Couple such restrictions with mass deportations of the non-white criminal class and creating an environment hostile enough to encourage most other non-whites under a certain age to self-deport, and freedom, shall we say, is going to take a hit.

I understand that this is scary for many people. It's scary for me. Once we start talking about bulking up government power and stripping freedoms away from citizens, we're suddenly gazing down that nice, steep, slippery slope to tyranny. Sure, a white ethnostate wouldn't necessarily force us to take the plunge (and I am willing to bet that it won't). But it would nudge us closer to the precipice and would remove the hand-rail and the little sign telling us to watch our step. In other words, in a white ethnostate, our leadership's room for error would be drastically reduced. All it would take is one power-mad strongman crossing the Rubicon, and suddenly we're not a democratic republic anymore. And if we look at history, we know very well that white people can be horribly oppressive to other whites when their political systems offer few safeguards against governmental power and abuse. This is the reason why the Founding Fathers declared war on England to begin with.

This must be said. It shows that we are not being flippant when we decide to cast our lot in with the Alt Right. It shows that we know the risks which are in store if we adopt any radical solutions to the troubles facing us today.

But you know what's even riskier? Not taking these measures, and instead thinking we can continue to cling to our precious freedoms as our world becomes more black and brown by the week. This is what conservatives do, and sadly, this is also what the Alt Lite does as it stretches itself too thin along the Spectrum Axis.

So I am going to put it in a way that nobody could possibly misinterpret. If current immigration and demographic trends in predominantly white countries continue, then the 21st century will mark the greatest loss of freedom for the white race in our history. This loss of freedom is coming whether we want it to or not. The choice of siding with the Alt Right ultimately boils down to whether or not we want to lose this freedom on our own terms or on the terms of our invaders.

For all the danger facing us, the choice couldn't be clearer.

Counter-Currents, May 3, 2017

1488 IS A GATEWAY TO THE ALT RIGHT, NOT VICE-VERSA

COLIN LIDDELL

The Alt Right is both a medium and a message. This is confusing for a lot of people. Don't blame them. It's tricky.

As a medium, the Alt Right is an aspect of the internet and social media that makes use of a number of simple psychological tricks and which exploits a number of factors, including youth, anonymity, boredom, egoism, and shock value. This translates essentially into memes, trolling, shitposting, Tweeting, and various forms of LARPing and (usually anonymous) signaling. Its operatives are typically anonymous individuals, except in cases where they have been too stupid to ensure this.

The *Alt-Right-as-Message*, however, is a collection of ideas and moral positions that, like any ideology, has an inherent tonality and consistency (or *not*, in which case it needs to work harder at this). These ideas and insights involve anti-liberal, anti-globalist, and anti-egalitarian positions on things like gender, race, identity, materialism, and even economics.

Compared to the anonymity of the *Alt-Right-as-Medium*, the *Alt-Right-as-Message* has a pedigree and is associated with actual named persons — people like Dr. Kevin MacDonald, Jared Taylor, Stefan Molyneux, Dr. Greg Johnson, Richard Spencer, and many others.

The *Alt-Right-as-Medium* is basically stupid, visceral, edgy, and fun. The Alt *Alt-Right-as-Message* is intellectual, cerebral, balanced, and hard work (especially for those with lower IQs or for those with high IQs narrowly focused — i.e. the autistes in our movement).

Understanding these two aspects of the Alt Right will save a lot of time and trouble in the future, as most of the controversies of the Alt Right are generated by an inability to understand this distinction.

Understanding this distinction will also help the leaders of the Alt Right behave more correctly, as sometimes the hard work done by the intellectual wing of the Alt Right can be damaged by lapsing back into LARPier territory. Rather than give actual examples, of which I am aware of several, imagine if the greatly respected Dr. Kevin MacDonald, no longer satisfied with just being called a "Nazi" by groups like the SPLC, was caught on camera *Sieg Heiling* and shouting "Race war now! Gas the Kikes!"

That would be a riot, and of course some would praise it as a forceful "rejection of Leftist moral framing," etc. But would it be effective? The obvious answer is *no*. Indeed, it would be highly destructive, as his lifetime's work would be easier to dismiss as the work of a "neo-Nazi nut job." So, ponder this hypothetical example next time you are unclear about these two aspects of the Alt Right and how they interrelate.

An interesting real-life case is that of RamzPaul who seems to be frequently embroiled in Twitter spats with what are known as 1488ers. As a talented vlogger, active Twitterer, and über-troll, who also seeks to hold an intellectually and morally consistent position that goes down well with young Eastern European women, Paul kind of straddles the divide between *Alt-Right-as-Medium* and *Alt-Right-as-Message*.

The problem however is not RamzPaul, the problem is the 1488ers, most of whom are simplistic and anonymous. Paul is routinely lambasted for not being purist and hard-core enough. He also picks up flack for his "normie" tone and for being soft on the Jews, even though he has frequently criticized Zionism and Jewish double standards.

There seems to be a misperception among 1488ers that they represent the hard core of the Alt Right and that those in the Alt Right who don't constantly signal a similar Vantard position haven't been red-pilled enough. When they do defend RamzPaul, as some of them do, they usually say things like, "He's a good entry point into the Alt Right for normies." People like Stefan Molyneux are viewed in a similar way, allowing the young, anonymous, autistic 1488er to have a sense of intellectual superiority.

In short, the 1488ers believe that they represent the core and a higher level of the Alt Right and that all other aspects of Alt Rightism—ancaps, the manosphere, pagans, trad-Caths, etc.—are merely lower levels of red-pilling for the normie masses leading to them. Is this view valid in any way?

It is early days, as most 1488ers seem to have only been 1488ers for around six months or less. I suspect that a great many of them—especially the more intelligent and balanced individuals—will mellow out and seek a morally and intellectually valid position instead of something shockish and sockish.

But we can also answer this question by surveying the general characteristics of the two kinds of Alt Righters.

The characteristics of the 1488ers' *modus operandi*—simplicity, repetitiveness, purity spirals, puerility, anonymity (sock value), virality (shock value), etc.—place it squarely within the *Alt-Right-as-Medium* part of our scheme, and suggest that it is strongly a lower and subservient form of Alt Rightism.

The main characteristics of the non-1488er's modus operandi—logic, evidence, insight, moral and intellectual consistency, the reliance on abstract thought, social outreach, a desire to exist beyond the basement, willingness to learn from successful political groups in Europe—suggest that it is the higher and more evolved form of the Alt Right.

So, does this mean that the 1488, shitposty, memey side of the Alt Right should just curl up and die? No, far from it!

Because of the way in which the mainstream media is skewed in favor of hegemonic liberalism, we need to have skilled skrimishers and asymmetrical warriors, even if they are obsessive, unwashed autistes in basements, who spend more time online than is healthy for them. It might even help for them to think they are the cutting edge and center of our movement as they find new ways to trigger the normies and push them in our general direction—as long as those really at the center of our movement don't get too carried away and make the same mistake.

Counter-Currents, April 11, 2016

NAZISM & THE ALT RIGHT:
AT PEACE WITH OURSELVES

ÉMILE DURAND

Time and time again the Alt Right gets dragged into disputes over the legacy of German National Socialism. They revolve around whether it should be denounced or embraced and whether it is expedient to display Nazi symbolism in public given the mainstream media's incessant attempts to demonize any kind of white racial consciousness by inextricably linking it to the real or alleged brutalities of German National Socialism.

What is often being ignored however is the existence of a deeper historical reason on the part of the Establishment for attacking white racial consciousness. Liberals attack and demonize the Alt Right, and any implicit manifestation of racial consciousness on the part of whites, not because they fear the emergence of violence. In fact, their obsession with Nazism is also not primarily rooted in its brutalities. There is a far deeper concern that animates the guardians of the established order and their lackeys. It is the fear of the ascendance of a radically different worldview, a paradigm that views race and heredity as core aspects determining the trajectory of society and historical processes. Even in the absence of the prospect of violence such a worldview is simply unacceptable to them.

Seen in this light, liberals should in fact be credited with good discernment and lucidity about what the Alt Right represents. They understand it even better than many race realists who frantically try to condemn "Nazism" and reject that label.

This confusion and dissonance arise indeed due to different meanings attached to the word "Nazism" by different parties. Those in the Alt Right who condemn "Nazism" comprehend the term in a narrow sense, as referring to a particular political movement that emerged at a particular time in Germany. The

Left however imbues the term with a more general meaning — i.e. the racial/hereditarian view of society and its organization along these lines.

In the Alt Right, therefore, everyone is Nazi, and no one is Nazi at the same time, depending on which meaning is attached to the term. In the narrow sense, none of us are Nazis since we function in a different historical period under different historical circumstances. In a wider sense, however, all of us are Nazis since we essentially subscribe to the same worldview espoused by that movement. The incessant branding of any racially conscious white as "Nazi" by liberals should therefore be seen as something more than sleazy attempts at defamation, but rather surprisingly as demonstration of better judgement than on our part about who we are. The Left gets it right for a change, surpassing many in our movement in its lucidity.

Therefore, I would like to argue that the way forward for the Alt Right should be unifying its worldview into an historically coherent whole, which obviously includes the National Socialist period in Germany. This can best be achieved by viewing that phenomenon in a macro-historical context, in other words through its historicization rather than politicization. Seen from this perspective, the crimes and mistakes of German National Socialism (real or alleged) simply become beside the point.

Every worldview has its own life history and manifests itself differently at different stages of its evolution. The form these outer manifestations take depends both on the immutable internal logic of its development and contingencies which accompany it at different stages, both of which are at least partly independent of its core message. A worldview should therefore primarily be judged not by its outer manifestations, but by its core philosophy.

Every newly emergent worldview is bound to appear on the political stage through violence, since it has to break through the gridlock of the old established order. And the liberal worldview was no exception. Liberalism first appeared on the political stage through the French Revolution and the ensuing Napoleonic wars, both of which wrought immense devastation throughout Europe, being responsible for the deaths of many people by the standards of the time. Liberals however do not denounce the French Revolution, not to mention the very Enlightenment ideals that brought it about, for the violence. They see it as a necessary and perhaps inevitable step in the ascendance of liberal, egalitarian worldview in the West.

Likewise, National Socialism in Germany was the first political manifestation of racial/hereditarian worldview, which had already had a rich history and strong intellectual support from many different angles. In the scientific/analytical realm this involved Arthur de Gobineau, Francis Galton, Cesare Lombroso, Paul Broca, and Charles Spearman, as well as such popularizers as Lothrop Stoddard and Madison Grant, and in philosophy the German Conservative Revolutionaries (although their views on race were more ambiguous).

Although eventually German National Socialism was brutally destroyed, and the racial/hereditarian worldview has been fanatically suppressed by the guardians of the old order, it continues to be corroborated by novel findings from the fields of psychometry, evolutionary biology, and population genetics.

In the same way that the roots of French Revolution and liberalism are traced back to Enlightenment philosophers of the 18th century, the National Socialist period in Germany will be regarded as the German Revolution by future historians, and its roots will be traced back to racial thinkers of the late 19th and early 20th centuries. The Alt Right in turn represents the continuation and modern-day manifestation of this same school of thought, drawing upon both pre- and post-WWII racial and traditionalist thinkers for inspiration.

One other reservation about Nazism that is often brought about, in fact by those racially conscious whites who view it positively in general, is the mistreatment by Nazis of some of the white nations. It all inevitably devolves into quibbling over details about whether this mistreatment invalidates or compromises the value of Nazism for White Nationalism. However, leaving aside the debate about to what extent these mistreatments are real or fabricated and whether they can be justified or not, a historicized approach to Nazism renders also such considerations moot.

Every grand historical development that is necessary and/or beneficial for a civilization on a macro scale will inevitably involve some aggrieved subgroups. Moreover, historical personalities that stand behind those grand events are more often than not guided by narrower interests and are not consciously aware of the larger significance of the events they herald. It may very well be that Hitler was guided first and foremost by narrow German interests in his undertakings, although plentiful evidence suggests that he had far broader historical vision with regards to the fate of Europe and the white race in general than his contemporaries, and that he had mistreated some European nations in the process. Likewise Bismarck, for example, was primarily guided by narrow Prussian interests in the process of unifying Germany, which inevitably involved mistreatment of many Germans who opposed Prussia (e.g. Austrians and Bavarians). This, however, in no way precluded the veneration of Bismarck by Austrian and Bavarian Germans imbued with a broad German identity. In the same way, the mistreatment of their ancestors at the hands of National Socialist Germany should not preclude present-day racially conscious Poles or Czechs from taking inspiration from it by viewing it with historical detachment rather than personal attachment.

The legacy of German National Socialism inspires, and its symbolism rouses many racially conscious whites today regardless of their nationality. Whatever one thinks of National Socialism and whether or not one believes the official narrative about it, it is part of the common history of the movement to which the modern-day Alt Right belongs, and it represented the same aspirations and longings that animate *all* racially conscious whites today. It was the first, and until now the only, time in modern western history when racial/hereditarian worldview reached the levers of power and was implemented politically, thereby providing inspiration for the future generations of all racially conscious whites. It is also the only time when whites confronted their present-day deadly enemies in a large-scale effort.

Trying to avoid any association with Nazism on the part of the Alt Right is therefore a highly demanding task and is bound to consume a huge amount of energy, which could be spent for other more beneficial purposes. The real issue is not whether it is expedient or not to avoid any such association in the public eyes, but whether or not this is an efficient use of our creative energies. The more the Left insists on its hateful and genocidal agenda, the more whites will be radicalized, and it will become more and more difficult for White Nationalists to abstain from invoking Nazi symbolism in public, given its rousing potential.

The moral burden therefore rests on the shoulders of liberals. The ascendance of the racial/hereditarian worldview in Western civilization is an organic historical necessity. The more they try to thwart it with their bigotry and narrow-mindedness, the more likely a violent confrontation becomes. They should be well aware that the excesses of Nazism were a direct result of the punitive Versailles Treaty forced upon the German nation and the emergence of Bolshevism in Europe.

The Alt Right in turn should come to peace with its roots and its history. Obviously, no one should be obliged to revere Nazism, but those among us who find inspiration in it should not be scorned or disowned. We will sound more convincing and more inspiring if we are coherent in our worldview and at peace with our past and with ourselves.

Counter-Currents, December 20, 2016

THE KURSK STRATEGY

JAMES LAWRENCE

Late in 2016, the "Hailgate" incident ignited a furious war of words on the Alt Right, centering on the use of Nazi rhetoric and imagery by people in our movement.

In my view, most people in the Alt Right took the correct line: viewing the incident as a failure, chastising those responsible, but not overreacting and cutting ties with the movement as a whole. Those who did try to distance themselves were wrong: four drunkards doing Nazi salutes in an audience of more than three hundred is pretty damn respectable, especially at a time when "mainstream" heads of state were puffing on Fidel Castro's dead mass-murdering Commie cigar.

Needless to say, those Hailgate defenders who accused people of "cucking" and "punching to the Right" were also wrong. The reason why the Left dominates cuckservatives is that Leftists see themselves as engaged in a *metapolitical war* (which, after all, they started), while cuckservatives see their political calling as a polite debate and business opportunity. People engaged in metapolitical war do not sell out their own side to the enemy, but nor do they coddle foolish and self-indulgent people who endanger their own side (this is why, in the first chapter of *Rules for Radicals*, Jewish subversive Saul Alinsky castigated 1960s Leftist agitators for burning the American flag). No-one who is serious about metapolitical war against the Left could object to the criticism of Hailgate voiced by most of the Alt Right.

My own view on the use of Nazi rhetoric and imagery is strongly negative. Whichever way you look at it, Hitler and the National Socialists are tainted: by the atrocities and massacres that morally besmirched their cause, by their catastrophic defeat, by the fact that most of Europe remembers them as invaders or enemies, and only lastly by the propaganda of the Left that has turned them into an archetypal bogeyman. I suspect that the defenders of Hailgate would rather have a "safe space" for weird and perverted tastes than a metapolitical fighting force, and would rather have the easy catharsis of "Roman salutes" than the harder Roman discipline needed to reconquer the West.

However, I am not interested in rehashing the post-Hailgate disputes, which focused intensely on the motives and personal records of pro-Nazi individuals in the Alt Right. To make a clean break with this, I will make no direct references to such individuals here—still less to allegations against individuals, or to details of individuals' personal lives.

What I want to do is to take a critical look at the "strategic" arguments for the use of Nazi rhetoric and imagery, of which I first became aware in the aftermath of Hailgate. I will say in advance that I consider these arguments to be mere verbal self-justifications. However, for the purposes of criticism, I will treat them as if they were serious and sincere. Having collated them from innumerable comments, articles and memes, I reproduce them as follows:

> Nazism is the essence of the Right, as far to the Right as one can go: when you call yourself a Nazi, nothing remains for the Left to call you. While weak-sauce intellectuals think they can get away from this term, the real Alt Right is full-Nazi: the popularity of sites with overt Nazi leanings is much higher than the popularity of sites that oppose Nazism.

> The media relies on the smear term "Nazi" to condition the public to reject Alt Right views. By deliberately using over-the-top Nazi imagery, and conflating it with the majority of the Alt Right's reasonable positions, we can trigger the mainstream media into overusing their smear term and hurling it at people who are obviously nothing of the sort. This makes them look stupid and dishonest and renders their precious smear term meaningless.

> The more we use Nazi imagery and rhetoric, and the more the media hysterically reports on it, the more ordinary people become desensitized to this imagery and no longer react violently against it. The deliberately shocking and extreme rhetoric of self-proclaimed Nazis makes eve-

rything else on the Right look reasonable by comparison, shifting the "Overton Window" towards the Right. Previously taboo and stigmatized ideas thus find a path to public acceptance.

We might christen this proposal the *Kursk Strategy*, after the 1943 battle in which Hitler's armies made the same strategic error that is being advocated here: using inferior forces to attack the strongest-defended and best-prepared part of the enemy front. Let us break it down into its three underlying myths and explain why it can only lead us to defeat.

MYTH #1: NAZISM IS THE ESSENCE OF THE RIGHT & THE FUNCTIONAL CORE OF THE ALT RIGHT.

In the Cosmopolitan and Jewish historical narrative, "Nazism" is an essence and an archetype: it is the eternal dark side of Western civilization. The militant Left is seen as the protector against this disease, whose own violent crimes (whether that of the Soviet NKVD or the modern antifa) are invariably "contextualized" as necessary evils that serve to keep the "Nazi" beast down.

This is an almost perfect inversion of the truth, which is that *the Left is the disease at the heart of the West*—and that its Rightist opponents are invariably defensive reactions, created by modifying the original order so as to meet the new threat. Rightist reactions (Burkean conservatism, the Fascist Uprising, the Alt Right) always postdate the Leftist assaults that gave rise to them (the French Revolution, Communism, modern Cosmopolitanism); and Leftist violence always dwarfs Rightist violence in quantity and intensity, a rule to which Communism and Fascism are no exception.

The Right and the Left are both underpinned by timeless principles (e.g., order as opposed to chaos). But the forms taken by Rightist reactions are always more closely bound to time and place, because they seek to defend a particular order, while their Leftist opponents seek only to reduce it to rubble. This is why the Right suffers so much more than the Left from political necrophilia—the error of confusing empty, defeated, and anachronistic forms for timeless principles—which, in the modern day, generally leads to what we describe as "LARPing."

So the first error that we see in the sentence "Nazism is the essence of the Right" is *necrophilia*, the confusion of a dead form with a living essence. The second, more pernicious error, which lies in the word "Nazism" itself, is the application of necrophilia to a distorted bogeyman created by Leftism, Jewish influence, and the Cosmopolitan establishment.

While hyper-sensitive to "lies" about their favorite ideology (many of which are quite true), pro-Nazis are happy to emphasize precisely those elements of Hitler's movement that are emphasized by the enemy, and to believe that they form a Rightist archetype because the enemy says that they do. In the Kursk Strategy, this dependence on the enemy's worldview is rationalized through the argument that "when you call yourself a Nazi, nothing remains for the Left to call you."

The elements of National Socialism (NS) selected for emphasis by the enemy—military expansionism, Nordicist racial supremacism, sub-Nietzschean megalomania, genocide—were mostly conditional to 1930s Germany, the idiosyncrasies of Hitler, and the fighting of the Second World War. These negative phenomena may have been strongly represented in NS, but they are not the "essence" of the Right—nor even of the Fascist Uprising, which was an early attempt to create a Rightist alternative to the "social justice" version of the managerial revolution. Those foolish enough to rattle on about them in the present day are flailing in a trap set by the enemy.

This is not some personal theory of mine. Those who took part in the Fascist Uprising were perfectly capable of distinguishing the *conditional* from the *essential*, which is why the various national movements outside Germany formed their own symbols and manifestos without reference to Hitler's movement (and why Mussolini, for example, castigated NS as "savage barbarism"). After the war, too, European Rightists were not so bowled over by Hitler's legacy that they could not assess the crimes and failures of NS in a critical way.[1]

---

[1] http://www.counter-currents.com/2013/05/julius-evolas-notes-

So whence comes the "Nazism" we know today—in which the figure of Hitler is idol-worshipped, the symbols and forms of NS are uprooted from their German context and treated as universal, and every German war atrocity must be rationalized away before we can even get around to saving Europe?

For the genesis of this *neo*-Nazism—or, to sacrifice politeness for accuracy of expression, *McNazism*—we must look to postwar America rather than 1930s Germany, and to George Lincoln Rockwell rather than Adolf Hitler. The break in filiation is hinted at in the name of Rockwell's party, the "American *Nazi* Party": a comparable name for a Leftist organization might be "The Commie Party" or "The Reds-under-the-bed." It was under Rockwell that McNazism acquired its defining qualities: the embrace of the hated Nazi bogeyman as a test of balls, the use of shock imagery to get media attention, the crude and gratuitous use of racial slurs.

Rockwell's trollish strategy—which he may have begun to abandon by the time he was murdered in 1967—did not work the way he intended, and only had the result of "selling" the Leftist caricature of the last Rightist uprising to credulous people on the Right. By the time I first encountered the nationalist element of the radical Right in the early 2000s, true-believing McNazis had mired it in an ineffectual purity spiral, and the smarter elements within it were doing their best to abandon half a century of swastika-addled failure. This project culminated in Richard Spencer's founding of the original *Alternative Right* in 2010—which is why it is such a pernicious lie to say that "Nazism is the core of the Alt Right."

Yet it is true to say that, around the same time, a more accessible movement in the younger generation turned the old stock of Nazi imagery to the new purpose of internet trolling. This Nazitrolling can be distinguished from McNazism by several factors: its cyberspace format, its insincerity and irony, its younger membership, and—of course—*the fact that it succeeds in its aims,* be these ever so modest as "triggering shitlibs and cuckservatives on social media." I find the rhetoric of Nazitrolling

on-the-third-reich/

distasteful in the extreme, but do not condemn it, because 1) it is not serious and 2) the Left deserves everything it gets.

We must always remember, however, that Nazitrolling is a fairly narrow Rightist reaction (more or less a direct response to SJW hypersensitivity) that depends heavily on several factors: anonymity, Millennial irony, and the structures of the modern internet. Once it crosses the line into serious belief or any amount of real-life LARPing, Nazitrolling reverts back into McNazism, as surely as Cinderella's ballgown turned back into scullery rags after the stroke of midnight.

Keep this in mind when you see a McNazi pointing to the vast numbers of people attracted to this type of trolling and trying to convince you that he is in command of some massive future human wave. Just as hits on Pornhub do not translate into political support for "Pussyhat Protests," clicks on Nazitroll websites say nothing about sincerity of pro-Nazi beliefs, or the willingness of large numbers of people to perform the NSLARP Ghost Dance in real life. All that we can say of real-life politics and culture is that, within them, Nazi rhetoric and imagery are still as toxic as ever.

MYTH #2: THE USE OF NAZI IMAGERY & RHETORIC TRIGGERS THE MEDIA INTO OVERSTATING THEIR POSITION & RENDERING THEIR OWN SMEAR TERMS USELESS.

This appears superficially plausible, because the FakeNews™ media is indeed descending into visibly ludicrous hysteria, and much of it does concern "Nazis." But the first thing to understand is that this self-discrediting of the media, and its resulting alienation from the public, is a natural process that can be left to run its course. The more the strictures of political correctness tighten their grip, the more "little Hitlers" are created and smeared by journalistic bigots, and this causes more and more people to tune the media out and resent their constant lies.

While triggering the media is certainly possible, in this favorable situation, we would be very foolish to abandon the principle of "never interrupting your enemy when he is making a mistake."

One Alt Right figure who appears to enjoy triggering the media is Richard Spencer. His public speeches (e.g., the second minute of this one[2]) have long included vague, ambiguous Nazi-themed references that are liable to be seized upon by a paranoid media but are sure to be greeted with indifference by the general public. If this is indeed a tactic used by Spencer, it is one to be used with caution—witness Hailgate—but we can at least credit it with being reasonably well thought-out.

What we want to do here is to highlight the dissonance between media portrayal and directly observed reality. In the case of Spencer, we want the media to publish ranting denunciations of the "Naziwhowantstokillsixmillionjews"; for curious normies to do Google searches on the target's name; and for said normies to find a soft-spoken and rather anodyne speaker saying perfectly reasonable things about white identity. Opening up little windows of doubt in the dominant narrative and bringing people to small realizations that they have been deceived, is the first step towards getting them to swallow the whacking great red pills in the Alt Right's arsenal of ideas.

But the Kursk Strategy does not just negate the tactic of triggering the media. In its folly, it also reverses the collapse of public trust in the media, helping out the enemy and making it less likely that normie awakenings will take place as a result of media lies.

Let's run our little hypothetical scenario again, removing Mr. Spencer, and substituting any old Rockwellian McNazi ranter. The media breathlessly denounces the "Naziwhowantstokillsixmillionjews"; normies do a Google search on the name; and what do they find but *someone claiming to be a Nazi and talking about killing Jews*. No dissonance between portrayal and reality; ergo, no awakening. Some might want to make an exception for the more blatant sort of Nazitroll irony here; but even in this case, normies attuned to irony will still tend to conclude that the media has good cause to portray things in this way.

This last point, the use of "irony" as a catch-all excuse for Nazi rhetoric and imagery, highlights a fundamental weakness of the Kursk Strategy: its assumption that Rightists can win the

---

[2] https://www.youtube.com/watch?v=FXGOWJbt2BU

metapolitical power of the Left through a blind, indiscriminate, cargo-cult imitation of Leftist ways. This clearly fails to distinguish the *vices of power* from the *means of attaining power*. It is like the behavior of a village idiot who spends all his savings on banquets, neglects his work to go hunting in the royal forest, and struts around ordering people about in the belief that he can thereby become a King.

Since the rise of the Millennial generation, and the total self-castration of the cuckservative non-opposition, the Left has comfortably indulged a fashion for "embracing negative stereotypes ironically." Notable results so far include "I Bathe In Male Tears," "Die Cis Scum," and sketches gloating over the prospect of oppressing future white minorities in the West.[3] Although these are, most likely, real expressions of hatred dressed up in a limp justification, the FakeNews™ media churns out excuses for them with the regularity of bowel movements.

So why can't the Right do the same thing? *Because we are not in power, of course!* We cannot afford to reopen doors, which we have strived for years to close, to warped and depraved elements on our own side; and we can still less afford to give a pass to sane and reasonable people who feign genocidal hatred as part of a ludicrous "strategy." It seems that even the Left, with the brainwashing apparatus of the media on its side, can ill afford the "irony" of its spoiled SJW members, as it is rapidly losing its moral hegemony and facing a popular backlash in the West.

MYTH #3: THE USE OF NAZI IMAGERY & RHETORIC DESENSITIZES THE PUBLIC & PUSHES THE OVERTON WINDOW TO THE RIGHT.

According to the theory of the "Overton Window," the extremist fringe of a political movement is a good thing to have around, because it makes the more reasonable body of opinions in that movement look anodyne by comparison. The pro-Nazis on the Alt Right, then, are supposed to act as a "bad cop" to the rest of the Alt Right's "good cop."

The serious mistake made here is, once again, cargo-cult imi-

---

[3] https://www.youtube.com/watch?v=_TMrJDHu_TU

tation of the Left. The fact is that the Overton window does not move equally for all men, for its movement largely depends on whether or not the media deigns to make a distinction between extremists and moderates.

One group who *can* usually shift the window are the Leftist "Black Bloc" anarchists. These violent thugs turn up at Leftist protests, smash everything, and next day the media is full of carefully-worded apologias differentiating them from the saintly peaceful liberals at the protests. The Left has long accepted these tactics in the knowledge that they stretch the boundaries of accepted opinion in their favor (while intimidating political opponents, of course).

One group who *may or may not* be able to shift the window are the Libertarians (who apparently came up with the concept in the first place). Having anarcho-capitalists around may make it easier for cuckservative big-business advocates to push selective "anti-statist" measures, because they can be sure that at least part of the media will support them in this. But the pro-statist wing of the media can, and does, try to scupper this by blurring the extremist-moderate distinction.

One group who *cannot* move the window are people who sexually molest the underaged. In popular parlance, the term "pedophile" encompasses *pedophilia* (attraction to children) and *ephebophilia* (attraction to adolescents below the legal age of consent), a distinction that can be identified with "extremism" versus "moderation." If the movement of the Overton window was some sort of natural law, we might expect constant media exposure of the horrors of pedophilia to make ephebophiles look respectable in comparison. But because the media, bowing to public disgust, does not deign to make a distinction between the two, what actually happens is that people use pedophilia as a reference point to condemn similar sexual misdeeds in the same way.

Now, muse long and hard on the fact that the FakeNews™ media in the West seems to be considerably friendlier to pedophiles than to us.[4] In light of this, what result does the Alt Right

---

[4] http://www.independent.co.uk/news/world/americas/self-

get when it tries to play games with the Overton window? Yes, you've guessed it: no distinction is made between the core of our movement and its lunatic fringe, just as no distinction is made between irony and sincerity with us, and every last one of us is parleyed into a *de facto* "Nazi."

This is not to say that the Overton window cannot shift in our favor *outside the remit of the media*, i.e., when normies come to our spaces and find reasonable people living cheek-by-jowl with ranting McNazis. But the media will never let "Nazis" live on their online reservations: once they are confident of being able to link them convincingly to the wider movement, they will always trot them out and use their rhetoric as a reference point to condemn the rest of us. Even if advocates of the Kursk Strategy are convinced by none of the arguments in this piece, they should at least think very carefully about why the enemy really, really, REALLY wants us to be identified as "Nazis."

Could it have something to do with the "desensitization of the public" referred to in the Kursk Strategy? Extreme NSLARP rhetoric might desensitize the public to the supposedly "extreme" positions of the Alt Right, but it is also likely to desensitize them to state crackdowns on free speech and resistance, which can now be justified by harking back to the heroic myth of the last war.

We are, after all, not the only ones trying to shift the Overton window. In the face of the populist reaction that is breathing a last flush of defiant life into hollowed-out democratic institutions, certain moves are being made from above to shift the Overton window towards a Committee of Public Safety, which would protect the Cosmopolitan project against the dangers posed by free speech and white majority resistance.[5] Public resistance to this would, of course, be ferocious; but one of the few things capable of splitting and overriding it would be a highly visible uprising of people claiming to be Nazis and appearing to

confessed-paedophile-todd-nickerson-tells-critics-youre-the-real-monsters-a6675946.html

[5] https://www.theguardian.com/politics/2016/jun/29/why-elections-are-bad-for-democracy

advocate genocide.

If Alt Righters who LARP as Nazis want the rest of us to silence our criticism on the grounds of "not punching to the Right," *then I suggest that they first stop punching for the Left.*

And no, this is not an accusation of bad faith directed at individuals (for what it is worth, I find most of such allegations made in the aftermath of Hailgate to be insufficiently convincing). It is true that *agents provocateurs* would, presumably, adopt the "Nazi" label that our enemies so fervently desire to pin on us. But I do not think that there is much more to the psychology underlying the Kursk Strategy than a form of harsh and angry verbal catharsis, made irresistible by the strong repression of white European speech in almost all aspects of public life.

The problem is that this sort of catharsis, like the shocking statements of well-paid degeneracy-advocates on the Left, comes under the category of the "Liberty of the Slaves."[6] It is speech that discredits the speaker, marking him as a person without civilized standards, and justifying his unfreedom of action under the managerial regime. Understandably, many of us are fed up with being civilized nowadays; but we must also understand that "racialist Tourette's Syndrome" is all part of our enemy's plan. Just as race-replacement policies give rise to the racial hatreds that are then used to justify suppression of white opinion, to give repressed and silenced whites a free hand for violent verbal catharsis on the internet is to give them just enough rope to hang themselves.

Our best defense against this is a good offense: we must forcefully push the Alt Right off the internet reservation and into public life, creating spaces where frank discussion of suppressed truths and opinions are possible, even if these must at first be small, low-key and even secret.

The pro-Nazi brigade will, of course, try to follow us; and the enemy will, of course, give maximum publicity to their antics. And this is why—for all that I have said here—I want to make it clear to those of like mind that we should never, *ever*, apologize to Leftist scum on account of pro-Nazi rhetoric within the Alt

---

[6] http://thermidormag.com/the-liberty-of-the-slaves/

Right, however unhinged it may be. *Simply attack, attack, and attack*—pointing out the hate and violence of the Left and the Cosmopolitan establishment, as well as the fact that they have created the racial divisions that they are now using to increase their power—and keep your honest opinions on NSLARP stupidity for those who do not question you with hostile intent.

Hopefully, over time, the psychological need for verbal catharsis will itself become obsolete—which means that self-justifications like the Kursk Strategy will also vanish like the mirages they are.

Counter-Currents, July 3, 2018

THE ALT RIGHT & THE ARTS

DAVID YORKSHIRE

THE ROAD TO ALT-RIGHT ARTISTRY

Since Hillary Clinton's mention of the Alternative Right in one of her speeches, there have been countless discussions about what the Alt Right is and represents, with everyone and anyone, no matter how inappropriate, suddenly declaring they are part of the Alt Right. I think it is quite easy to define what the Alt Right is: it is the postmodern manifestation of what Julius Evola termed the True Right.

The True Right has been almost completely disprivileged from the mainstream arts scene in the present day. The political Left, meaning firstly the Whiggish Left and then the socialist Left, realized as early as the late 18th century the power art had to shape political discourse by altering the masses' perceptions of the world. They thus sought to seize the artistic mainstream as a means towards political power.

The Right was quick to counteract this in Britain, and High Tory magazines like *The Quarterly Review*, *Blackwood's Magazine*, and (initially) *Fraser's Magazine* were founded to combat Whig influence on the literary scene. The ones founded later that were associated with Charles Dickens like *Household Words*, *All the Year Round*, and *Bentley's Miscellany* not only continued the tradition, but really brought it into the mainstream, shaping the values of high Victorianism, even if those values were often broken by mean Whig mercantilism, which was heavily criticized or satirized in the works of Dickens, Gaskell, and Thackeray, who all also wrote lengthy novels.

Modernism was not invented by the Jews, as so many people seem to think, but by white Europeans. The first modernist painter was undoubtedly J. M. W. Turner, hence the misuse of his name on an infamous postmodernist prize for anti-art in the UK. The first modernist novel I would posit is Herman Melville's *Moby-Dick*, and it is perhaps quite appropriate that the first country formed under Western modernity should have this novel as its epic. Yet artistic modernism in its early attempt at a break with tradition was certainly of the Left and one notes Turner's liberal worldview and *Moby Dick's* multiculturalism.

This Leftist reaction was exacerbated by the First World War, the aftermath of which saw almost a transvaluation of values, as the surviving remnants of the flower of England and beyond resented what was seen as a generational betrayal by their elders. The two eminent one-time Fabians, George Bernard Shaw and H. G. Wells, entertained and indoctrinated a willing audience in Britain, while Dadaism, cubism, and readymades, pushed by (often Jewish) Leftists that included the likes of the Frankfurt School, who saw the potential of modern art to literally revolutionize culture, gained currency over classical line and form on the continent.

A Rightist riposte came in the 1920s, as the politics of Italian fascism became intertwined with the aesthetics of futurism. In Britain, Wyndham Lewis and Ezra Pound drifted ever Rightwards, just as they had drifted around the entire occidental world, influencing the arts scene wherever they went. Sadly, Hitler's complete antipathy to modernism, no doubt influenced by his rejection by the Viennese Academy, meant not only the stunting of German Rightist art, as German artists became afraid of exploring new paradigms of expression, but also allowed the Left to tighten its grip on modernism.

It also meant that the Leftist version of modern art could be construed by the Extreme Left as an antidote to National Socialist neo-classicism. Deconstruction and Frankfurt School Critical Theory also pushed the idea that traditional forms of European culture had led to the gates of Auschwitz, regardless of the Soviet Union's philo-Semitism and favoring of artistic realism. Sadly, too few in the arts attempted to combat this, with the likes of T. S. Eliot turning to writing poetry about cats. The lack of moral courage shown by the Right in politics since the Second World War has been reflected in the arts and has meant all cultural texts and their creators that could be construed in any way, even mildly, as Rightists have slowly been purged from mainstream culture.

With the Right's cultural structures broken, the Left has continued its course towards complete nihilism in the arts, just as it has spiritually, politically, morally, and philosophically. The Left is the great negation. Yet this has left a vacuum, and Nature abhors a vacuum.

THE EMERGENCE OF ALT-RIGHT ART

As everyone knows, the Alt Right has really emerged out of the internet. The invention of the internet has facilitated an ease of networking around the Occidental world. This has enabled artists and writers to advertise their work without the need for exhibitions, university lectures, or book reading events. Rightist publishing houses like Counter-Currents and Arktos largely owe their success to the internet, their nucleus being their websites.

Writers that would be shunned by the mainstream publishing houses, not for any lack of ability, but for their lack of ideological congruency with the mainstream, like Juleigh Howard-Hobson, Ann Sterzinger, and Tito Perdue, are now able to get their work in print and advertised. Equally, the Leftist hegemony in cultural criticism, through its all but complete control of academic institutions, has been broken by websites like the *Alternative Right* and *Counter-Currents*, where articles can be posted online and made available to everyone.

The freedom of the internet as a new public space for artists has also broken Leftist hegemony in the galleries. Make no mistake, when Charles Krafft's exhibition was announced at Stolen Space in London in November 2015, the gallery was threatened with violence by Leftist activists. Whenever necessary, the Left enforces its hegemony through violence. It is easy to forget that among the street theater and happenings organized by the Left in the 1960s Cultural Revolution, there were explosions and gunfire delivered by groups like the Weather Underground.

Yet art has by no means been reduced merely to the virtual space of the internet. As stated, print books are issued by the aforementioned publishing houses, and I also created *Mjolnir Magazine*, a print magazine to showcase the talents of artists and writers from both the Alt Right and the Occidental Right in general. Equally, the general public are growing weary of the nihilism and vacuity of the Left, and art galleries are becoming more willing to exhibit alternatives. Stolen Space was willing before it was threatened, but Charles Krafft still managed to put on a very successful exhibition at Zoya Tommy earlier in 2016. The sculptor Vig Scholma has also found little difficulty in exhibiting his work.

Yet being deemed a Rightist artist is not without its dangers. The artists Dan Park and Jerzy Szumczyk, the former of Sweden, the latter of Poland, have both been arrested because the current ruling elite have disapproved of their art. Szumczyk erected the sculpture *Komm Frau*, which memorialized the rape of hundreds of thousands of German women by the Red Army during the latter part of the Second World War. He was fortunate, and no charges were brought against him, although his sculpture, depicting a Red Army soldier threatening a prostrate German woman with his pistol, was carted away by authorities back in 2013.

Dan Park was less fortunate. In addition to his works that had been on display at the Rönnquist & Rönnquist gallery in Malmö having been destroyed by the state, Park was also sentenced to six months' imprisonment in 2014 for "defamation and inciting hatred against an ethnic group." The gallery owner, Henrik Rönnquist was fined and received a suspended sentence. In May 2016, he was again arrested by police. Park's works highlight the crimes committed against the native Swedish population by ethnic minorities. One must remember that until recently, Malmö was the rape capital of Europe, before Rotherham in Britain took its place. It is encouraging, however, that artists are still willing to suffer for their art, to suffer for Truth in the face of political correctness.

Politically, the Alt-Right cultural movement is, to borrow an oft-abused word, diverse. It ranges from the most Left-leaning positions of Andy Nowicki and Ann Sterzinger to the stauncher Rightist worldviews of Tito Perdue and Colin Liddell. For all their online shitposting and memes, the National Socialists in the Alt Right have yet to make an impact in the arts, and this may be to do with their tendency to remain psychologically and spiritually stuck in a previous era of their imagining, rather than towards a willingness to create something anew.

Geographically, the artists are concentrated in the Anglosphere particularly America, but not exclusively so. The aforementioned Vig Scholma is Dutch, Park Swedish. Guillaume Faye provides a link between the Alt Right and the French New Right and is more known for his philosophy than his literary works. Also in France resides the musical ensemble *Les Brigandes*, whose lyrics are very much Alt Right, even if, as I revealed in my interview with them for *Mjolnir Issue III*, some of them are quite unsound as regards the racial question.

THE ARTISTRY OF THE ALT RIGHT

As perhaps already remarked, the content, range, and media are as diverse as the ideology. Of course, humor plays an important role, for the Alt Right is playing the Left's old game and winning. As the Left has tied itself in knots with political correctness, it has created a quasi-religious puritanism of perversity that denies humor. It has therefore become a perfect target for mockery, and I, for one, delight in lampooning the Left through characters that are perhaps not as caricatured as real-life social justice warriors.

Leading the way is Charles Krafft, the artist who probably most embodies the Alt Right. His ceramics marry traditional form and technique to postmodernist irony, satire, and ridicule. Such are the levels of irony in the Leftist artworld that Charles was able to pass off his windmills with swastika sails and mock-National Socialist *Bierkrüge* as "darkly ironic," and one of his Hitler teapots was even sold to a Jew! Yet Charles' humor transcends mere politics and his Disasterware™ and Spone™ *objets d'art* display humor blacker than coal!

I once said in an interview that the *Gesamtkunstwerk* of film was probably beyond us for now, yet that has not entirely proven to be the case. The animation team known as Murdoch Murdoch have been creating the most cutting satire reminiscent of (ironically) the 2003 to 2005 BBC cartoon *Monkey Dust*, although the team themselves claim their influences as *South Park*, *Akira*, and Adult Swim. The collage-style animation has a deliberately self-deprecatory tone about its own quality, as per *South Park*, with images often containing the Shutterstock logo or the characters' mouths suddenly changing to animated form during speech.

The Alt Right has even encroached on the music scene, largely concentrating on parodies, the best of which are probably those of *The Right Stuff* team. These cover versions see a replacement of the original lyrics with humorous ones about the white experience usually in relation to other races like the Jews and Negroes. As with the "dank memes," the lyrics often mock the Left and false Right's shibboleths, like the Holocaust™, "gender equality," or "white privilege." Take this opening from The Daily Shoah's *Summer of '88*, for example (to the tune of Bryan Adams' *Summer of '69*):

> I got my standard pool t-shirt
> From those fucking Teespring kikes,
> Wore it on Memorial Day, 'cause
> It's the summer of '88.

Yet every movement cannot consist merely of a reaction against something. It must also represent something, and, amidst the laughter, there is serious consideration. The arts too reflect this. As with the original songs by *Les Brigandes*, Ann Sterzinger's short stories and novels transcend the humorous and serious, the profound and profane, and her "loser lit." could be seen as postmodern tragicomedy. If there is a flaw, it is that Ann is distinctly anti-human, and her anti-natalism comes out quite strongly in her writing.

Andy Nowicki also writes within the genre of "loser lit." and comes from the same religious background as Ann, both being Roman Catholics—more lapsed in Ann's case—which to a greater or lesser degree, informs their morality. Andy's novels are often much darker in tone, however, and there is often an element of horror in his critiques, particularly those of feminism—albeit dramatic horror, as opposed to the zombie fiction of K. Bartholomew, whose short stories and novels satirize everything from government to celebrity culture through schlock horror.

Indeed, Ann and Andy share their flair for dramatic hyper-realism with Tito Perdue. Tito tends to have a more positive outlook on the world, and his chief protagonist Lee Pefley succeeds through his adherence to tradition. There is also an innate spirituality to his novels that transcends Christianity, just as Vig Scholma's artwork transcends any fixed religion, yet is racially bound. Juleigh Howard-Hobson's poetry is grounded in her Heathenism, and is therefore inherently racial. The spiritual dimension of culture is important, for one cannot have a spiritual revival without it. In negating the spirit, the Left has been left flogging readymades for over a century now and is unable to create anything fresh and radical — a plastic meaningless culture for a plastic meaningless age.

There is, then, much promise for a flourishing in Alt Right art, and, certainly, I have been approached by many artists and writers wishing to showcase their work in future editions of *Mjolnir Magazine*, which is a good starting point for writers cutting their teeth in short fiction before attempting something longer for *Counter-Currents* or Arktos. It is also a vehicle for existing writers and artists to pass on their skills to the next generation, and I have here mentioned only the most well-known. I believe we are witnessing merely the first sparks of a cultural inferno.

If I can offer two last pieces of advice for budding Alt-Right artists, it is this: honor the tradition that has gone before, but do not copy it slavishly, for one must always renew and reinterpret tradition for each new age; remember that the love of your own people and culture should always come before your disdain for those who wish to destroy them. The future is a blank canvas waiting for our artists to fill with the images of their choosing.

Counter-Currents, November 2, 2016

TOWARD AN ALT-RIGHT RELIGION

F. C. STOUGHTON

I

We in the Alt Right tend to regard our internal religious debates as pointless and divisive. Atheist or Anglican or Asatru, we feel, target each other for denunciation or proselytization only to the detriment of our cause. Thus we often adopt a playful cynicism when dealing with the subject of religion so as to avoid intragroup strife and hurt feels. Consider, for example, one of our Twitter stalwarts' wry play-by-play of a recent Alt-Right religious kerfuffle: "'ChristCuck' attacks 'dirt-worshipper'; according to rescue workers, *thousands of opinions feared unchanged.*"

Despite pervasive reticence, however, many of us continue to dream of mapping out some kind of Alt-Right religious system or systems. We question the commonplace idea that people are best served by rejecting organized religions out of hand, though at first glance this advice seems well-intentioned and even sound. Westerners of course do not typically wage *jihad* to coerce people's beliefs to fall in line under a single, unifying gospel; we've all been reared on the secular precepts of cultural and moral relativism, in which everyone is right in their own special way and everyone only glimpses contingent truths for-the-moment and for themselves alone.

But what results from such attitudes in the long term? Around us we see what should be a heuristic paradise, but *nothing connects with nothing.* We are all these solitary pseudo-shamans claiming a discreet, personal, atomized angle on the truths of the universe, each equally valid but equally irreconcilable with those of another. There is no community, no continuity. There's nothing to learn from your ancestors or teach your kids since everyone should just, like, work it out for themselves . . . or not.

Against this laissez-faire, anything-goes mindset we hold

that the only experience worth having, religious or otherwise, over the long term, is one that can be shared with likeminded folk. Interconnectivity of experience and belief reinforces a people's identity and steels them against strife, stupidity, and genocide. The stone endures while disconnected, particulate sands scatter in a limp breeze.

II

Besides, the idea that "anything goes" in the modern West is a thin facade. Scratch its surface and find a codex of religious dogmas as rigidly prohibitive as any verse of Leviticus or *sura* of the Koran: anti-essentialism, cultural Marxism, secular materialism, hate speech codes, social justice, and radical egalitarianism. Masters of these strict protocols claim as their sacred mission the destruction of mean, oppressive, hierarchical power structures. But this, too, is total bullshit: in the act of toppling the old order they've simply installed *themselves*. Now new Pharisees in government, academia, the mainstream media, and the commercial sphere mutter shibboleths of "fairness" and "diversity" only to perpetuate their power grab. The universalizing crypto-church they've raised holds, for us, no hope of salvation; it demands only our non-existence.

As if this weren't bad enough, there is another global religion out there demanding our non-existence. While the self-righteous egalitarians gleefully deconstruct our identity with their magic words, jihadists simply want us dead; they relish deconstructing our neck vertebrae with their knives and our nightclubs with their AKs and our Palmyras with their C-4. That the egalitarians zealously welcome this latter group into our homelands in large numbers means the endgame of their professed tolerance is nothing but a two-tiered intolerance towards us, a rhetorical and actual death sentence.

So, while we in the modern West like to brag about being "beyond all that religious stuff," in truth we're increasingly crushed between the armies of Leftist Egalitarianism and Islam, religious ideologies that could not be less similar except that they work in concert against us.

III

It is through realizing the threats we face, both demographic and spiritual, from these twin death cults that many of us have been redpilled into to the Alt Right's ranks from normie secularism or atheism, cucked Christianity, or autistic Libertarianism — seeking a climate less comfortable and more bracing. Let's face it: when jihadists chanting *Allahu Akbar* recently decapitated Fr. Jacques Hamel in the middle of morning Mass in Rouen, Pope Francis could have done with a bit more harshness, perhaps a wee bit of pushback. But no, he could not bring himself to condemn the sawing-off of his underling's head. He offered boilerplate more in line with the Church of the Globalist Egalitarians than with the church he purportedly heads: *All religions want peace!*

Yawn. This was never true. But now that jihadists live in Western societies in large numbers, the lie is ever more apparent. The basis for Western religious tolerance — that rosy, libertarian, Jeffersonian notion that it does us "no injury for my neighbor to say there are twenty gods or no god" since "it neither picks my pocket nor breaks my leg" — seems no longer to apply. Godless Marxist zealots pick our pockets while monotheist Muslims break our necks and hymens. We can no longer afford the breezy indifference of an open, tolerant, unaffiliated mind.

IV

So what to do? What to *believe*? We would ask it this way: what do we want our beliefs to do? For the religion of the Alt Right, in all its forms, is refreshingly pragmatic.

We have already touched on the ramifications of collective belief: get everyone reading from the same script to consolidate your power, as Constantine knew at the Council of Nicaea and as ISIS knows today. And it is almost true to say that the Alt Right is only interested in religion insofar as it satisfies such political exigencies. But not quite: the social and political effects of a belief are a sum of its effect on *individuals*. The social cohe-

sion elicited by shared belief is no good if it turns us, individu-
ally speaking, into sad robots, cowards, or cuckolds—which
would, in turn, render the collective nothing to be particularly
proud of.

So though any manner of collective worship may unify us,
we refuse to be unified in self-defeat. We refuse to honor alien,
universalizing gods who don't honor us back, who appear to
think that we are fungible with other individuals and peoples.
We refuse to abase ourselves before a jealous god—it is *we* who
should be jealous of a god who puts others before *us*. We condemn the migrant-loving, pathological altruism of the Current
Year's pope. We blast the Evangelical Israel-firsters of the pastor Hagee stripe. We scoff at notions of endemic, original sin
("white guilt" or "white privilege") and their groveling atone-
ments in the virtue-signaling cult of childless volunteers in the
South Sudan. We reject even the belief in a personal savior who
is supposed to have already done the work of squaring up our
shortfalls with the divine—turning us into idle, passive observers, i.e. cucks. Any such shortfall we claim as effortspace for
own great spiritual work.

Beyond that, we're flexible. We would believe in the divini-
ty of a smug green frog or real estate mogul if we thought he'd
reward our affections by blessing us with *virtù* and hale prolifi-
cacy.

V

Considering this pragmatic bent, many of us appear to
want, in terms of an Alt-Right religion, something more or less
along the lines of the following, posted by an anonymous
commenter on our forums: "We need some esoteric, occult shit
for the elites and some low level, low grade crypto-ancestor
worship/glorification of the past for the proles. See where it
goes from there."

To this a more "no-nonsense" Alt-Righter provides the inevitable retort: "You love your mother for no other reason than
she is *your* mother. If that's not a good enough reason for you,
all the esoteric bullshit in the world isn't going to help you."

Both positions are valid. But the objection of the latter only proves the former's point. Our religion must accommodate the range of outlooks and inclinations one gets even in a homogeneous population—of cops and provocateurs; of soldiers and statisticians and poets. Some of us are literal-minded Gradgrinds by nature, and there is nothing wrong with that or any getting around it. Such types, looking in justified horror at how our enemies' religious sophistry has gotten many in the West to supplant their natural love of kin with "universal love," would think "occult esoterica" only likewise clouds and complicates a straightforward, inviolable issue—endangering further supplantation.

To this the former commenter would say that esoterica, and religious symbols in general, are not scaffolding to prop up or enshadow our love, but are expressions of it. There is a tradition in the West, especially among the pagans of Classical antiquity, to see such symbols, in stone or in song, as projections of the artist's inner qualities rather than as merely depictions of distant, pre-existing ideals, gods, or objective realities. This is why the classical poets from Hesiod to Ovid could take such liberties when giving their own version of their respective culture's religious theogonies. Xenophanes went so far as to suggest that if cows and horses had hands and could draw, they would make their gods look like cows and horses.

VI

Feuerbach and Marx seize upon this idea that the gods might be mere projections as a reason to reject religion. But they would ask a poem to prove its merit using only addition, subtraction, and bags of onions or cement, and then sigh patronizingly when the poor poem fell short. Their critique of religious belief—that it has no recourse to concrete evidence or empirical data—tries to bully us into accepting that the only worthwhile accounting to be made of anything comes through means that religion cannot provide. But no human phenomena—no feelings of desire, curiosity, dread, love, hate, awe, purpose; no flight of fancy or invention—translate into the hard sciences without being stripped of the qualities that make them make sense to us. What good is it to say that because these things can't survive the trip they are *untrue*? Being pragmatists in matters of religion, we feel there is no meaningful distinction to be made between the objective existence of the Parthenon, which is a "mere" projection of our aspirations to commune with the divine, and the existence of Athena herself. She exists through her effects, i.e., the Parthenon.

We are not a rigidly dogmatic people. Inventiveness is, for us, a potentially sacral act. Nietzsche held the invention of gods to be, rather than an act of self-delusion, *a priceless exercise of self-sovereignty*. Our desire to commune with the infinite by creating anew, and the successful projection of that desire in productions glorious and rare — from megaliths and myths to dank memes — is, for us, and as William James would say, *the positive content of religious experience*.

(Please. We are not here to say whether or not the gods really exist as ontic entities, or whether the actual holds primacy over the possible or vice versa — these are painfully autistic questions to be asking in light of our current crisis.)

VII

So the Alt Right provides a wide table, accommodating heterodox theologies and hermeneutics. Here a worshipper of Lord Kek or God Emperor Trump could break bread with a devout Rodnover; a Mormon may toast his fruit punch — *skál!* — with a mead-chugging Asatrur/Odinist and a wine-sipping materialist atheist.

Do we sound friendly and flexible to a fault? Too much like the current secular dispensation of unaffiliated, easy-going slouchers? Whence comes the unifying, bracing rigidity we claimed to need in the face of the current Islamist and liberal-egalitarian *jihad*?

It comes via an ethical question — the iron question: *is it good for Europeans?* On this point we are *fundamentalists*. With this as a first principle, one can — to quote another of our commenters — implement a Kantian categorical imperative *without being a faggot*.

For too long we in the West have been conditioned to ask only how we might be good Europeans, which was assumed to be
tantamount to asking how we could best benefit non-Europeans.
The Merkel-style semi-man can never say *no* when browns demand gibs; he would offer up his chair, wallet, wife, law, history, and future in hopes of signaling, if only for one glorious
moment, his virtue. What a beacon of selflessness he is! A holy
advocate and catalyst of perpetual Third-World smiles!

This pathological deference takes many forms. It has altered
the demographics of our neighborhoods and nations, over-
hauled the personnel and programming of entertainment and
news networks, and changed what passes for (((higher education in the humanities))). The list goes on. Nowhere in the West,
it seems, is safe from the "Great Erasure," from Europeans' crusade against themselves.

The Alt Right practices radical pushback against such cuckoldry
as a sacred duty and an act of religious devotion.

VIII

Our devotion takes at least as many forms as the chimera of
pathological deference we must slay. The green shoots of our
first principle we gather and bind into three fasces: *Procreation.*
Education. Invention.

Unless we keep ourselves healthy and strong, and produce
healthy, strong children, any other consideration quickly becomes kinda irrelevant; we will fade and die and become a
memory, until we cease to be even that. Thus we honor non-
degenerate Motherhood and Fatherhood. We unabashedly encourage stable families and eugenic breeding practices as a religious principle.

Unless we religiously instill in ourselves and our children
the story of our ancestors and their achievements (and even
make lessons of their failures), we endanger the future to the
great *oubliette.* An uncultivated, trivial mind is susceptible to
distraction and amenable to enemy propaganda. So while
modern SWPLs in yoga pants practice meditation or mindful-
ness, devoutly clearing their heads in order to better contem-

plate their momentary feels or their caramel macchiatos, we relentlessly cultivate in our mental spaces the seeds we inherit from our ethno-genetic and civilizational past.

Against cultural relativism, deconstruction, SJW spin, and the ravages of digitized prolefeed we thus honor as a religious principle the thoughts and deeds and creations of our forebearers — artistic, scientific, martial, poetic, philosophical. With William Gayley Simpson we hold that the great works of the West provide us with the most holy *scripture* – Nietzsche our nobler Leviticus; Shakespeare our subtler Ecclesiastes. An Alt Right Civic Religion would cease to teach the bland, universalizing "love thy neighbor as thyself"; we would sooner draw lessons from Odysseus' vengeance on the upstart suitors.

The fragments of Heraclitus; *Being and Time*; *The Rite of Spring*; the longship; the Lunar Rover; the battle of Thermopylae; the Pantheon; *L'Apothéose d'Hercule*; *Götterdämmerung* — these speak from us and to us. They are our sacred texts and divine monuments. We will never take them for granted, heartbreakingly rare as they are amid the dumb, frozen desolations of the universe.

IX
Templum Deorum

But we do no honor to our forbearers if we are so busy honoring them we become past-oriented, dogmatic, and uncreative. We must avoid being Emerson's "meek young men" who "grow up in libraries believing it their duty to accept the views which Cicero, which Locke, which Bacon have given, forgetful that Cicero, Locke and Bacon were only young men in libraries when they wrote those books."

A religious revolution must be made by and for its moment. Every new generation, if they are in touch with the pulse of the day and draw from the infinite, will make high art and occult shit and myths and gods anew. Fortuitously, providentially, Keks and Trumps will arise at the opportune moment and in the nick of time. Genius will regenerate, as of old.

We thus find the Alt Right is not merely the "Alternative

Right." Though it is a new movement, it is part of the revolutionary, creative, inventive instinct that is ancient in us. Indeed, there something very *Alt* (i.e., German for "old") in the *Alt Right*, i.e., we are the Old Right made anew to displace the erstwhile Right-wing, the neocons, cowards, and cucks, to revive our old civilization with new fervor, focus, and love.

Counter-Currents, September 9, 2016

WHAT WOULD AN ALT-RIGHT ADMINISTRATION LOOK LIKE?

LAWRENCE MURRAY

One of the many paths to power for Alt-Right ideas would be to control substantial elements of the federal government. This scenario has major limitations given the Constitution and the inertia that exists in the American system due to the nebulous divisions of sovereignty it imposes. It's also hated by purists, who think the United States has to go. And perhaps it will eventually, because there is no method of totally fixing it from within. But controlling blocs of federal power is a scenario in which executive orders, acts of Congress, and Supreme Court rulings could be made with the intention of *not making things worse*. Because that's exactly how things are for us under occupation – *worse every year*.

This makes more people resent the system but it also . . . makes us worse off. We shouldn't rule out the idea of having policy positions for the current system of government; that door is not entirely shut yet. Planning for collapse scenarios is all and well, but having policies which could plausibly be enacted tomorrow rather than the day after tomorrow has rhetorical value. It shows we aren't just LARPing about the ethnostate and that there are short- and medium-term applications for our ideas. So here are some areas that an Alt-Right administration could tackle:

IMMIGRATION

The United States has a history of turning away the world's huddled masses, so yes, anti-immigration is an *American value*. Before the 1890s, and more so before 1880, most immigration was from places like Ireland, Germany, England, Scotland, Scandinavia and so forth. From 1880–1920, most immigration came from Italy, Poland, Russia, and other non-Northern European countries, bringing with it large numbers of Jews. The 1924 Immigration Act, also known as the Johnson-Reed Act, set up a national origins quota for who could enter the United States as a reaction to this change. The law replaced the 1921 Immigration Act, which was less strict, passing the House of Representatives by 308 to 58 and the Senate 69 to 9. The 1924 law limited entry visas to two percent of the total number of people of each nationality in the United States as of the 1890 national census; 1921's law referred to 1910. The quota system greatly favored Northern European countries over Southern and Eastern European countries, in addition to further restricting immigration from Asia (Asian immigrants already could not become naturalized citizens in most cases).

If Congress were to pass a new immigration act revising the (((Hart-Celler Act))) of 1965, it could also use an old census to set up a new quota system. Like the old Immigration Acts, it would also be aimed at conserving the ethnic and racial character of the United States. If we were to set up new national origins quotas based on the 1960 Census, the only countries with any substantial number of visas would be Germany, Italy, Britain, Canada, and Mexico. That wouldn't be terrible.

The president also has the authority to block whatever countries he wants and deny entry to their nationals:

> Whenever the president finds that the entry of any aliens or of any class of aliens into the United States would be detrimental to the interests of the United States, he may by proclamation, and for such period as he shall deem necessary, suspend the entry of all aliens or any class of aliens as immigrants or nonimmigrants, or impose on the entry of aliens any restrictions he may deem to be appropriate. — U.S. Code § 1182 (Inadmissible Aliens)

The problem with executive orders is that they can be rescinded by the next administration with the stroke of a pen. In the long-term it would be better to institutionalize immigration restrictions into the laws of the land and retain enough of a legislative majority to prevent them from being repealed. Such is the way our legal system works.

MARRIAGE & FAMILY

You can't legislate behavior, but you can definitely incentivize it. Our laws regarding marriage and divorce are completely dysgenic, anti-family, and anti-natal, and they need to be changed. There are two crucial reforms necessary. First, the legality of no-fault divorce must be abolished. The ability to get a divorce without having any valid reason was first introduced into the United States through a 1970 law signed by none other than California governor Ronald Reagan, who remains beloved by conservatives for some reason. By the 1980s, almost every state had enacted no-fault divorce laws, in a decade which also remains beloved by conservatives for some reason. For people who claim to care about family values, conservatives have neglected the family itself.

Intact families with replacement-level fertility rates are the building blocks of our civilization and integral to having a healthy society, and so any laws which facilitate the destruction of such families and degrade the value of child-bearing marriages are antithetical to life itself. The family is the ultimate expression of future orientation. Feminism, by "smashing the patriarchy," has rather smashed the family, and produced broken homes and a record number of miserable childless catladies and single mothers. This is a disaster that needs to be brought under control before we permanently go off the demographic cliff. And conservatives have been complicit in it.

Secondly, we need a revised version of the Defense of Marriage Act (1996) put in place and the Sanhedrin ruling that overturned it, *United States v. Windsor* (2013), totally dropped. Homosexual marriages, to the extent that they exist, are a parody, and even some LGBT academics reject them as being "heteronormative." The drive for homosexual marriage is entirely the work of a lobby that plays off the nurturing instinct of women and the ideology of a regressive egalitarianism, and doesn't reflect the reality that most homosexuals are not monogamous. In other words, it is less for the benefit of monogamous homosexuals and more to the benefit of those who want to deconstruct the ideal of the nuclear family by destroying its legal definition. It is evident that we have to prioritize what is best for childbearing couples over what is best for a minority of the homosexual minority.

Marriage is between a man and woman, and not only should those couples be entitled to the legal benefits of marriage, but couples which produce children should be given further entitlements. Just as we need to get immigration under control to maintain our society and culture, we also need our people to reproduce themselves. And while there is nothing we can do to instantly overturn the collapse of family-centric culture, we should do everything we can to incentivize its return. We need to make childcare, education, and home-ownership easier for nuclear families, who are, again, integral to the continuity of our society. We should consider even taking drastic discriminatory measures against the willfully childless, especially childless couples (without fertility issues) and single people in their thirties and onward. Nothing else we do or build will matter if it is not inherited by our people because they failed to reproduce.

FIREARMS

The purpose of gun ownership is two-fold: to empower self-defense in a society with deteriorating security, and to promote the ideal family provider-defender role of the citizen. As the United States increasingly comes to resemble the Third World, the right to defend ourselves will only become more valuable. Hobbes said that life was "solitary, poore, nasty, brutish, and short," and nowhere is this more true than outside of the global north (Greater Europe and East Asia). Since 1965, most population growth in the United States has been of Third-World origins thanks to the scrapping of our national origins immigration quotas by the (((Hart-Celler Act))). You're going to want a gun if your neighborhood looks like Brazil or South Africa. Or if you are geographically surrounded by places that look like Brazil or South Africa. And that is the future as of now — most births in this country are non-white. In vibrant New York City, 90% of violent crimes are committed by the black and mestizo population, and private gun ownership is severely restricted. More people died in Chicago from gun violence the last eight years than American soldiers in Iraq and Afghanistan during the same period. A gun-free future is anarcho-tyranny.

Diversity breaks down trust and social cohesion in two main ways: first it balkanizes society into competing ethnic groups, and secondly it erodes trust between members of the same in-group, since they are accustomed to not trusting people in the first place. In a low-trust society, you need to arm yourself because you can't count on your "fellow citizens" to behave, and you can't rely on the police to protect you.

In terms of legislation, there should be as few restrictions on firearms ownership as possible. Ownership should be regarded as a civic virtue—to be ready to defend home, hearth, and fatherland—and there should be ongoing educational campaigns to promote gun safety and responsibility. Like marriage laws, our laws regarding guns should be aimed at incentivizing and uplifting the model citizen, not creating the model dependent. The model citizen is capable of self-defense of his family. Concealed-carry permits enable this and should be issued and valid in all states, which would require either a federal law or arm-twisting to get all states to pass permit laws (as was done with driving laws).

FOREIGN POLICY

Much of US foreign policy is really out of the hands of the government proper and remains unchanged no matter who is elected. Revolutionary action would ultimately be needed to alter some of our foreign relationships and institutions. That said, there are things an Alt-Right administration could do from within Congress or the executive branch. Programs that send "development aid" overseas can be cancelled. Attempts at "developing" the entire world to Western levels of consumption are an ecological disaster waiting to happen and currently responsible for explosive birthrates in the global south, which thanks to our medical technology and the local aversion to birth control are driving immigration pressures and creating an unsustainable demand for resources. Furthermore, there are plenty of economically depressed areas in our own country which should inherently be put first and benefit from investment and infrastructure improvements.

Military bases that are irrelevant to our missile defense systems should be closed, leases cancelled, and the land returned to the countries they are located in. All military personnel not on reserved bases should be withdrawn from countries which we have not declared war against. Additionally, only countries which we are allied with in a lawfully-declared war should be eligible for military aid. That means no more billions for Israel each year. The *casus belli* of "humanitarian war" should also be renounced, as toppling autocratic governments in the name of democracy is a waste of time, treasure, and blood, in addition to forcing one of the worst forms of government on populations which will be unable to weather it. Forcing democracy on the Middle East and North Africa is especially dangerous, since democracy leads to the rise of Islamist parties and religious sectarianism (see Libya, Egypt, Syria, Iraq, etc.). Another important foreign policy realignment would be de-escalating the (((neocon))) standoff against Russia, which is a natural ally against the global conflict with the Islamic world, since the Russians are quite literally on the front-lines of it.

ENERGY & THE ENVIRONMENT

The United States should become energy independent or limit imports to countries which are aligned with our values and civilization. We should not be making the Islamic monarchies of the Gulf rich. We should be making use of our natural resources here in the United States — such as coal, oil, and natural gas — and promoting the use of efficient, emission-free alternatives like nuclear energy. This will also create domestic jobs. If climate change predictions are correct, and predictions that change will occur regardless of how much we cut our current emissions, the sane energy policy should be to make sure our energy supplies remain secure and sufficient to meet our consumption needs regardless of global shifts, by promoting energy independence and autarkic production. Additionally, since climate change and rising sea levels would cause cataclysmic migration pressures and coastal flooding, we need to strengthen our borders accordingly and develop the technologies necessary for protecting our ports. If people actually care about the impact of climate change and our energy policies as opposed to virtue-signaling about them, they will think about the long-term repercussions and allow the government to undertake the multiple administration-spanning projects necessary to mitigate them. This is not something we can solve in one or two terms, and it won't be solved by making unenforceable carbon-capping pacts with other countries.

TRADE

We need to encourage as much domestic production as possible in order to create quality jobs for American workers so they can start and sustain families. The United States was built on the strength of its internal marketplace and having high quality exports. A country as massive as ours should not be relying on Third-World sweatshop slave labor to produce many of its most basic goods, from clothing to food to household appliances. This is unethical and spatially absurd; the product of historically anomalous free trade laws and the cheapness of exploiting overseas labor.

We will be judged by history, both for hollowing out the economic base of our own country and for supporting modern-day slavery. Why do we ship clothing all the way from Bangladesh or Indonesia to the United States? Why do we both pour money into foreign Mexican production and import Mexican workers into our domestic workforce? At some point, these countries are going to have labor laws or unionization, and the costs of producing overseas will go up anyway. In terms of pure balance sheet costs alone, it is cheaper to manufacture overseas. But when we consider the costs of all the inputs in this supply chain, from feeding and housing foreign workers, to fueling the container ships, to trucking the goods to retailers and warehouses in the United States, there are huge costs not factored into the price we pay at the register. If protectionism is opposed for economic reasons by globalists, economists, and anti-nationalists, perhaps they can be convinced to support them on moral or environmental grounds. Producing locally is better for the environment and means a slave-free supply chain. Why our supposed liberals ignore this is a source of fascination to me. But for nationalists the solution is clear, to support as much domestic production as we can sustain, and this can be done through legislation.

EDUCATION

The American education system needs a lot of work. State-run universities and federal and state student loan programs need to be rethought to serve the needs of our nation rather than being sponsors of Marxist academics and producers of brain-dead, debt-laden, unemployable drones. The liberal arts are valuable when taught properly, but people should not be going deeply in debt to get a liberal arts education, especially since it's become a source of anti-civilizational values. How insane have we become that we encourage our children to believe that college is the one true path to status and enlightenment, despite most students learning nothing of value in what have become glorified high school classes. We need more support for STEM and trade school education, not more Intersectional Feminist Basketweaving. We need the liberal arts brought under better oversight, and financing for those who wish to "study" them restricted. The electrician and the plumber build the country as much as the engineer and the philosopher. The education system in this country fills a large amount of young people's heads with racial and gender mythology and supplies unemployed Marxists at the taxpayers' expense. This can be fixed.

You get more of what you incentivize and less of what you don't. The tech sector says we need more scam H1B1 visas for less-expensive foreigners because there aren't enough qualified Americans to do QA testing for smartphone apps. Why couldn't we change that in four years? We need to figure out which policies would incentivize the best to do their best and which would channel the mediocre into less academically or scientifically rigorous, but still productive, work. Currently, we have a blindly pro-college culture and loan system of generating profits off ignorant people by leading them into debt for meaningless degrees. This has to change, and it could start from the top-down. Something has to be done about student debt, because debt makes home-ownership harder and delays family formation. A society where the young have negative wealth and low birthrates is going to die. It is a testament to how wildly irresponsible, i.e., evil, the current system is that it inches us closer and closer societal collapse in the name of progress.

CONCLUSION

An Alt-Right administration in the United States would not be able to save the United States. The authority needed to totally save our civilization does not exist in the American system. That doesn't mean we should reject the rhetorical value of having policy proposals. Audiences want to know what we would do, not just what our theories are. Conversely, we have to keep in mind that policy proposals are never going to be enough. But someone needs to pull the emergency brake. If we don't do anything to change our values and way of life—or try to create conditions that would lead to change—we aren't going to magically emerge from the rubble of its collapse better off. Accelerationists would do well to remember that. If we ever have the opportunity to rewrite the laws we should take it. Let's make sure when we step out of the Weimerica Shopping Center, we do so from a position of strength.

Counter-Currents, August 3, 2016

SEXUAL LIBERATION &
RACIAL SUICIDE

F. ROGER DEVLIN

What is "sexual liberation"? It is usually spoken of by way of contrast with the constraints of marriage and family life. It would seem to be a condition under which people have more choice than under the traditional system of monogamy. Hugh Hefner's "Playboy philosophy" seemed to offer men more choices than just sleeping with the same woman every night for fifty years.

Feminism promised women it would liberate them from "domestic drudgery" and turn marriage and motherhood into just one among many lifestyle choices.

On the other hand, there was always an element of free choice even regarding marriage: one may choose whether, and to a certain extent whom, one will marry. Indeed, marriage is perhaps the most important example of a momentous life choice. But on the traditional view you cannot make your choice and still have it. Once one takes the vow and enters into the covenant, *ipso facto* one no longer has a choice. In other words, marriage is a one-way nonrefundable ticket. Your wife *is* your choice even if she eventually displeases you in certain ways, as all mortal wives necessarily must. Keeping your choice of mate open forever is called "celibacy."

Ultimately, the ideal of sexual liberation rests upon a philosophical confusion which I call the *absolutizing of choice*. The illusion is that society could somehow be ordered to allow us to choose without thereby diminishing our future options. Birth control, abortion, the destigmatizing of fornication and homosexuality, arbitrary and unilateral divorce — all these have been pitched to us as ways of expanding our choices.

Now, I am in favor of giving people all the choice they can stand. But I would like to be careful about what this means:

analysis will reveal that the term "choice" has distinct and part-ly contradictory senses which may not be equally applicable in all contexts. In other words, choice is not a single thing which can be expanded indefinitely at no cost; the appearance of greater choice in one area can be shown to entail reducing one's possibilities in another.

One perfectly legitimate sense of choosing is doing as one desires. When we are asked to choose a flavor of ice cream, e.g., all that is meant is deciding which flavor would be the most pleasing to us at the moment. That is because the alternative of chocolate or strawberry involves no deep, long-term conse-quences. But not all choices can be like this.

Consider, for example, a young man's choice of vocation. One of the charms of youth is that it is a time when possibility overshadows actuality. One might become a brain surgeon, or a mountain climber, or a poet, or a statesman, or a monk. It is natural and good for boys to dream about all the various things they might become, but such daydreams can breed a danger-ous illusion: that, where anything is still possible, everything will be possible. This is only true in the case of trivial and in-consequential matters. It is possible to sample all of Baskin-Robbins' thirty-one flavors on thirty-one successive days. But it is not possible to become a brain-surgeon *and* a mountain climber *and* a poet *and* a statesman *and* a monk. A man who tries to do so will only fail in all his endeavors.

The reason for this, of course, is that important enterprises demand large amounts of time and dedication, but the men who undertake them are mortal. For every possibility we real-ize, there will be a hundred we must leave forever unrealized; for every path we choose to take, there will be a hundred we must forever renounce. The need for choice in *this* sense is what gives human life much of its seriousness. Those who drift from one thing to another, unable to make up their minds or finish anything they have begun, reveal thereby that they do not grasp an essential truth about the human condition. They are like children who do not wish to grow up.

Now, sexual choices, especially for women, are analogous to a man's in regard to his calling. Inherently, they cannot be made as easy and reversible as choosing flavors of ice cream. But this is what sexual liberation attempts to do. The underlying motive seems to be precisely a fear of difficult choices and a desire to eliminate the need for them. For example, a woman does not have to think about a man's qualifications to be a father to her children if a pill or a routine medical procedure can remove that possibility. There is no reason to consider carefully the alternative between career and marriage if motherhood can be safely postponed until the age of forty (as large numbers of women now apparently believe). What we have here is not a clear gain in the *amount* of choice, but a shift from one sense of the word to another—from serious, reflective commitment to merely doing as one desires at any given time. Like the dilettante who dabbles in five professions without finally pursuing any, the liberated woman and the playboy want to keep all their options open forever: they want eternal youth.

The attempt to realize a utopia of limitless choice in the real world has certain predictable consequences: notably, it makes the experience of love one of repeated failure. Those who reject both committed marriage and committed celibacy drift into and out of a series of what are called "relationships," either abandoning or being abandoned. The lesson inevitably taught by such experiences is that love does not last, that people are not reliable, that in the end one has only oneself to fall back on, that prudence dictates always looking out for number one. And this in turn destroys the generosity, loyalty, and trust which are indispensable for family life and the perpetuation of our kind.

Most of those who have obeyed the new commandment to follow all of their hearts' desire do not appear to me to be reveling in a garden of earthly delights. Instead I am reminded of the sad characters from the pages of Chekhov: sleepwalking through life, forever hoping that tomorrow things will somehow be changed for the better as they blindly allow opportunities for lasting happiness to slip through their fingers. But this is merely the natural outcome of conceiving of a human life as a series of revocable and inconsequential choices. We are, indeed, protected from certain risks, but have correspondingly little to gain; we have fewer worries but no great aspirations.

The price we pay for eliminating the dangers of intimacy is the elimination of its seriousness.

In place of family formation, we find a "dating scene" without any clear goal, in which men and women are both consumed with the effort to get the other party to close options while keeping their own open. There is a hectic and never-ending jockeying for position: fighting off the competition while keeping an eye out for a better deal elsewhere. The latest "singles" fad, I am told, is something called speed dating, where men and women interact for three minutes, then go on to someone else at the sound of a bell.

Sex belongs to early adulthood: one transient phase of human life. It is futile to attempt to abstract it from its natural and limited place in the life-cycle and make it an end in itself. Sustainable civilization requires that more important long-term desires like procreation be given preference over short term wishes which conflict with them, such as the impulse to fornicate.

The purpose of marriage is not to place shackles upon people or reduce their options, but to enable them to achieve something which most are simply too weak to achieve without the aid of a social institution. Certain valuable things require time to ripen, and you cannot discover them unless you are faithful to your task and patient. Marriage is what tells people to stick to it long enough to find out what happens. Struggling with such difficulties—and even periods of outright discouragement—is part of what allows the desires of men and women to mature and come into focus. Older couples who have successfully raised children together, and are rewarded by seeing them marry and produce children of their own, are unlikely to view their honeymoon as the most important event of their marriage.

People cannot know what they want when they are young. A young man may imagine happiness to consist in living on Calypso's Island, giving himself over to sexual pleasure without ever incurring family obligations; but all serious men eventually find such a life unsatisfying. The term "playboy" was originally derogatory, implying that the male who makes pursuing women his highest end is not to be taken seriously. The type of man who thinks he's hot stuff because he's able to have one-night stands will never raise sons capable of carrying on the fight for our embattled civilization.

Confusion about one's desires is probably greater in young women, however. For this reason, it is misleading to speak of women "wanting marriage." A young woman leafing through the pages of *Modern Bride* does not yet know what marriage is; all she wants is to have her wedding day and live happily ever after. She may well not have the slightest notion of the duties she will be taking on.

Parenthood is what really forces young men and women to grow up. Young men whose idea of the good life was getting drunk, getting laid, and passing out suddenly start focusing on career planning and building capital. They find it bracing to have a genuinely important task to perform, and are perhaps surprised to find themselves equal to it.

But without the understanding that marriage is an inherently irreversible covenant, both men and women succumb to the illusion that divorce will solve the "problem" of dissatisfaction in marriage. They behave like the farmer who clears, plows, and plants a field only to throw up his hands on the first really hot and sweaty day of work, exclaiming: "Farming is no fun! I'm going to do something else!" And like that farmer, they have no one to blame but themselves when they fail to harvest any crops.

Understanding the marriage bond as an irreversible covenant similarly influences the way economic activity and property are understood. Rather than being a series of short-term responses to circumstance, labor and investment become an aspect of family life transcending the natural life span of any individual. From a mere means to consumption, wealth becomes a family inheritance. In Burke's fine words: "The power of perpetuating our property in our families is one of the most valuable and interesting circumstances belonging to it, and that which tends most to the perpetuation of society itself." By contrast, the characteristically modern view of property finds its clearest expression in the title of a bestselling 1998 financial planning guide: *Die Broke*. This amounts to a scorched earth policy for our own civilization. Perhaps someday the author will favor us with a sequel entitled *Die Alone* or *Die Childless*.

But not everyone is equally receptive to this kind of message. Women in parts of West Africa are averaging over eight children apiece. The revolt against marriage and childrearing is an overwhelmingly white phenomenon. It is primarily in white countries that the birthrate has fallen below replacement level. It would behoove racially conscious whites, therefore, not to ignore the sexual side of the revolt against our civilization, nor shortsightedly to limit our attention to the single issue of miscegenation. The homosexual bathhouse view of sex as merely a means to personal pleasure attacks our race from within and at its source. As much as with inimical races and racial ideologies, our survival will depend upon our ability to organize effective resistance.

When we look around at all the forces arrayed against our race, it can be daunting. How can we fight them all? Are circumstances right? Would we be ready even if they were? And what to do in the meantime? The situation becomes a lot less daunting when we realize that the first battle, and the first victory, must take place within ourselves.

TOQ Online, April 8, 2010

A PLACE FOR WOMEN
IN THE ALT RIGHT

WOLFIE JAMES

It's no secret that historically, men have harnessed intelligence, drive, pride, and anger to lead and conquer, while women have been empathetic supporting characters who provide vital biological services. For the most part, it's a model that works, and Alt-Right arguments for traditional female roles are legitimate: there's tremendous value in having women devoted to raising many healthy, happy, stable children amidst a well-tended home. But there may also be room for woke women in the Alt Right, despite widespread opposition to an open-armed welcome. The movement can consider, with some reservation, incorporating women without being feminized or co-opted.

The truth is that men are better suited to the cause. After all, what makes women caring also makes them crazy; the stability they instinctually seek can also be irrational. These emotionally-driven characteristics that enable the creation and rearing of beautiful white babies are often at odds with the tenets of the Alt Right: confident intellectualism and literacy, reliance on statistics, righteous hatred, unassailable positions regarding immigration and Jewish power, clandestine friendships, late-night trolling, love of offensive memes, and reverence for a certain frog.

Further, Alt-Right men have unlocked the power of disregarding what normies think of them. They're also growing bolder in declaring themselves White Nationalists versus the Alt Lite safe space of civic nationalism, and have an increasing supply of comrades in case they alienate friends and family with their salty truths. What's more, their belief in the cause is so strong that such losses might even be a relief. Being declared a racist or a Nazi is the new compliment. And while the ladies in their lives can hear their arguments, clear and potent as moonshine, women are justly afraid of what taking the red pill might mean for themselves.

Feminists can spew their drivel about fair pay, consequence-free sex, or growing out all their body hair while demanding government-subsidized birth control and abortions. But the true core of the female ethos is a need for stability. And, if truly and properly embraced, the Alt Right is a dangerous and unstable proposition.

The only constants in the Alt Right are Pepe's knowing smile and a rejection of the existing order; otherwise, the path forward is uncertain. It requires commitment to viewing the environment through a crystal-clear truth lens, even though the world is filthy. It's the terrifying realization that your people are being deftly dispossessed, and knowing that it's impossible to return to blissful ignorance of the reality of diversity. It's the embarrassment of having been pulled along on puppet strings by Jews who'd eradicate you as easily as employ you. And for women, this path forward is far more worrisome than for men, for whom racist loathing and suspicion can, remarkably, be passed off as endearing, idiosyncratic personality quirks.

White women, particularly mothers, are pressured by progressives in the same way blacks and mestizos are to vote Democrat—fall in line, or be maligned. Many women who openly identify with traditional gender roles or demonstrate a desire to be surrounded by their own ethnicity will get black-balled; ironically, those who are usually crying racist are living well in their own white enclaves. It's typical liberal logic: they claim the moral high ground and the title of most tolerant . . . until you disagree with them.

A man's risks in going public as a member of the Alt Right are mostly financial. It's horrific to lose your job over your (totally correct) assessment that race, specifically the white race, matters. If a man's NAXALT-rhetoric buddy from the soccer league or his batty aunt turn their backs on him . . . no great loss. But a woman's risks in going Alt Right are largely social, and without the availability of Standard Pool Parties to fall back on, a woman has no social safety net.

A woman can lose everything by going public with her desire to avoid people of color and the fact of her preferring the
company of whites, because her relationships with other people are a large part of her identity. If she is openly referred to as
a racist, a traitor, or a doormat, it will hit her emotional well-
being harder than it would a man. Her reaction may be weak
compared to a guy's, and the Alt Right doesn't deal in propping others up when they demonstrate weakness or ineptitude.
But as women thrive on a sense of community, it's valid to
acknowledge that the threat of having their social standing
stripped from them in favor of a crusade that is still in its in-
fancy is undoubtedly petrifying.

There aren't enough women who publicly align with the Alt
Right at present in order for the newly awoken to find that new
community. A man can thrive as a lone wolf, but a woman will
wither from loneliness. So while many in the Alt Right want to
keep it a boy's club, the women around them will suffer if
they're not given some meaningful way to interact with or par-
ticipate in the movement. Supporting them as they learn the
lingo and how to properly troll could mean all the difference as
they lament the likely loss of numerous long-standing relationships. It may sound trite, but for a movement as important as
White Nationalism, there is strength in numbers, as whites are
a rare breed as it is. Turning away women because of their
emotionality is reckless and shortsighted.

Consider the sad scenario of a man being part of the Alt
Right and not indoctrinating his woman before they commit
themselves to each other. Women are vastly more important
biologically than men, and with today's white, liberal / independent / apolitical woman, he'll be lucky to get a single child
out of the relationship. She'll continue to signal the virtues of
being a career woman, and instead of performing the most important function the Alt Right espouses by having many white
children, he'll maybe end up with a single weird kid, two un-
happy parents, and three ambivalent cats. Instead, a wife who's
a White Nationalist is far more likely to push for procreation.
That's win-win, folks.

In the Fourteen Words context, it's also illogical to keep

women at arm's length: as the most fervent supporters of their kids' well-being, it makes sense to bring women into the Alt Right. The people who would literally die for their children should be the ones entrusted with protecting their interests in education, relationships, and lifestyle from birth. Keeping your women in the dark regarding the realities of race might unintentionally fuel the multicultural fire that's being stoked in today's school system. Without someone there to keep tabs on the "lessons" your kid's getting at school (if she can't home-school), he'll be fully down with the brown and indoctrinated in their ways in no time.

If your kids and the future existence of the white race are the most important and costly investment you'll ever make, is it cheaper to raise them (alt) right with both parental influences, or to fight the system for eighteen or more years with half your household disarmed and clueless, hoping to red-pill your kids at some point in the future? For anyone who's ever been stuck in a depressing conversation with a twenty-year-old Bernie supporter, it should be easy to acknowledge that it would have been preferable to teach them race realism and the importance of national identity years ago.

The Boomers made many critical mistakes, and not least among them was to let their kids choose their own paths: seeking a useless liberal education, leaving them ignorant of the reality of race, and tossing aside their racial identity in favor of systemic compliance. In the meantime, the Jews laughed and promoted their own children into the financial sector and other influential fields, thus solidifying their control even further.

So while Hillary Clinton's shockingly tone-deaf Alt Right speech brought a lot of cucks and Jews to the movement's door, it's actually the women who might just boost the movement to the next level. While the Alt Right has thrived in part thanks precisely to its exclusionary nature, it's only reasonable to assume that a movement has to expand and evolve in order to gain greater influence. By embracing the opportunity that an exceptional woman can provide, a man can do more to propel his genetics and the white race than he could alone via the Internet and Pool Parties. It's not a strategy available or sensible for all men, but it should be a consideration for those who wish to become involved in—and promote their current and future family members' involvement with—the movement.

Counter-Currents, January 24, 2017

SEXUAL SERFDOM & THE SEXUAL COUNTER-REVOLUTION

GREGORY HOOD

EQUALITY & HIERARCHY

Every egalitarian movement ends with the establishment of a new hierarchy. As it solidifies, caste and status crystallize on the social ladder until the class structure is as rigid as in feudal Japan. Eventually, those of talent, originality, and ambition conclude they have nothing to gain from the system's preservation. This is how we get revolution.

Today, "privilege" theory is the ideology of the System. Though egalitarian, it pathologizes white male heterosexuals as morally flawed because of their inherent characteristics. The ideology is rife with contradictions—suggesting homosexuality is a matter of choice will result in moral condemnation, while stating the obvious truth that someone is born with a particular sex will result in similar fury from those who tell us that "gender" is actually fluid. Who you decide to screw is inherent and sacred—but the makeup of your body is just a social construct. Race doesn't exist—except when it does. Still, if there is one sociological truth, it's that facts never get in the way of Belief and a redemptive social Narrative.

While it was once held that white males could transcend their position in an oppressive society through participation in social justice movements, even this is increasingly untenable. It's now a cliché that every "anarchist" or "anti-racist" conference will eventually collapse into infighting and vitriol because of the mere presence of these undesirables, no matter how enthusiastically they attempt to cuckold themselves. The Occupy Wall Street rallies quickly abandoned a focus on economic inequality to embrace goofy racial stage theater, making sure that white males spoke last at any of their meetings. Unsurprisingly, after an initial surge, it collapsed as struggling American

workers quickly concluded that they would rather be financially raped by Wall Street sociopaths than be represented by self-
hating, sexually confused lunatics with graduate degrees in
Ethnic Studies who think the best way to raise wages is
through unlimited immigration. Of course, what prevents such
movements from being entirely made up of "People of Color"
is the inability of the more vibrant denizens of the American
Empire to self-organize without having their hand held by
white or Jewish babysitters.

THE SEXUAL CLASS SYSTEM

But if the rhetoric surrounding race is heated, that surrounding sex is bordering hysteria. On college campuses, the testing
ground for what is being developed for the entire country, a
curious duality has developed.

On the one hand, standards of what were once called deco-
rum and sexual restraint are all but absent at most universities.
Co-ed dorms, pornography showings and sex toy exhibitions,
and the general prevalence of the "hook up culture" satirized by
Tom Wolfe in *I Am Charlotte Simmons* make it easy for American
college men to obtain casual sex in a business-like fashion.

In fairness, the prevalence of "hook-up culture" among
American females may be exaggerated—#NotAllWomen are
behaving this way. However, this is of relatively little importance, and what would once have been called shameful or
"slutty" behavior no longer has any moral sanction, meaning
that *enough* are behaving this way such that your average "bro"
can confidently expect sexual exploits that would have seemed
worthy of Casanova to a prior generation. The result is the relative unimportance of the sexual act among an entire generation
and the prevalence of various arrangements including "friends
with benefits," hook up calls, and small-scale harems possessed
by generally unremarkable men. "Slutwalks" in defense of all
this are already clichés in SWPL cities and on campuses, despite the fact that it enables men to view these kinds of women
(accurately) as sexually disposable. Anything to stick it to those
stuck-up Christians I suppose.

On the other hand, college campuses are practically a *de jure* (if not *de facto)* police state when it comes to sexual relations between men and women. From the moment they step on campus, women are cautioned that every man they meet is a potential rapist and the statistic of "one in four women is raped" is widely deployed—even though it's wrong. Student handbooks are fodder for unintentional comedy, as some schools mandate elaborate procedures to obtain permission before initiating sexual behavior. Sexual assault is defined so broadly as to criminalize innocent behavior. The presence of *any* alcohol, practically inevitable, can be held to render consent impossible, essentially making a huge percentage of sexual encounters some variety of "rape."

Any kind of flirting can be technically criminal, and hapless college males find themselves before disciplinary tribunals that ignore the presumption of innocence, deny the right to counsel, and punish the accused even before the truth is established. Every male college student is furiously lectured to *never* question a female student's claim that she was raped, but more than one college or even high school student has quickly learned that girls may magically transform a drunken hook up into a "Morning After Rape" on the "Walk of Shame" home.

Filming casual sexual encounters should be considered shameful in a normal society—but men have actually used it to free themselves from false acquisitions, as brave, independent, and strong "rape survivors" are revealed to have enthusiastically participated in group sex before deciding to ruin their partners' lives the next day. The fact that men are advising each other to clandestinely film sexual encounters to protect themselves from rape accusations speaks for itself.

BETA MALES, GAME, & ENTITLEMENT

Amidst the miasma of slut walks, Women's Studies, and various women's activist groups, the wise college man learns to exploit the sexual carnival while taking measures to protect himself. After he graduates, he takes a similar tack in navigating a broken culture. Sexual politics are reverting to a strange combination of the caveman era and Tumblr. Blunt physical attraction is all it takes to acquire sex in most cases, but if any sexual act draws the attention of the media or legal system, a man is instantly condemned, regardless of the truth. Therefore, he reacts with an attitude of amused mastery toward "modern women" and their elaborate rationalizations — taking what he can get and not expecting anything. With luck, he can find the diamond in the rough worthy of marriage — but fewer and fewer believe such a thing even exists or that marriage, like war, is anything other than a racket.

But what of the "beta males" — the so-called nice guys who want one girlfriend to be faithful to, marry, and have children with? We can all think of exceptions who pull this off — but in the modern era, adultery, divorce, and affairs are so shamefully common that our grandparents' tales of marriages lasting 50 years or more prompt astonishment or even awe. Nonetheless, the beta male still has a certain expectation that this is what women in some sense *should* do. When he finds that many women are not receptive to his buying dinner and sending flowers and flowery messages, pining can become resentment.

This is the basis of the "entitlement" culture condemned by feminists and the media following Elliot Rodger's killing spree. Linked to "privilege theory," the general thrust is that men (especially white men) believe that they are entitled to a faithful wife, ready access to sex, and a middle-class lifestyle simply by virtue of the fact that they are males. According to this theory, the relative loss of cultural, economic, and political power is something that white men cannot deal with, and react to with violence and unacceptable political beliefs. Therefore, we get the familiar canard in the media that members of the Tea Party (or for that matter, White Nationalists) don't actually care about or understand politics — they are simply acting out their resentments.

Certainly, Rodger's manifesto reeks with *ressentiment.* If it were not for the loss of life, it would take a heart of stone not to laugh at his indignant moan that girls would rather rut with people other than himself, the "Supreme Gentleman." Dissident Right commentators including Steve Sailer noted that this resentment was particularly focused at blondes. Rodger did not identify as white and spoke bitterly against whites, especially white girls. Indeed, white advocates such as those at the Council of Conservative Citizens attempted to create momentum behind the meme that Rodger's attack was just another example of anti-white racism akin to the Knoxville Massacre or the Knockout Game.

Needless to say, it didn't catch on. Rodger may not have been white, but that doesn't matter—after all, neither was George Zimmerman. Nor did the fact that Rodger killed more men than women significantly derail the narrative that massacre was just another incident in a never-ending war of aggression against women, in which the White Man is the eternal antagonist.

The #YesAllWomen hashtag that served as the moral panic of the week was used to prove that all women—yes, all of them—are the "survivors" of sexual assault via act, word, or institutional oppression. Various apolitical women seized on it, relating stories about how a "creepy" guy hit on them, or someone had the temerity to make a disrespectful comment about their sexual behavior.

The purpose of this was not to establish truth or falsehood. It was to assign women to a victim class designated by their sex (or, presumably, transfer into the gender via surgery). It was to fortify the social hierarchy. As influential blogger Roosh V has observed, feminism is rapidly approaching a point where it will be literally impossible to criticize a woman for anything, be it adultery, slovenly appearance, or even acts of violence, murder, and the utmost cruelty. Even Bill Maher, before he became a tiresome Democratic hack, pointed out this double standard. As he put it, it's politically incorrect "just to be male." And, in something he would never say today, "You cannot reform biology."

ENTITLEMENT & GAME

For many of us, simple experience wakes us up from any naïveté that all women are somehow innocent victims besieged by sexually voracious and aggressive men. Acknowledging reality means destroying ideas deliberately promoted by both the egalitarian left and the reactionary American Right about the inherent evil of the male sex drive. While the Left praises the female sex drive as good in and of itself (slut walks) and the reactionary Right seems to deny its existence, science suggests it is simply different from men.

In evolutionary terms, women *qua* women are attracted to those men who appear able to provide them with the most resources and social status (at the time) as well as physical appearance, which is a proxy for genetic quality. In game terms, it means if a man can exemplify (or fake) the qualities and attitude of a man with social standing and resources (alpha), he will reap female attraction. In the biological program running in the background for all of us, men value fertility (youth and beauty) and availability, and women value social protection (social value, money, strength). It's from these basic biological realities we get some of the most important elements of the sexual marketplace dynamic. This is why women constantly feel the need to create complicated rationalizations to explain away what they are doing ("I never do this, I swear!") and why other women are the most unforgiving critics of "sluts."

Similarly, it is also why we get the almost entirely one-sided spectacle of men self-destructing because of temporary sexual urges or the need for simple physical release. It's easy to think of powerful leaders who spectacularly sabotaged their careers for sex from a woman often less attractive than their own wives. It's extremely hard to think of female equivalents. Can anyone imagine Hillary making the mistake(s) of her husband? And are there any males out there willing to be a male Monica Lewinsky? How else we can explain the behavior of an Arnold Schwarzenegger who betrayed his Kennedy wife for his homely maid?

However, technology and state policy are changing the equation. In a culture where birth control, abortion, prophylactics, and a dizzying array of welfare programs and "advocates" exist for women, many of the consequences of sexual promiscuity are removed. At the same time, laws regarding divorce, child support, alimony, and other aspects of what is still ironically termed "family law" play out in a largely consequence-free environment for women's sexual choice. The result is the introduction of a class system that allows women to, theoretically, have their cake and eat it too. The legal and societal structure actively punishes chastity, rewards adultery, and subsidizes irresponsible behavior. Is there any more stereotypically "modern" figure than the single mother? Perhaps Dan Quayle's comments about *Murphy Brown* were prophetic after all.

While female sexual desire is praised and encouraged to run rampant, male sexual desire is pathologized by the media and academia. Indeed, the shrieks are already upon us that "traditional masculinity must be destroyed." Of course, it already has been destroyed, and not necessarily because of deliberate social conditioning. Arguably, the nation where this rot has sunk in the deepest is Japan, where young Japanese men known as "grass eaters" abandon even the pretense of masculinity. While it could be argued that even this may be a feature, not a bug, of mass capitalism, genetically modified food, and urban living, we have to consider the possibility that this just may be an unintended side effect. After all, it can hardly be charged that the Japanese political culture is beholden to feminism, mass immigration, and ethnomasochism.

Of course, modern society doesn't just turn men into Last Men—it turns women into Last Men too. And not everyone wants this. On paper and by the modern standard of the "pursuit of happiness," there's no reason for traditional families and households to continue to exist at all—but they do, and they are reproducing more than everyone else. Nonetheless, a formidable system is in place, with all the financial incentives and sinecures that come with it. And any class system will generate its defenders and hack intellectuals, eager to justify the sinecures and entrenched privileges that sustain them.

SCIENCE, TRADITION, & SEX

But there's a catch. Chase Nature out with a pitchfork, and you'll end up alone in a house full of cats in a majority non-white neighborhood. Modern childless women, regardless of their careers, are not particularly happy. This manifests itself in, at best, Left-wing moral crusading and, at worst, insane and pitiable behavior. As for single women, all the SNAP cards in the world don't substitute for a father, and the grim objective reality shows that a traditional family outperforms strong womyn who think they can "have it all." The cold tale of demographics suggests that feminism is simply a transition stage between the end of a decadent society and the takeover by a more vital, patriarchal one. The results are in—and feminism is revealed as a failed social experiment sustained only by a vast assemblage of propaganda, subsidies, and legal protection.

Enter feminism, especially its obnoxious online variety. The feminist critique of entitlement is projection at its most crude, as fundamentally modern feminism is about defending ingrained privilege and propping up the crumbling System. Contemporary "strong women" feel entitled to abort their children without the interference from the father, obtain financial rewards after cheating on their husbands, and receive sexual attention even after they grow fat, old, or unattractive.

More than that, a host of television networks, magazines, academic studies departments, and media figures tell them that they are heroic figures for giving in to their lowest desires. Of course, it doesn't take much to be a hero in modern America, and you don't have to be particularly brave for the media to call you "strong"—if you are part of the right social class. Women who actually display real strength—the type who bear children, defend their families, and, in the most literal definition of "strong," lift weights and stay in shape—are condemned as traitors to their sex.

What is occurring is the decadent phase of an outdated social system. In an age of technological growth, social evolution occurs remarkably fast. The low intelligence shoggoths inhabiting women's studies departments today are equivalent to the degenerate French aristocrats who long since abandoned the life of the sword to indulge in the decadent ideas that would destroy them. Feminists are outdated. As a culture and as a species, we no longer gain anything from their existence, and their presence is a burden to the productive. They are simply parasites, feeding on the social capital they are actively destroying—until they are swept away by the next sexual revolution, or perhaps I should call it the sexual restoration, whose vanguard are the theorists and practitioners of game.

THE SEXUAL COUNTER-REVOLUTION

Game is the male revolt against the sexual caste system imposed by feminism. The "red pill" is simply an acknowledgement that what women say they want, and what they actually want, are two different things. Even some women who say that they want a "traditional" relationship are not willing to do what it takes to get this by actually behaving like a lady, staying in shape, or not detonating a relationship over trivia. By definition, game is men learning what actually works with women and using it to fulfill their primal needs for sex, companionship, and, ultimately, fulfilling relationships and family life.

When a member of the Parasitic Class like an affirmative action journalist or Women's Studies professor gives his or her opinion on something, it behooves the reader to ask himself, "How does this person benefit if I believe what they are telling me?" The feminist rage against game is the rage of the effete fop against his uppity peasants. Game shifts the frame on sexual politics by allowing men to reclaim sexual power, punish female misbehavior, and pursue their own interests. It is aspirational, teaching people to look above their station, and in that sense, it is a destabilizing force within the social system. It teaches men to break free of their assigned place as the *kulaks* in the modern social order, responsible for subsidizing everyone else.

Notably, while "men's sites" like *Return of Kings* focus on self-improvement, learning skills, and physical fitness, recent feminist writing has focused on justifying or even promoting moral flaws such as obesity, adultery, and fraud. The manosphere promotes excellence; feminism promotes equality. The default feminist rhetoric on sexual politics seems to be an inexhaustible series of variations on the theme of "Wow, just wow." It's not surprisingly that in such an intellectual desert even somewhat juvenile articles on "text message game" seem like an oasis.

Moreover "game" fits into the subset of Dissident Right

movements that recognize there is no contradiction between Traditionalism and science. "Game" heaps scorn on the "pedestaling" behavior of many religious conservatives and reactionaries who want to treat women like medieval princesses. Instead, game recognizes that women are sexually voracious in their own way, that they derive much of their self and societal value from their sexuality, and that many of the conservative beliefs about chivalry and virtuous women only make sense in a social context that privileges patriarchy, families, and fidelity. If there is one Christian teaching I can agree with, it is the doctrine of "total depravity" for both men and women.

It's not that "science" is an enemy of Tradition—it's that certain small "t" traditions arose because human beings act with an evolutionary program running in the background. The impulses of sexual selection, competition, and attraction are rooted deep within the unconscious of the species. So-called "social constructs," like prizing female virginity, or the willingness of men to sacrifice for women, are rooted in biological and empirical realities, not religious mysticism.

What defines the real modern Right, as opposed to the reactionaries, is understanding that objective realities are reflected within ancient mythologies and practices. The traditionalist teachings of thousands of years ago are more applicable to modern society than a Ph.D.'s eminently credentialed and empirically flawed ramblings on *Jezebel*. We should be cautious about modern intellectuals casually dismissing the wisdom of millennia as "outdated" when these same people will mock religious beliefs while holding far more absurd (and less empirically supported) beliefs about racial equality.

CLASS STRUGGLE

Heterosexual men are, as a class, a designated oppressor group in the system that is developing. By teaching men to question their place in this order, and leading them to more subversive conclusions about tradition, human biodiversity, and racial realism, the "manosphere" is declaring itself an enemy of the system.

But this isn't just an ideological challenge. The personal is political, and nowhere is the new hierarchy being enforced with more fanaticism than in sexual politics. Of course, the corollary is that every challenge, no matter how small, takes on new importance. In every nightclub, bar, and coffee shop, a man approaching a woman using game has been elevated to a political act. Men recognizing a desire and acting on it using knowledge about social dynamics is a challenge to the sexual serfdom that demands that men accept their place—under women. And that can lead to further rebellion.

Of course, unless it leads to other things, "game" is merely a means, not an end. And while "game" is based on highly subversive and inegalitarian premises, the ends are hardly revolutionary. After all, meaningless hook ups between immature boy-men and proud "sluts" is hardly a challenge to the consumerist culture. The value of game is that it even though it is directed towards profane ends, it can be the first step on an upward path of rebellious ascension.

KNOW YOUR PLACE

A telling example of the Left's attitude towards game is the reaction of one Chris Gethard, a functionary for the Culture of Critique. He posted a video telling men to avoid these ideas and was praised for it by Lindy West of the female affirmative action outlet *Jezebel*. Gethard flaps his weak hands and insists that men who practice game "should be legally bound [to] never find love." But more importantly, he tells men to accept that they need to shut up and do what they are told by the media. After all, "One day you'll be, like, 37, and you'll have a mortgage, and you'll be totally okay with that. You'll be completely fine."

Needless to say, one look at his face and you know every opinion he's ever had and why none of them are worth listening to. As for "Lindy West," her mere physical appearance (trigger warning) warrants the return of the patriarchy, the immediate overthrow of the American government, and an Axis Victory in the Second World War, among other things.

What is important is the revelation of the end game of feminism and progressivism—don't protest, accept your fate, and be happy you have your big screen TV that you bought with your credit card. Far from being a movement of liberation, progressivism is the handmaiden of consumerism. Don't question these beliefs, swallow the pretty lies, and we'll let you play your video games. *Know your place.*

It's more than an ideology—egalitarianism is a system of control. What the Dark Enlightenment terms the Cathedral imposes a set hierarchy of groups, along with codes of behavior. And while the punishment for deviating from codes of behavior isn't quite as severe as what samurai meted out to impudent peasants, the principle is the same. All the sophomoric arguments, expletive-filled feminist ranting, social network shaming, and insufferably self-congratulatory #hashtags are simply the enforcement arm of this social structure.

THE BRIDGE

For all the "metapolitics," all the essays, all the conferences, and all the books and speeches, the White Right has only succeeded in creating a subculture, and a fairly closed one at that. No one casually enters white advocacy. The costs can be great, and so are the rewards, but once you are in, you don't go back (unless you turn traitor). What it has largely failed to do is build a "bridge" to ordinary white people, who have largely been intimidated from participating in street demonstrations, attending conferences, or even speaking publicly about their beliefs.

Game, in contrast, has succeeded as a bridge to subversive ideas. While some men can tell themselves they don't need white identity, *every* straight man needs to appeal to women, and not every man knows how. Game meets an existential need. More importantly, game meets the two essential characteristics of the real Right. It is rooted in empirical reality and scientific truth while still respecting Tradition, and it challenges the official orthodoxy about egalitarianism.

It's no accident that the Southern Poverty Law Center attacked the "manosphere" as a "hate," leading to widespread mockery. More importantly, after this occurred, many of the most important manosphere sites and commentators have been speaking frankly about racial realist concepts and ideas. Discussions on forums within this subculture are well-informed and more grounded and less ideological than the raging abstract arguments that plague White Nationalist websites. The process of radicalization (or, more accurately and charitably, waking up) is taking place amongst a huge segment of the population that this movement has never been able to reach. And regardless of what White Nationalists think about "game," the System perceives game as a threat.

ENDGAME & REVOLUTION

Why does this absurd system exist, something so paranoid that it panics over shy men trying to learn pickup lines? The same reason most things exist—someone is benefiting from it. The more deracinated society becomes and the more families are broken down, the more relationships become a simple function of the consumer economy. A hookup culture provides no barriers between the individual and the market. The fact that many Western women believe slaving away in a cubicle and participating in a garbage culture is "freedom" while raising children is "slavery" testifies to the power of social conditioning. This conditioning is part of the process of turning sex and relationships into products to be sold—or rationed out—by an increasingly totalitarian system of control. "Equality" is just part of the scam—in the end, this system is based, like any other, on the reality of power.

The solution to sexual serfdom is not revolution from the periphery, but rebellion from the center. Ride the tiger. Recognizing equality as a scam is the first step. No one believes in equality—especially in the bedroom. Act accordingly. If people are insistent on turning themselves and their bodies into a product, treat them that away, take advantage of it, and use what works. We must approach the world not as serfs, but as barbarians. We have no stake in what they have built except to take what is ours. What should fill you is not a sense of entitlement, but aggressive contempt, and a desire to conquer.

Both men and women can use what the manosphere preaches. Equality is a scam—always be seeking to rise. And in your upward path, find those few men—and women—among the ruins. They are still there in the wasteland, and shared contempt for egalitarianism is as strong a foundation as any. Together, as comrades, lovers, and eventually families, men and women can forge a new people and create something worth preserving. This culture and system sure as hell isn't it.

Counter-Currents, June 16 & 17, 2014

MEN GOING THEIR OWN WAY

SPENCER J. QUINN

Many organizations and movements on the Right can be construed as push-back against Cultural Marxism. While the Alt Right certainly does do this, I wouldn't include it in this group. In a world without Cultural Marxism, you can still have an Alt Right (although at that point, we'd probably drop the "Alt"). This is because we stand *for* things more than we stand against them, for example, a positive white racial identity, peaceful ethnonationalism, and more or less traditional, commonsense values beyond that.

But what about organizations that are almost entirely blow-back against Cultural Marxism? I believe that folks on the Alt Right should foster positive relations with as many of these groups as possible. One such group is Men Going Their Own Way, or MGTOW.

Essentially, MGTOW consists of "meninists" or men who have to differing degrees checked out of traditional monogamous heterosexual relationships. This is in large part a response to the growing power and autocracy of the feminist Left, which has, indeed, sabotaged the Western men when it comes to marriage and raising children. Some of these men belong in the manosphere and aim for little more than ephemeral dalliances with women. Others, like cynical, once-bitten monks, have sworn off women entirely. Furthermore, I detect little homosexuality in the MGTOW. As advertised, it is about men going their own way . . . but without women.

Here is their statement of purpose from their website:

M.G.T.O.W — Men Going Their Own Way is a statement of self-ownership, where the modern man preserves and protects his own sovereignty above all else. It is the manifestation of one word: "No." Ejecting silly preconceptions and cultural definitions of what a "man" is. Looking to no one else for social cues. Refusing to bow, serve and kneel for the opportunity to be treated like a disposable utility. And, living according to his own best interests in a world which would rather he didn't.

My first impression upon researching this topic is a feeling of solidarity with the men involved. Sympathy too, but certainly *not* of the condescending kind. (Lord knows, if a few things had not gone my way in life, I might be "going my own way" as well—I consider myself *very* lucky in that regard.) The MGTOW website provides a history of the movement, a nice round-up of the manosphere, a blog, videos, testimonials, links to books on Amazon, and, shockingly for me, a live chat(!).

Of course, the official literature of the movement clearly spells out what MGTOW is all about. All of it is reasonable and well-researched. Particular essays I liked included Schopenhauer's take on women, the "Sexodus," Parts 1 and 2, and one entitled "The Water Fountain," which uses a playground as an analogy for some of the more self-defeating aspects of chivalry in the modern world.

But it is in the forums where one finds the quickest route to the Truth. Some conversation topics are quite positive and involve technology and gadgets and other cool things that men in general like to riff on. Others, however, include "Blue Pill Hell," "Marriage and Divorce," and the aptly-named "Relationshits." In these, one will find the starkest anti-woman, anti-marriage pronouncements possible. A prominent warning reads: "The MGTOW Forums are for registered red-pill Men only. There are no exceptions. All females may exit immediately."

Not sure if this is meant literally, this being the anonymous internet and all.

Anyway, here is where men vent, and they vent a lot. A good deal of it is grotesque hostility towards women, yes, and fairly indefensible too. Here is a typically lurid quote: "So sure, get married and have four kids. BOOM you are now $1 million in the red and stuck with lazy, stay at home land whale with a vagina stretched beyond recognition."

Money gets brought up a lot as well. One poster's signature reads "Marriage is grand. Divorce is 500 grand!" Another poster once posted a meme comparing over-the-hill Hollywood actresses when they were young and hot versus how they are now. No misogynistic epithet is off the table here, it seems. MGTOW also has derogatory terms for men who still adhere to the normative culture of marriage and kids and don't realize they are being had, namely, "manginas," "beta simps," "white knights," and others. This is similar to how some on the Alt Right disdainfully refer to mainstream conservatives as "cuckservatives." When a professor named Brad Wilcox from Prager University tried to criticize MGTOW last May for its anti-marriage stance, the scorn and derision on the forums had no end. Most notably, they referred to him as a "turd-flinging monkey." These are men who will not be swayed.

I admire that about them, even if I don't quite agree with everything they say. Because behind all the cynicism and resentment is equal parts truth and pain. Cultural Marxism and feminism *have* enabled women to the detriment of men when it comes to marriage and child-rearing. And many of these women do not hesitate to use their ill-begotten power to the fullest. The MGTOW forums are rife with these kinds of stories: men dealing with divorce, separation from children, garnished wages, tax difficulties, and a general loss of rights and prestige in our society. I have personally known two men whose lives for a time were all but ruined due to the whims of unstable wives. I have no doubt there is much justice behind the decisions of the MGTOW crowd to simply say no to women, to "tune in and drop out" to appropriate part of a Timothy Leary slogan. Because feminism presupposes a class-like struggle between men and women, men are now actually starting to fight back. And according to some of them, it's the best thing they have ever done. Once free from the matriarchy some of them find they are more productive, more active, healthier, and in general, happier. Furthermore, they are now untouchable by the enemy. How can a feminist attack a man who refuses to have contact with women?

Despite this, however, I find the rise of MGTOW troubling. I cannot speak for everyone on the Alt Right in this case (especially since there is some overlap between the two movements), but I would imagine that many would share my apprehension. Most on the Alt Right share a white racial identity and a concern for the future of whites as a race. If enough white men drop out of the gene pool, especially young men who are bright and literate enough to appreciate all the literature found at mgtow.com, then the race faces an additional threat to its survival.

There is something else, too. The MGTOW forum reminds me a lot of the 1980s television program *Married . . . with Children*, only without the laughs. The forum is not funny, of course, but the ignominious pratfalls from grace that many of these men have suffered coupled with the abject dysfunction of their former lives and the crude *contempt* with which they hold their ex-spouses is, by nature, comic.

Here is a snippet of dialogue from *Married . . . with Children* which I will take to my grave with me. After getting Husband to say something she wants to hear, Wife whines, "You don't sound like you mean it." The husband then grimaces and says, "That's because I *don't* mean it!"

Cue the laugh track. You have the classic send up and smack down of a good joke. Wife fancies herself something special, then slips on a banana peel and goes splat on her bottom. It's funny. But imagine actually *living* in such a circumstance. Imagine having such loathing for your spouse that you can't even be bothered to conceal that from her. This is what it is like reading through some of the conversations on the MGTOW forum.

Comedy as truth is a terrifying thing.

A 1950s science fiction author could do a lot worse for an apocalyptic novel than by making the very last men on Earth a Pythagorean cult of he-man woman-haters who categorically refuse to get busy. A plot could be contrived to have a some of the last few nubile women to infiltrate the cult and seduce the religiously reluctant men. Of course, one of the women falls in love with one of the men. They consummate, but soon a second woman falls in love with him as well and steals him from the first woman. The first woman, in a fit of jealousy, then becomes swayed by the idea that humanity *needs* to go extinct and works with the elder cultists to achieve this nefarious end. As a result, the adulterous couple and their sidekick robots must race out of Techno-City to the site on Venus where the computer-operated thermonuclear rocket bombs are programmed to . . . well, you get the picture.

I assume also you see where I am going with this. If taken to its professed extreme, the Men Going Their Own Way crowd must end up as villains, and not even charismatic ones. As intolerable and obnoxious as Leftist, feminist women have become, we still need to ask the question: are we going to propagate as a race, or not? It seems that the MGTOW crowd already has their answer, and it is not yes. And that is terrifying.

Of course, I would not *dare* lecture any of these men on what they should do with their personal lives. If eschewing the company of women makes them happy, fair dinkum. But what I would like to do, as a person who hates cultural Marxism as much as they do, as an avowed enemy of their enemy, as a potential ally on the Alt Right, is to ask them something.

Is it really a good idea to proselytize? People in the forums have been exulting about how the MGTOW movement has been growing as of late, especially after their little dust up with Prager U. But perhaps the goose and the gander are a tad at odds here. I can see MGTOW as a necessary haven for some unfortunate men who've been married with children and then victimized by an increasingly anti-male and, let's face it, anti-white society. But when they brand themselves as a positive alternative for the broader population of men, especially young men involved in the manosphere, that's when they start to step on the toes of the Alt Right. They seemed more concerned with themselves in the here and now rather than the future. They're defining themselves by the very thing to which they are reacting. They seem more anti-woman than pro-man. And the very idea of being in favor of *both* men and women is laughed out of the room. Good relations between the sexes is *only* way to keep the race going, and they don't seem to care. It's almost like they're giving up.

The Alt Right is concerned with white populations who are not producing at replacement levels and living in countries that are being swamped by waves of non-assimilating immigrants. This is a really important thing to be concerned about, and you don't need a GPS to figure out where our future is headed. It's bad enough that many young white men are effectively wasting time with sexual hijinks in the manosphere while their Muslim or Hispanic counterparts are busy having kids at age twenty. The last thing we need is for them to start spouting "marriage is slavery" or some other nihilistic mantra from MGTOW and effectively not having children.

Again, this is not saying that what the MGTOW crowd is doing with their own lives is wrong. Rather, it would be wrong if all or even most white men did what the MGTOW crowd is doing. I think this is a reasonable assertion. On the website's history page, one can find the following pronouncement: "Great men of history have already given enough, so the modern man can afford to take a century off."

No, we can't. At least the white ones can't. If enough of us were to take this century off from reproducing ourselves, you can bet your $500,000 divorce we wouldn't live to see the next one.

Counter-Currents, October 3, 2016

DOES THE MANOSPHERE MORALLY CORRUPT MEN?

GREG JOHNSON

For several years now, the website I read more than any other has been *Chateau Heartiste*, formerly known as *Chateau Roissy*. I also read Roosh V from time to time. Both men are highly intelligent, and Heartiste is also a brilliant stylist, with a wicked sense of humor.

But, for all the pleasure and knowledge I have derived from these and other manosphere writers, I am increasingly drawn to the view that the net result of the manosphere is to morally corrupt men.

Paradoxical though it may seem, I also think the manosphere is actually a mechanism by which *women* morally corrupt men. The manosphere is touted as a way for men to emancipate themselves from the tyranny of feminism, but in reality it functions as a subtle instrument of female domination.

No normal, healthy man would want his daughter or sister to be emotionally manipulated and sexually exploited by a man who is narcissistic, sociopathic, and Machiavellian—or just a garden variety jerk.

However, the manosphere informs us that science, history, and copious anecdotal testimony show that when women are allowed complete choice in the sexual realm—particularly if they can have sex without the threat of pregnancy—they do not simply gravitate toward biologically and mentally healthy men with "Alpha" traits but also to a whole range of "false positives," ranging from emotionally aloof and unavailable men to jerks and cads to men with severe "dark triad" personality disorders: narcissism, sociopathy, and Machiavellianism.

A healthy, well-ordered society punishes jerks and cads. Ideally, it should simply weed out people with severe personality disorders by preventing them from reproducing. Thus, emancipated female sexual choice morally and psychologically corrupts men. Not because sex is evil or "sinful," but because emancipated women reward anti-social behaviors and pathological personality traits with sex. Furthermore, emancipated female sexual choice harms the women who fall victim to jerks and sociopaths. Finally, since a great deal of personality is genetically determined and thus heritable, emancipated female sexuality is dysgenic, because it helps perpetuate jerk genes.

To correct these problems, we need to roll back sexual liberation by reestablishing social shaming for female promiscuity and, most importantly, involving the family—particularly fathers and brothers—in the process by which women choose suitors and husbands. Involving the family in her deliberations can expand a woman's awareness and sharpen her judgments by bringing other perspectives into play. Men, furthermore, are better than women at discerning good men from evil ones, and, as I said above, no decent man wants his sister or daughter to be exploited and victimized by bad men. (For all the same reasons, mothers and sisters should involve themselves in the process of selecting suitors and mates for the young men in their families.)

Now, I suspect that manosphere gurus like Heartiste and Roosh are actually with me so far, even agreeing basically with my conservative political agenda.

So why do I think that the manosphere works as a tool by which feral feminine desire corrupts men? Because the manosphere simply takes emancipated female sexuality as a given. Then it teaches young men to adopt the behaviors and mimic the traits that appeal to such women. Young men not only learn about healthy masculine traits but also admiringly analyze "jerkboy" game and "dark triad" cads.

In sum, my concern is that the manosphere teaches young men to emulate anti-social and pathological traits. Women then reinforce these traits with one of the most powerful inducements of all: sex. And, over time, otherwise good men become the kind of men they would never allow around their own sisters and daughters. This is moral corruption. Namely, moral corruption by teaching men to conform to emancipated female desire rather than to correct it.

The manosphere provides the New Right with all the *theoretical* premises necessary for a patriarchal sexual counter-revolution that reinstitutes traditional and—it turns out—biologically sound norms and institutions to govern sexuality, thereby promoting the individual happiness of men and women and the common good of society and the race in general.

But in *practical* terms, the manosphere does not promote such a restoration, but instead urges an ethic of "riding the tiger" (or perhaps the cougar), i.e., to personally wallow in—and thus to amplify and advance—the decadence that we are supposed to combat.

Counter-Currents, February 25, 2015

WHIGGER *SHARIA*

DONALD THORESEN

One can quickly gauge the depth of infiltration of any given colonizing force by measuring the extent to which the subject peoples incorporate the ideological framework and symbology of their oppressors into their own thought processes. White Nationalists tend to be highly perceptive and thus particularly sensitive to the ubiquitous narratives of our displacement and marginalization. We are quick to spot examples of anti-whiteness wherever they are found, from pop culture to politics, and do a supremely admirable job of exposing such things so that others can judge our claims for themselves.

However, try as we might, we remain (for the time being) physically and mentally embedded in an anti-white system, and so cannot help but absorb some of its effects. This includes the notion that non-whites are somehow morally and racially healthier, abler to be themselves, and are justifiably liberated from the burden of self-effacement. Unable to be freely and unapologetically white in our very souls, unable to harness the cultural and demographic trajectory of our own countries, whites often turn submissively to other races for identity, for that glimmer of rootedness which we have been denied. We see this in others frequently and rightly call them out on it (e.g. "cucking" for Israel), yet White Nationalists—those who should be acutely aware of this type of thought process—sometimes fail to see how it infects their own behavior. This is the psychological underpinning of the "white *sharia*" meme.

As is the case of those who find personal meaning and community by subsuming themselves into the racial "other," those who advocate "white *sharia*" are merely shining a light onto a tragically empty space in their souls. They have yet to mentally decolonize themselves. Rather than channel their anger towards the real enemy, and rather than reflecting on their own personal level of anti-white indoctrination, they lash out uncritically and valorize non-white culture for its perceived organic health and its "edginess." It is yet another of the subtle effects of Jewish cultural control.

What is "white *sharia*"? It is a rejection of and a reaction to feminist excesses and the resultant diminishment of the male self which takes Islamic religious law as its model (whether used literally or not is irrelevant). Though there are other dimensions to the idea of "white *sharia*," this, coupled with a general dislike and/or distrust of women, seems to be its primary manifestation. Looking critically at feminism is healthy. There are, however, so many resources to which one can turn to find the truth about the "wage gap," "rape culture," and other such absurdities that there is no need to rehash any of it here. It is sufficient to say that feminism as understood today is yet another aspect of the Jewish long con against white men and women. On this, most of us would certainly agree. What interests us here, however, is not that particular idea but rather the bizarre way in which some White Nationalists have reacted to it, and what this reaction suggests about the level of pressure placed on us by our Jewish overlords. Advocating "white *sharia*" is, in most cases, probably just a childish troll but, given the gravity of our situation and the importance of getting the solutions right, *everything* needs to be critiqued and contextualized. Damaged thinking cannot go unremarked.

What is it that compels those who are otherwise pro-white to resort to fetishizing the culture of barbarous foreign peoples? The same thing that causes a "patriot" to simultaneously believe that one should not be a minority in the country his ancestors built while advocating death and destruction for any group which threatens the integrity of Israel: it is carefully inculcated self-hatred from above and the internalization of white subservience. "White *sharia*" is an implicit admission that what is authentically white has little value and is intrinsically incapable of dealing with contemporary historical contingencies.

White Nationalists have intellectually freed themselves from the toxic idea that whites do not have a right to exist on our own terms in our own countries, but the psychological effect of a lifetime of living in a system designed to prevent it will manifest itself in many areas of one's life so that thought and action do not always converge. White Nationalists must struggle daily to create this convergence on an individual and collective level. One of the undertakings necessary for this to occur is the questioning of one's personal, often subconscious, entrenchment in the system. In the case of "white *sharia*," those arguing for it (again, whether in jest or not is irrelevant to this discussion) need to ask themselves why they are attracted to the brutality of the Islamic world. What is it that compels them to turn towards foreign religious law as a model for white advocacy?

Just as a white man might seek "traditional" Asian women, a white woman might seek "hyper-masculine" black men, or a white teenager might see black culture as more authentic and "cool" than his own, those who are attracted to "white *sharia*" are driven to it because they cannot find the corresponding values they seek in the white community. Why? Because whites have been taught that whiteness has no value, that that which is white is pedestrian and facile, that excitement and vitality are only to be found by embracing the cultures of non-whites. Our culture is being deliberately destroyed. We are everywhere confronted with messages claiming that we are unworthy of collective self-defense and that our traditions and values are pathological. White Nationalists are in a position to know this and remedy this problem, but some (a minority, fortunately) seem to have abandoned such things either for the sake of humor or because they *actually* believe that the primordial, mystical savagery of Semitic peoples can be transposed onto white societies and channeled into sound political action. Saving the white race is not a joke, and incorporating the social norms of desert-dwelling primitives into white societies is a colossal strategic mistake. It is neither sustainable nor desirable.

Any White Nationalist who engages in talk of "white *sharia*" needs to do some serious self-reflection. Is it necessary to ape non-whites in order to attack the imposed system of white destruction, that can be critiqued on entirely rational grounds using white, Western traditions and conducted within the bounds of white ethics? Absolutely not. We can and should attack the system *on our own terms*. Is the advocacy of a white version of a non-white idea based upon admiration or jealousy of that particular non-white culture? If the former, there will inevitably be a white intellectual tradition from which to draw deeper and more nuanced inspiration; if the latter, then one should question the factors by which value is sought in non-white cultures rather than from within one's own racial tradition. And most importantly, of course, what precisely do advocates of "white *sharia*" want? A perusal of some of their texts would suggest that they want sheer brutality in place of order, blind rage in place of targeted anger, anarchic childishness in place of seriousness, and that policing white behavior is more important than defending white communities from invasion. None of these furthers our cause. Encoded in the word "*sharia*" are images of rape, stoning, torture, genital mutilation, acid attacks, honor killings, *purdah*, and a distinctly non-white incivility and mercilessness. Is this really a sound strategy for white advocacy? These are not things to which whites are naturally attracted. Indeed, we are repelled by them. We generally try to end such barbarity wherever we go—even when doing so does not directly benefit us. The "white man's burden" is an idea that is unlikely to be all that prevalent in our future global dealings, but it originates from our innate, biologically-based drive for justice and order. It is both a blessing and a curse, but *it is who we are*.

"White *sharia*" is nothing more than advocating for the subjugation of white women and others as punishment for their having been victims of Jewish lies and deceptions. It is yet another manifestation of the "white suicide meme" posing as a new paradigm for racial salvation. This kind of internal behavior will in no way convince anyone but sociopaths of the righteousness of this movement, let alone of the problems in feminism or any other "ism" being used as a tool for white displacement. Most White Nationalist women seem to readily accept that they have been victims of Jewish lies, and they are doing a noble job in advocating on behalf of white women. But we need more of them, and this will not happen if they are alienated by the unleashed anger of some loud, reactive young trolls who do not seem to understand the importance of growing this movement and who find something valuable in the superficial "edginess" to be found by incorporating the behaviors and symbols of our enemies into White Nationalist discourse.

If "white *sharia*" does not sound as ridiculous to you as "white Zionism," then it is time to take stock of who you are and for what, exactly, you are fighting. In doing so, not only will you naturally arrive at a more workable political strategy, but you will have eradicated one more remnant of anti-white indoctrination from your core being. There is no reason for whites to see themselves only through the ideological lens and cultural filters of the colonizers. Whites who push this meme are still stuck in the nauseating muck of anti-whiteness, subconsciously constrained by the forces they wish to resist, and will ultimately fail in their project because "white *sharia*" cannot be anything other than a joke and a distraction. It is an unfortunate but necessary reminder of how much we still have to do within our own movement to eradicate the residual poison of Jewish occupation.

Counter-Currents, June 7, 2017

GAY PANIC ON THE ALT RIGHT

GREG JOHNSON

The Alternative Right is subject to occasional gay panics. Throughout most of human history, politics and war have been exclusively male occupations, and in those realms of culture where women took part—such as religion and education—the sexes were still separate rather than mixed. Since this is a political movement, it is naturally attractive to men. Since it is a dissident political movement, it also tends to scare off women.

However, in the present age, all predominantly or exclusively male institutions are routinely slurred as "gay." The purpose of this charge is to lower trust and raise conflict within male groups and to encourage them to integrate women, whose presence will supposedly provide insurance against future charges of being "gay."

Generally, this slur originates from the Left, where homosexuality is supposed to be a good thing. But gay panics presuppose "homophobia," one of the Left's sins. The Left is quite happy, however, to exploit such sentiments to weaken any male institutions that make individual men or society as a whole stronger, from male gyms and sports leagues to men's clubs and the military—and now the guardians of the white race.

Unfortunately, the Left is not the only source of gay panics in our ranks. The most recent examples are self-inflicted.

For instance, after the Halloween 2015 National Policy Institute conference, the Two Matts, Parrott and Heimbach, made up the story that Heimbach was disinvited from NPI because a "gay mafia" disapproved of his Old Testament opinions on homosexuality. Their motive was narcissistic rage, and their aim was simply to harm NPI by starting a gay panic, a troll so divisive that it was eagerly promoted by the Southern Poverty Law Center which shares the same destructive agenda. Naturally, there followed a great deal of squeaking and spinning in the smelly hamster cages of the internet movement, which generated a great deal of distrust and ill-will but did nothing to stop or slow down our race's programmed march to extinction.

The most recent gay panic agitation comes from Sinead "Renegade" McCarthy, whose black marks include linking White Advocacy to flat earth and anti-vaccine cranks, slurring people who think there is more to activism than crazy-eyed women passing out flyers (e.g., Richard Spencer, Angelo Gage, Nathan Damigo, etc.), and basically demanding that the movement capitulate to feminism. Her motives in pushing the gay panic button seem to be equal parts narcissistic rage and feminist entryism.

Which brings us to the question of the proper role of women in "the movement." First of all, "the" movement is not unified and monolithic. There are multiple groups and platforms, and if you don't like what is in the offing, you can create something more to your taste. Andrew Anglin thinks women have nothing to offer *The Daily Stormer*, and that is his right. At *Counter-Currents* I publish women like Savitri Devi, Juleigh Howard-Hobson, Margot Metroland, and Ann Sterzinger not "because they are women," but because they do good work. I have done interviews with Lana Lokteff because she does good work. I am also grateful for female donors and organizers, again because they add value to the movement. Finally, I am increasingly intolerant of gamers, MGTOWs, and woman haters, because their ethos is no more compatible with the healthy sexual order we want to create than the feminism they oppose.

But I completely reject the feminist notion that gender parity should be a norm and that we should welcome women — any women, even women who add no value or who objectively detract from the cause — just because they are women. This is war, not ballroom dancing. In my corner of the movement, women who add something to the cause are welcome. I have no time for men or women who add nothing. And men who do nothing but harass or repulse women who *do* add something need culling.

Gay panics weaken the movement, so how can we armor ourselves against them? There are basically only two options:

(1) get rid of all homosexuals or (2) stop caring about them.

The first option cannot work, for the simple reason that gay panics do not require the *actual presence* of homosexuals but the *mere possibility* they are present. A male group may be 100% heterosexual, but that cannot prevent a malicious and dishonest person from spreading rumors, making charges, and starting a gay panic anyway.

This means that the endless "purge" threads on internet forums are pointless.

- ❖ First, there is no point worrying about homosexual entryism, because they are already inside. When I first arrived on the White Nationalist scene in the year 2000, it was apparent that a number of discreet and open homosexuals like Martin Webster were already well-ensconced.
- ❖ Second, the most enthusiastic purgers are themselves "outsiders" and would-be entryists who are in no position to purge anyone.
- ❖ Third, the movement is not a monolithic, centralized, Bolshevik party, so talk of purges makes no sense anyway. Again, there is nothing to prevent people from creating their own groups and platforms according to their own ideological tastes.
- ❖ Finally, as I said before, even if the purgers get what they want, it still does not protect them against gay panics, because the problem is not the presence of homosexuals, but the *specter* of homosexuality, the *mere possibility* of homosexuality, which will never disappear.

This means that the only way to protect a group against gay panics is *simply to stop caring about it*. When someone tries to make an issue of Jack Donovan speaking at NPI or James O'Meara writing for *Counter-Currents*, nothing stops them deader than simply saying, "I don't care." Meaning: I'm not tainted by it. It doesn't make me dirty. There is no guilt by association. You can't catch cooties off the internet. So I just don't care.

Of course, what makes most people care about homosexuals is the Bible, which treats homosexuality not just as abnormal but as an offense against God. This is the source of the intense and irrational anxiety and the sense of moral contagion involved in gay panics. Thus it follows that the more Christian an organization is, the more fragile it is in the face of gay panics. Which implies that the less Christian an organization is, the less susceptible it is to this form of subversion.

This also implies that the recent gay panics in the Alt Right might eventually strengthen it, or at least certain segments. If Parrott and Heimbach hoped their "gay mafia" slur would split those susceptible to gay panics away from NPI and attract them to Trad Youth, the net effect will only be to make Trad Youth more brittle and NPI more resilient. Because Trad Youth is overwhelmingly if not exclusively male too. Which means that they can be hoist by their own petard. (Someday some jerk is going to suggest that the dust up with NPI was merely a gay spat between bear and twink factions.)

This brings up the question of the proper role of homosexuals in "the" movement. Again, I can only control my little corner of the movement, but my view is that White Nationalism should be "straight but not narrow," meaning that we should uphold and defend heterosexuality as the norm but also recognize that not everyone fits that norm. But as long as homosexuals uphold healthy norms and have something positive to contribute, they can and do make our movement stronger, *if we stop worrying about it.*

Counter-Currents, March 18, 2016

THE ALT RIGHT:
OBITUARY FOR A BRAND?

GREG JOHNSON

It is ironic — or maybe just sadly fitting — that Richard Spencer, the man who launched the Alternative Right brand, may have just destroyed it. But that seems to be fallout of his speech at the recent National Policy Institute conference, which he ended with the words "Hail Trump! Hail our people! Hail Victory!" Spencer then raised his empty liquor glass in a toast. Some people in the audience, however, predictably responded to "Hail Victory!" (*Sieg Heil*) by giving Nazi salutes.

This was, also predictably, caught on video by *The Atlantic*, which had been invited into the conference to make a documentary about Spencer and the Alternative Right. When the video was made public, it was of course rapidly propagated. For years, the Left has been pushing the increasingly tired slur that Jared Taylor, Peter Brimelow, Kevin MacDonald, etc. are just "suit and tie Nazis." But Spencer breathed life into this charge by furnishing visual "proof." There was surely rejoicing in the offices of the ADL and SPLC, as well as the *Washington Post* and *New York Times*.

Now I do not wish to split hairs about the motives and culpability for this public relations disaster, except to say that I do not believe the charge that Spencer was intentionally sabotaging NPI and the Alt Right. Instead, I wish to comment on the consequences of this affair and how we should respond to it.

First and foremost, Donald Trump, when confronted with the video, naturally condemned and disavowed the Alt Right. He's not a Nazi, after all, and he probably found it as embarrassing as I did. This is a pity, because Trump has to know that almost no mainstream intellectuals and commentators defended his candidacy and vision. But people on the Alt Right did.

Moreover, we have an enormous pool of talent and brainpower. Our public writers and activists are only the tip of the iceberg. The vast bulk of our people are secret agents, with clean public records. My hope was that during the first Trump administration, the Alt Right could start mobilizing this talent to craft policy proposals to help show that Trump's ideas about immigration, trade, and foreign policy are morally defensible, politically desirable, and practically feasible. In fact, I rather hoped that the National Policy Institute would take a hand in crafting some of these national policies.

It was always a long shot, of course. Over the past two years, there has been a massive influx of talented people into our movement, but our organizing and fundraising have lagged far behind. We honestly don't know what to do with all these people. We have a lot of work ahead of us if we are going to actually influence policy, and the way forward is not always clear. But when you are at a loss about what to do next, at least do no harm. Spencer really had one job: not to embarrass us or Trump, and he blew it. Now there is zero chance of any proposal coming from NPI being taken seriously.

But there is no reason why the rest of us have to share Spencer's fate, which is why various Alt Right and Alt Lite figures have distanced themselves from him. Mike Cernovich and Paul Joseph Watson have been most vociferous and strident, accusing Spencer of intentionally sabotaging the Alt Right. Stefan Molyneux recommended Cernovich's take. Vox Day does not think Spencer is controlled opposition but that he nevertheless behaved in a self-aggrandizing manner and made a serious public relations error. Ramzpaul declared the Alt Right brand irreparably damaged, so he is now simply going to refer to himself as a man of the Right.

Those who actually spoke at NPI made more measured comments. In an interview, Jared Taylor declared, "I was very surprised. I was very saddened by it. I think it's a terrible, terrible pity. I don't endorse any form of National Socialism. I think that's a completely inappropriate and crazy model for the United States." Peter Brimelow at *VDare* and F. Roger Devlin at *The Occidental Observer* both rejected the Nazi brand, attributing Spencer's words and the salutes from the crowd to "juvenile bravado" and "rowdy behavior on the part of a few overzealous and partially drunken young men." In an interview, Matt Tait basically endorsed the analysis offered by Colin Liddell and described Spencer's final gestures as "snatching defeat from the jaws of victory" and "undoing what is good about the Alt Right."

Spencer's defenders have been pushing the line that we should not air our differences in public (of course). But there are problems with this. First, if Spencer speaks and we remain silent, people will assume that he is speaking for us. Second, criticizing Spencer is not about changing his behavior. It is about social signaling: communicating our differences to the public we are trying to persuade. So obviously it cannot be confined solely to back channel whispers. Finally, it presupposes a false unity to the movement. Literally the only thing that unifies us is common goals (and with Spencer I am not even sure about that). But if our movement is inherently pluralistic, colonizing every niche in the cultural and political ecosystem, then the only way to establish and maintain our different approaches is to criticize one another. Of course it can go too far. And there are some people who spend all their time attacking movement people rather than our enemies. But with healthy pluralism comes healthy dissent and debate.

Richard Spencer does not speak for me either. Spencer has damaged the Alt Right brand—perhaps irreparably—by associating it with Nazism. The Alternative Right began as a particular brand, the name of Spencer's webzine. But it quickly became a generic umbrella term encompassing a range of different alternatives to mainstream Republicans and conservatives.

But from its start, the *Alternative Right* webzine was an entryist tool for White Nationalists. It was a platform for outreach and conversion of people who are closer to the mainstream. It created a safe space where "normie" conservatives could encounter human biodiversity, ethnic nationalism, the Jewish question, paleomasculinity, etc. without having to adopt stigmatizing labels like "Nazism." But after Spencer's NPI speech, there is good reason to think that will no longer work.

What's wrong with branding the Alt Right as Nazi? Here are a few thoughts.

❖ What is White Nationalism based on? Is it based on objective facts about human nature and politics, facts that are true in all times and places? Is ethnonationalism a political system that is good for all peoples, not just the white ones, much less just the Axis nations? Or is it based on what happened in Germany between the World Wars? If ethnonationalism is objectively true and universally valid, then why bring the Nazis into it at all? Particularly because:

❖ Regardless of the truth about National Socialism, our enemies have invested decades of work and billions in capital in turning it into the ultimate political taboo, a toxic stigmatizing brand — the kind of brand that is seared into your flesh. If the NPI audience had broken out into cries of "Hail Satan!" we wouldn't even be having this conversation. Some of our people conclude that all these defenses must hide the enemy's greatest weakness. I think that is silly, but even if it were true, *only a fool attacks the enemy's best defended spot*, especially when they are incredibly weak elsewhere, e.g., denying the reality of racial differences, proclaiming diversity is a strength, supporting open borders, free trade, hate speech laws, etc.

❖ Even if there were nothing wrong with the Nazi brand at all, it would still have been wrong for Spencer to in effect foist it on people like Jared Taylor, who choose not to use it and trusted Spencer because they thought he understood this.

Please don't give me the tired argument that they'll call us Nazis anyway, so we might as well become them. First, some of us really aren't Nazis. Second, even if you are, we're only fighting against the whole damn world, so why take on additional and needless burdens? Third, just because your enemies are out to get you doesn't mean that you should make their work easier. (Compare the press coverage of the recent NPI conference to the coverage of the NPI press conference back in

September, then explain to me how the saluting made no difference at all.) Finally, they'll call you Jews, informants, and fags too. Do you want to own those labels as well?

Please don't tell me that all publicity is good publicity. There really is such thing as bad publicity.

Please don't tell me that Spencer's critics are all simply trying to make friends with an implacably hostile press. First, our concern is obviously not persuading our enemies but reaching people who are sympathetic or neutral. Second, if the press is implacably hostile, why is Spencer so focused on courting it?

The great irony here is that I have published quite a bit about Hitler and National Socialism at *Counter-Currents*, whereas literally the only thing Nazi-like about Richard Spencer is his haircut. This is why everyone found this gaffe so surprising—some pleasantly, others unpleasantly. When I first met Spencer in 2008, he was dating an Asian woman (something now public because of an article in *Mother Jones*). The only foreign regime he strongly identifies with is Putin's Russia, which is valiantly battling against "Nazis" in Ukraine. As long as I have known him, Spencer has been chummy with Jews like Paul Gottfried. NPI, like *American Renaissance*, has always played patty-cake with certain Right-wing Jews. Before Spencer came on board, NPI had published Edward Rubenstein, Byron Roth, and Michael Hart. But, unlike *American Renaissance*, they published Kevin MacDonald as well. Spencer has continued in that vein, publishing additional books by Roth and Hart, plus Richard Lynn's *The Chosen People*, and various essays and introductions by Paul Gottfried. Before long, Spencer will be back to business as usual, which means that most of his new-found friends will simply go silent—or be back at this throat.

Literally everything about this controversy, from Spencer's "Nazism" to the press coverage to the adulation of the Nazi troll army is at best superficial and at worst fake. But that's the stuff of which politics and publicity are made. The negative consequences, however, are real.

Now some Alt Rightists are rejoicing that Spencer's gesture has caused Alt Light poseurs and "cucks" to abandon the Alt Right brand. But that is self-defeating. Outreach efforts only work by attracting people who don't already agree with us. These people are only a danger if we fail to convert and assimilate them. But apparently some people don't want to be bothered with converts.

I do want to end on a hopeful note. There is no question that the Alt Right is a useful brand, and because of that, it may well revive. But even if the Alt Right is dead, White Nationalism is still very much alive and growing. What happened at NPI was foolish and self-defeating. And there is always a danger that too much self-defeating behavior will add up to a simple defeat. But our progress has always been two steps forward, one step back. So let's just learn from this setback and keep pressing forward.

Counter-Currents, November 29, 2016

GOD EMPEROR NO MORE

GREG JOHNSON

Never betray your friends to court the favor of your enemies. If you betray your friends, the most principled and perceptive among them will drop you, leaving only the delusional and venal. That is not a good trade, given that the approval you gain is bound to be fleeting and contingent, whereas the contempt and distrust you create will be permanent. The people you betrayed may come back to you out of sentimentality or self-interest, but their trust and respect will never return. They will always regard you as a traitor.

Why is such a simple lesson so hard for politicians to understand?

Donald Trump's dizzying about-face on Syria has won the temporary applause of his enemies, but he has forever lost the respect of his most ardent supporters on the Alt Right, the people who actually believe in and defend his nationalist-populist message, including his America First foreign policy.

I thought Trump's willingness to fight a two-front war against the Democrats and his own party was sufficient proof that he was sincere about his America First foreign policy. But he ditched it at its first real test.

I no longer trust Donald Trump.

But it is worse than that. I no longer like or respect Trump either. Trump didn't just betray us. He betrayed us over something utterly stupid. We've seen this all before. We've seen pictures of dead or injured Syrian children on CNN (although not the victims of US-backed forces). We've heard stories of Assad "gassing his own people." We've seen the same vulgar emotional manipulation and ginned-up storms of social signaling. We've been asked to start wars based on what some little Syrian Anne Frank allegedly says on Twitter. We know that the press, politicians, and intelligence agencies behind this are trying to topple Assad. We know that they are liars, because they are the same people who lied to get us into the Iraq War. And Trump has seen it all too. *He knew better.* We know he knew better, because of a long history of Tweets about Syria, which now make him look like a feckless hypocrite. So, for him to fall for the warmongers this time frankly makes me question his intelligence, his character, even his sanity.

Beyond that, attacking Assad exacerbates our problems. We want Assad to win this war. We want him to destroy ISIS and other Islamist terrorist groups. We want peace and stability in Syria, so we can send millions of refugees back home, whether they want to go or not. And we certainly do not want heightened tensions with Russia.

Furthermore, Trump's intervention in Syria is now being used as an argument to admit more Syrian refugees.

Then, there's the little problem that Trump's strike was unconstitutional. Wouldn't it be poetic if Trump gave the establishment the Syrian war they have been trying to start for years—as well as grounds for impeaching him before he manages to slip up and do something good for America?

Finally, why are we even *debating* retaliations for atrocities committed by Syrians in Syria? Obviously, because no matter what side you come down on, Jews and Israel benefit. They benefit when we actually promote chaos and regime change in Syria. And they benefit even if we end up doing nothing, simply because we *not* debating, say, retaliating for atrocities committed against whites by Muslims all over Europe, or against whites by blacks in South Africa, or against whites by mestizo invaders in America. Let's debate regime change in South Africa or Germany or Sweden or Mexico, shall we?

Or better yet, why not focus on America First? Trump has his work cut out for him effecting regime change in Washington, DC.

Some have suggested that Trump changed his Syrian policy out of Machiavellian calculations:

- ❖ To impress/intimidate the President of China, who was dining with him in Florida
- ❖ To impress/intimidate Putin, to make him more

tractable in future negotiations

❖ To impress/intimidate Kim Jong-un in North Korea

❖ To undermine the "Trump is beholden to Putin/the
Russians 'hacked' the election" narrative that Democrats have been pushing because they are incapable
of taking responsibility for Hillary Clinton's disastrous candidacy

❖ To placate Jewish warmongers and their lapdogs like
McCain, Rubio, and Graham, as well as their chorus
of media shills

❖ To get his faltering Presidency back on track by doing something popular with the establishment that
opposes him

❖ To convince the world that he is a dangerous madman, to make other powers more tractable to US de-
signs

We are also told that the ineffectual nature of the strike was
actually part of the plan. The Syrians and Russians were fore-
warned, expensive equipment was removed, etc. Missiles were
allegedly deactivated in flight. (Certainly, more comforting
than believing that Russian technology shot a lot of them
down.) Trump does not want to actually harm Assad. There
was no risk of escalation with Russia or Iran. Trump just wants
to do one or all of the above.

Frankly, I'm not buying it. None of these theories are half as
clever as purported.

❖ Russia, China, and North Korea would not be im-
pressed or intimidated by a mere expensive fire-
works display that risked nothing. But if Trump
tried to hurt Assad and failed, that is hardly impressive or intimidating either, and saving face would
require escalation, perhaps into outright war.

❖ If Trump warned the Russians and Syrians and did
nothing to hurt Assad, it would support, not undermine, the Trump-Russia collusion narrative. It is a
meme that the Democrats would rather court nuclear

war than take responsibility for their own failure. If Trump actually tried to hurt Assad and risked real escalation with Russia, one has to ask: Is it worth a nuclear war to shut these people's lying mouths? Trump would have to be mad to think so.

❖ If the establishment can get Trump to do its bidding by blocking his policies, it will only continue to stymie Trump until more *Danegeld* is extorted. Trump surely knows better. It is far too early to declare Trump's administration a failure. Realistically, I expected him to be stymied by liberals and cucks for a full two years, until the 2018 elections. Trump was never deterred by bad press. How many times was he declared finished in the primaries and election? He didn't listen before, so why would he start now?

❖ Trump has already convinced a significant percentage of the world that he is a dangerous madman. But the Syria pivot does not support that perception. It supports the conclusion that he is a mercurial, hypocritical buffoon who cannot be trusted to maintain his most basic promises. How, exactly, does that make him a more formidable negotiator?

The most plausible explanation for the Syria pivot comes from Seventh Son at *The Daily Shoah* (Episode #145). When Trump was asked about the gas attack by a reporter at the news conference with King Abdullah of Jordan, he saw it as an opportunity for abusing Obama as a weak little girl for declaring a red line in Syria and then backing down when Assad crossed it rather than acting decisively. When asked if this attack crossed any red lines for him, Trump of course had to agree and amplify, lest he too be a weak little girl like Obama.

In short, Trump painted himself into a corner with his big mouth, his adolescent alpha posturing, and his fixation on denigrating Obama, and since acknowledging mistakes has never been Trump's strong suit, it was child's play for the establishment to spring into action and funnel him into launching airstrikes. The politicians, pundits, and masses are well-programmed with Jewish talking points. All they needed was an opening, then all the tools started whirring for war.

Let's hope that Trump has realized his mistake and decides to declare victory and turn back to real priorities. Let's hope that the other players in this game, like Syria, Russia, and Iran *let him*.

I think Seventh Son's analysis is correct, and it helps us decode Trump's whole foreign policy. For a long time, we on the Alt Right were scratching our heads about the great anomaly in Trump's America First platform, namely Iran. Trump constantly repeated the rankest, most gefilte-fishy neocon talking points on Obama's Iran deal, which threatened to cause a terrifying outbreak of peace in the region. My hypothesis was that Trump took this stance simply to contradict and abuse Obama.

But, *goyische kopf* that I am, I assumed that the rest of Trump's foreign policy—the stuff I agreed with, of course—was sincere. Now I am not so sure. Is Trump's entire foreign policy agenda simply based on negating Obama's? What about his domestic policy agenda? Does Trump base his policies not on a sober assessment of what is good for America, but simply on some sort of egomaniacal desire to one-up and put down Barack Obama and his ilk? Granted, doing the opposite of Obama and Hillary is generally a good guide to policy. But you'd have to be an overgrown adolescent chimpanzee to run a country that way. Could this be why Donald Trump is idolized by rappers?

If this is the Trump code, you can bet I am not the first one to crack it. Which means that the establishment now knows how to play Trump. History is one long record of the triumph of the cunning over the macho. Which means that all bets are off for the MAGA agenda. Sure, we might still get some of what he promised, but now a new enemy has emerged from the shadows, perhaps the most formidable one yet: no, not the "deep state," but Donald Trump's own adolescent egomania. (Yes, I know cat ladies have been saying this for years, but they say that about anyone with a scrotum, so they are not to be taken seriously.)

For the Alt Right, it's Mourning in America. We believed in

this guy. We liked this guy. And now he just seems stupid. Frankly, so do we. The day Trump launched his strike, I received the proof copy of my new book *In Defense of Prejudice*, and I cringed my way through the chapters on Trump. Sure, I can tell myself that it was still right to support him, that Trump is still better than Hillary. So why is he enacting Hillary's foreign policy? Maybe Martin Heidegger really was the last philosopher with sound political judgment.

I'm a little suspicious at how quickly we on the Alt Right moved to condemn Trump. As soon as I heard that missiles had been fired, my feelings changed completely. The cloud of confusion and anxiety that was building over the previous days suddenly erupted in lightning and thunder. It was a catharsis.

But in truth this break has been a long time in coming. I think that we all felt that Trump was faltering out of the gate, especially with the health care bill. And when people feel that a relationship is doomed, it is quite common to search for a principled pretext to give it a *coup de grâce* and move forward. It is psychologically easier that way. One maintains one's sense of agency, which is an important component of one's self-worth. In short, it is just another case of what I call honorable defeatism.[1] In this case, however, it is a good thing, for two reasons.

First, a lot of us were too emotionally invested in Trump. I thought I had a pretty realistic view of Trump, but this betrayal still came as a brutal blow. It must be a lot worse for the souls who actually thought the Alt Right was responsible for putting Trump into office, who felt that we owned a piece of him. The Alt Right's relationship with Trump was always a one-way man crush, based largely on projections. Ending such a relationship is a healthy thing.

Second, it helps us refocus on our mission. When Trump was elected, I argued that the Alt Right needs to see itself as Trump's loyal opposition, the opposition that wants him to succeed in spite of himself. After all, Trump is not one of us. He's a populist and a civic nationalist with generally good in-

---

[1] Greg Johnson, "Honorable Defeatists," in *In Defense of Prejudice*.

stincts. But he's not terribly articulate or intellectual, which is one reason he seems to have been so easily misled by the Jews and cuckservatives that opportunistically crowded into his administration. It is our job to offer an intellectually sound and emotionally compelling case for nationalist populism, to help Trump advance his policies, and to help as many Trump supporters as possible advance beyond them to White Nationalism.

Now that the God Emperor has fallen to earth, we need to remind ourselves that Trump was never the end game. He was—and remains—an immense opportunity to smash the current globalist establishment and unleash nationalist, populist, and racialist forces that will be raging into the future, long after Trump is dead. It is our movement, not Trump, that represents the real long-term interests of our race, and we have to start acting like it.

Counter-Currents, April 8, 2017

IDENTITY VS. IRONY

GREG JOHNSON

The Alt Right embraces and revels in irony. But this is problematic, because ironism is a form of cultural decadence.

What is irony? By "irony," I do not mean the trope whereby one intends something different from, or opposed to, what one literally says. Nor do I mean situations in which what actually happens is very different from, and sometimes opposed to, what one expected. For instance, when Oedipus vows to find the cause of the plague, not knowing that it is he himself. Nor do I mean Socratic irony, which is a kind of dissimulation and condescension in speech.

Instead, by "irony" I mean a refusal to take serious things seriously, an attitude of detachment and condescension towards things that one should look up to with respect or adoration.

Detachment from small and silly things is healthy. But ironic detachment from great and serious things is a sign of decadence, because we need ideals. Ideals are what raise human beings above animals. Men without ideals are just clever animals, whose reason is subservient to the satisfaction of their natural desires.

When irony becomes an ethos, I call it "ironism."

Ironism in the postmodern sense means relating to culture, ideas, and especially ideals without committing to them, without owning them, without making them a part of you, and especially without opening yourself to their power to transform you. In his book *Postscript to The Name of the Rose*, Umberto Eco describes this postmodern ironism brilliantly:

> I think of the postmodern attitude as that of a man who loves a very cultivated woman and knows that he cannot say to her "I love you madly," because he knows that she knows (and that she knows he knows) that these words

have already been written by Barbara Cartland. Still there is a solution. He can say "As Barbara Cartland would put it, I love you madly." At this point, having avoided false innocence, having said clearly it is no longer possible to talk innocently, he will nevertheless say what he wanted to say to the woman: that he loves her in an age of lost innocence. If the woman goes along with this, she will have received a declaration of love all the same. Neither of the two speakers will feel innocent, both will have accepted the challenge of the past, of the already said, which cannot be eliminated; both will consciously and with pleasure play the game of irony. . . . But both will have succeeded, one again, in speaking of love.[1]

What Eco means here by "innocence" is sincerity, earnestness, and commitment. Barbara Cartland wrote lots of torrid romance novels, which, whatever their flaws, were brimming with sincere professions of passion. But the couple in question would feel silly speaking of love in such a naïve and straightforward way. They can't own or commit to such emotions. Yet they must speak of love. But they also feel the need to communicate that they think themselves above it. So they speak of love ironically and condescendingly. They put "love" in scare quotes. They put love in the mouth of a ladies' romance novelist.

Eco says this is a solution to the problem of speaking of love while still being hyper self-conscious. Unfortunately, I don't think that's a solution at all, because to be hyper self-conscious is unhealthy, and it is especially unhealthy in relation to things that we should take seriously, like moral and political ideals and our racial and cultural identity.

How is self-consciousness subversive of identity? First, we will deal with identity, then with self-consciousness.

Some things are us, and some things are not us. Your identity is what you are. The rest of the world is what you are not.

---

[1] Umberto Eco, *Postscript to The Name of the Rose*, trans. William Weaver (San Diego: Harcourt Brace Jovanovich, 1984), pp. 67–68.

Some things that are not us can become us. I am going to use neologism for this process that is so ugly that even Heidegger scholars have rejected it: "enowning." Enowning means making something part of you. Enowning is more than just ownership, since the things we own really aren't part of us, although we can more or less invest ourselves in them.

Conversely, some things that are us can become no longer us. I call this process "disowning."

When we eat and drink, we are enowning — literally incorporating — things that are not us. When we learn a language or a skill, we are enowning something that is not us. We are becoming the vehicle through with a tradition of practices stretching back into unrecorded history lives and perpetuates itself. When we adopt ideas, really believe them, and live accordingly, we are enowning them. When we cut our hair or trim our nails, we are disowning parts of ourselves. When we decide that ideas are no longer true and values no longer good, we disown and disavow them.

There are, however, some things that you can enown but cannot disown, chief among them your mother tongue and the culture instilled along with it. If your brain is your hardware, your mother tongue and culture are your operating system. If our genes constitute our first nature, our language and culture constitute our second nature, which provide the context and framework for all subsequent experience. No matter how many other languages you learn, no matter how widely you might travel, no matter how rootless and cosmopolitan you might aspire to be, these new acquisitions do not erase your mother language and culture. They are simply added on top of them. You can never fully uproot yourself from your mother tongue and culture. You cannot get rid of them. It's like trying to run away from your own shadow. It always follows you. It's always there, whether you own up to it or not.

Self-consciousness is a form of consciousness. Consciousness involves a distinction between the *act* of consciousness and the *object* of consciousness — between seeing the painting and the painting that we see, between hearing the melody and the melody that we hear. As conscious beings, we are first and foremost conscious of things other than ourselves. We are like the sun, with rays of consciousness streaming out in all directions, revealing all manner of objects. We are agents, not objects, of awareness, who are involved with the world, not with ourselves.

But if there is a difference between consciousness and its objects, how can be become self-conscious? Self-consciousness is a turning inwards, which is possible because we can first *disengage our consciousness from the world*, then *introduce a split in ourselves* between agent of consciousness and object of consciousness, then contemplate this objectified fragment of ourselves.

If self-consciousness presupposes *disengagement from the world* and *self-objectification*, one has to ask: Is self-consciousness healthy? Yes, within limits, it is. Life can be viewed as a constant process of enowning and disowning, both things in the world and aspects of ourselves. For conscious beings, self-consciousness is healthy as a tool of self-criticism and self-improvement. Self-consciousness allows us disengage, objectify, and then either improve or disown beliefs and patterns of feeling and behavior that might otherwise harm us.

But there are limits to self-consciousness.

First, there are limits to its utility. One can be too self-conscious — too disengaged from the world, too self-objectified, too much of a navel-gazer — to lead a good life. Life can be improved by self-consciousness, but self-consciousness is not life itself, and being hyper-self-conscious is self-defeating.

For instance, you might be a highly practiced speaker or musician or warrior. The acquisition of these skills requires self-consciousness as a means of self-criticism and self-improvement. This is, for example, why gyms, dance schools, and martial arts academies are filled with mirrors. This is why we have teachers, trainers, and friends: to see ourselves through their eyes, in the hope of improving ourselves.

But when the time comes to actually perform, we have to thrust self-consciousness aside and simply engage with our task. And if, at that point, self-consciousness creeps back in — "Am I saying this right? Am I pronouncing this right? Am I communicating this right? Does this finger go here?" — you are disengaging from your task, objectifying your performance, and thinking about yourself rather than the matter at hand. You are second-guessing yourself. You are withdrawing energy and focus from the task. And you will start slipping up. You will start getting tongue-tied and stammering. You will start hitting the wrong keys. Your defense and attack will slacken. You will lose your edge. Because you're no longer fully present, no longer in the moment, no longer performing these acts anymore. You're reflecting on then. Even the most accomplished master can trip himself up simply by starting to reflect on what he's doing, because then he's no longer really, fully, committedly doing it. The performer must be engaged, not disengaged. His self must be one, not split. He must be fully into the task, not half in it, half out of it. He must be fully an actor, not in part a spectator viewing himself from the stands.

Second, there are metaphysical limits to self-consciousness. J. G. Fichte once enjoined his students, "Gentlemen, think the wall." Then he said, "Gentlemen, think he-who-thinks the wall." In other words, disengage from the wall, objectify yourself, and think about it instead. But who is performing that act? Obviously, the thinker is another part of you. And by asking that question, I have now objectified him as well. Now we are thinking he-who-thinks he-who-thinks the wall. But who did that? Yet another part of you. Obviously, this process can go on forever, mincing up the self into tinier and tinier pieces.

But the self can never be fully objectified, because there always remains a distinction between the *act* and the *object* of consciousness. Thus complete self-consciousness is not possible, for every act of self-consciousness presupposes splitting the self into subject and object, and as long as the subject is a subject, it is never an object. Your consciousness only *works* when you are not looking at it. Consciousness is the looker, not the object. Yet mankind is often enthralled by the delusion that we can monitor and control our own consciousness, even though the subject always recedes beyond every attempt to objectify it.

When I was a child, I sometimes suffered from insomnia, and one of my hippy cousins told me that it would help me relax and fall asleep if I focused simply on my breathing and my heartbeat. So I would shadow each of these automatic processes with self-consciousness. But then the absurd idea would steal through my head that maybe these processes would stop if I no longer reflected on them, which would induce a feeling of panic that would stave off sleep even more. These morbid, obsessional thoughts were, however, quickly banished by induction. For I would eventually fall asleep, and yet I have woken up every morning since. Our consciousness, like our heart and lungs, is at root an automatic biological process that does not require the shadow of self-consciousness to operate. This makes sense, for man is part of the animal kingdom, and consciousness exists in animal species that show no sign of self-consciousness at all.

How is the hyper-self-consciousness of ironism subversive of cultural identity? Irony as a cultural form is all about is stepping back from your culture, severing your commitment to it, severing the seriousness that is at the root of that commitment, and objectifying it—even discarding it.

There is a sense, though, in which one's deep identity is actually immune to ironism. Your mother tongue and native culture are acquired before you are self-conscious. They exist on deeper level of your mind than self-consciousness. They are one of the conditions that make self-consciousness possible in the first place. Self-consciousness can spiral in on itself and try to uproot itself from its origins, but the effort is futile.

Such efforts are not, however, without consequence, for although they cannot change your deep identity, they can alienate you from who you really are and lead to a shallow and inauthentic existence. You have no choice about your deep identity, but you do have a choice to embrace it or flee from it, to own up to it or disown it, to be authentic or inauthentic, to be real or fake.

The true destructiveness of ironism can best be appreciated when civilization faces the test of barbarism. In "The Second Coming," W. B. Yeats brilliantly describes a decadent culture on the brink of collapse. Two lines are especially resonant: "The best lack all conviction, while the worst / Are full of passionate

intensity." The best are the defenders of civilization. The worst
are the rabble that would tear it down if given the chance.
What happens when the best no longer feel a passionate attachment to civilization? What happens when they are detached and ironic toward their identity, willing to enact it only
in "scare quotes"? More to the point, what happens when such
men face off with a rabble animated by passionate intensity?
Obviously, other things being equal, the rabble will triumph,
and civilization will fall.

One of the reasons why ironism is rife today is because our
culture is dominated by Jews, who are outsiders. Jews do not
feel an identity with our civilization. They are all too happy to
appropriate the best of its products, but they spend far more
time mocking and degrading the rest of it. Jewish ironism
makes perfect sense, because this is not their culture. Unfortunately, they have the power to mainline their ironism into the
rest of us. But it makes no sense for us to accept it, since this
really is our culture. Moreover, while Jews teach us to lack all
conviction toward our culture and interests, they cultivate a
passionate intensity toward their own, which is how whites
have lost and Jews have gained control over our society.

It is important to understand the dangers of ironism, because the Right today is rank with it—the whole "LOL dude,
it's just a meme," "I'm only being ironic" culture.

There's a place and a role for irony. People are not overly
eager to commit to new things, especially if they are radical
and marginal. This is why we have changing rooms at clothing
stores, so you can try clothes on and see if they look good on
you before you buy them. This is why we let people test drive a
car before they commit to buying it. This is why merchants
have 30-day money back guarantees. If you don't have to fully
commit upfront, then you're more likely to try something, and
if you try it, then you are more likely to buy it.

Ironic spaces where people can encounter White Nationalist
ideas perform an important function for our movement. They
allow people to try on radical ideas for size before committing
to them. Irony gives them deniability if mom looks over their
shoulder. They can just jump back and say, "Whoa! I'm just

playing around here! Don't take this seriously! I'm not committed to this. I disavow! I was just being ironic!" The more people who feel safe trying on our ideas without committing to them, the more people who will ultimately come on board.

But we must never lose sight of the fact that, in the end, we have to close the deal. The salesman who lets you take a test drive can't let you remain non-committal. The shop girl who lets you try on a shirt can't let you remain non-committal. When people are exploring our ideas, we can't let them remain non-committal either. This is not a game. We are not just playing with ideas, we are fighting for the survival of our race against cunning and ruthless enemies who are out to exterminate us. If you are detached and bemused about that, you haven't gotten the message. This is war, and there is no room for ironists in foxholes.

The ironists also need to recognize that ideas inspire actions. So we must ask ourselves: What is more likely to inspire a movement that actually changes the world for the better: a worldview that is based on objective reality and calibrated for practical success—or a grab bag of edgy memes, drunken pranks, and sound drops from TV shows? People are going to take ideas seriously regardless, so we need to provide them with serious ideas.

Irony is useful as a tool, but ironism as an ethos is decadent. Thus the great problem of our movement is to move people from an ethos of ironism to an ethos of commitment. We must move from play to seriousness, bemused detachment to passionate intensity, smirks to sincerity, evading responsibility to assuming it, self-indulgence to self-sacrifice—from being children to being grownups. It is time to put away froggy things and act like men. For in the end, the people who are going to save our race must be 100% committed to the struggle because it is a matter of identity, of who they really are, not a pose they can jump back from and pretend like it's all just a game.

Counter-Currents, August 23, 2017

THOUGHTS ON THE
STATE OF THE RIGHT

JAMES LAWRENCE

There's no sense in mincing words anymore: the Alt Right has hit a wall and is presently faced with the hard task of pulling back and searching for a new course. The enemy media are (prematurely) claiming victory. Many progressives are hastening to vindicate the "antifa" domestic terrorist movement,[1] discarding the pretense that liberal misgivings about organized political violence hinge on anything more than crass utilitarianism.

My purpose here is to offer some thoughts on what has happened and how our side can hope to recover its ground. I do not wish to exaggerate the present difficulties, nor blame people in the Alt Right for suffering what is essentially a form of state repression outsourced to volunteer paramilitary groups and powerful corporations. However, repression by those in power is a constant for us; what has changed is the *effectiveness* of this repression, which used to meet with a fluid, agile, and durable target, and now increasingly enjoys a sluggish, clumsy, and brittle one. One major reason for this is that prominent figures in the Alt Right, protected by a widespread culture of hooting down internal dissent, took strategic and aesthetic decisions that ended up turning an antifragile movement into a highly destructible one.

Where the Alt Right was once proudly decentralized, it now seeks unification (and is, of course, more divided than ever). Where it once contained a constellation of anti-progressive elements, it is now reduced to an isolated ethnonationalist core spitting fire at everything else around it. Where it once em-

---

[1] https://www.theguardian.com/world/2018/mar/19/the-Alt Right-is-in-decline-has-antifa-activism-worked

ployed intellectual quality *and* transgressive trolling to equally great effect, these polar opposites have lately been merged into a dull and stagnant rehash of Rockwellian neo-Nazism.

As many of these changes were made precisely so that certain individuals could enjoy leadership, it would be perverse to allow them to shirk responsibility for the results. That said, I am not accusing anyone of deliberate sabotage: those who employed these methods certainly believed that they would work. This is why a true analysis of the present state of affairs must look beyond mere personalities and decisions and identify the deeper fault lines in the ideological fundament of our movement.

YOUR BRAIN ON LIBERALISM

To understand why the Alt Right is failing, we can start by asking a simple question: *how do most people in it envisage the victory of the movement?* I would anticipate receiving three basic answers: 1) a mass white awakening provoked by anti-white depredations; 2) the rise of a reactionary post-Millennial youth wave; and 3) a collapse of modern Western civilization that will destroy the ruling power structure at a stroke.

None of these scenarios correspond to reality. Anti-white depredations that would have seemed unimaginable a few decades ago have not provoked ordinary people into rebellion. "Generation Zyklon" might be fairly conservative, but they have little social and political power, and many cradles in the West have already been filled by the children of the imported neo-proletariat loyal to the Left. As for a civilizational collapse: even assuming that such a thing could happen, it would likely favor those who already possess disproportionate resources and entrenched power structures. The big winners of the Western Roman collapse were the barbarian invaders, the Christian Church, and (sometimes) the late Roman landholding elites who got to merge with the invaders; the *bagaudae* rebel groups in the provinces were simply suppressed by old and new rulers alike.

All of these Alt Right victory fantasies bear a common stamp of origin: they are *liberal* fantasies. This fact should not surprise us in the least, given that liberalism enjoys near-complete intellectual hegemony in the West, and forms the common ideological bedrock of progressivism and post-1945 conservatism.

One of the fundamental pillars of liberalism is what we might call a *democentric* view of things. In this view, men are born free, then choose to enter into a "social contract" and set up a ruling authority in order to secure their interests. This implies not only that the ruling authority is the servant of the people, *but that the initiative to drive history is in the hands of the people;* those in power can only choose to fulfil or deny the popular will. Although the ruling elites may disregard their obligations and repress popular demands, this can only prove ineffective in the long run, as the will of the people "inevitably" takes the course of insurrection and restores the original social contract.

Contrast this with the anti-liberal view, which we can call *cratocentric* or "rule-centered." In this view, all men are born into subjection (i.e., as children under the sway of parents); society arises from the expansion and agglomeration of families, as the cities of antiquity arose according to Fustel de Coulanges; and the authority of the ruler is no more dependent on popular consent than is the rule of a father over his children. The masses can assent to the commands of the ruling authority, or else negate them, but they do not and cannot take the initiative to change society. Repression by authority usually works as advertised, and where successful insurrections do take place, they do not spring from a spontaneous popular will but from the power schemes of a rival authority.

Although democentric ideas may possess ideological hegemony over the modern West, cratocentric ones still possess their ancient hegemony over human nature. And when we critique democentrism from a cratocentric viewpoint, we understand that it is not really an expression of "anti-elitism," but an ideological weapon to serve the long struggle of liberal elites against the traditional elites of the West. Democentrism is toxic to the legitimacy of an aristocracy, and hazardous to that of a monarchy; but it is a useful smokescreen for anonymous plutocrats, and a positive elixir of health for the managerial elites whose business it is to control society in the name of the people.

What does all of this have to do with the present state of the Alt Right? Well, let's come to the point: *the liberal managerial class ruling the West preserves its own legitimacy by using manipulation and patronage to construct a democratic facade for its own exercise of power.* When it wants to destabilize a foreign government, it funds a color revolution, or encourages an internal rebellion. When it wants to impeach a renegade US President, and anticipates the need to disarm his conservative supporters, it comes up with a media-constructed assault on public opinion masquerading as a spontaneous protest by school shooting survivors. When it wants to strengthen that impeachment effort by getting hold of some juicy photos of brown children being shot dead by border guards, it whips up a caravan of illegal migrants to storm the US border. And so on.

As these examples suggest, this manipulation does not always succeed, at least not directly. But it has created a strong illusion of unlimited popular agency that infects even the self-described enemies of liberalism, fooling them into a false view of how power is achieved and exercised. The tactics pursued by the Alt Right since Hailgate can be compared to a *cargo cult*, in the sense that they rely on recreating the democentric facade of liberal movements. Protest marchers chanting racialist slogans are our Black Lives Matter, street brawlers are our antifa, and neo-Nazis are our trannies and homosexuals demanding public acceptance for their shocking private fetishes.

Everything is in place—except, alas, for the decisive factor, *which is the patronage and toleration of those in power.* And needless to say, when these tactics fail, the defeated upstarts start to get depressed about the inability of their people to spontaneously defend their own interests. Liberalism is a potent drug indeed!

THE FASCIST PATH TO POWER

In light of this, it is worth taking a brief look at the ways in which the fascist movements of the early 20th century achieved power. Many of those pushing liberal cargo-cult tactics in the Alt Right believe that they are imitating fascism, and they hold out hope for a "white awakening" because they know that Hitler and Mussolini rose to power on the back of popular movements. However, a closer look at the history of these movements refutes the popular myth of a fascist rise to power by pure mass revolution.

Robert O. Paxton's *Anatomy of Fascism* is of great use here. It discusses not only the successful fascist movements in Italy and Germany, but also the unsuccessful ones elsewhere, and distinguishes all of these from conservative authoritarian regimes that did not rely on the same radical and populist methods. It also separates out the stages through which a fascist movement must cycle in order to assume power. The aid of established power is needed at several points on the way.

The first stage begins long before the fascist movement is founded, and consists of the social, intellectual, and political developments that contribute to making it a possibility. As everyone knows, the Great War and the rise of Communism in Russia were the most important preconditions for the original fascist movements. Less often appreciated is the role of what we would now call "metapolitics": a longer process of mental preparation going back decades, in which the failings of liberalism and democracy were exposed and the decline of Western civilization was discussed. This smoothed the way for the creation of fascist movements in the wake of the Great War, but it did not guarantee their success (for example, fascism did not take power in France, although the French had experienced the longest period of mental preparation for it).

The next stage begins once the fascist movement is founded and consists of a process by which it roots itself in the social and political system — or, alternatively, fails to do so. Initially, the fascist movement seeks to maximize its popular appeal by creating a loose and amorphous "antiparty," which serves to attract all sorts of people who possess wildly divergent interests but are united by a vague discontent. Later, although the movement continues to rally the people, many of these early followers end up being pruned off as alliances are made with existing social and political interests. In Mussolini's case, this was achieved when the *squadristi* in rural Italy made themselves an indispensable ally of the big landowners, who were being squeezed between the *laissez-faire* liberal state and the socialists agitating their workforce. In Germany, Hitler managed to attract small businessmen and a few large ones to his cause, although most of these stuck with traditional conservatives (and certainly did not bankroll the NSDAP to the extent claimed by the Left). It is important to emphasize the toleration of both of these fascisms by elements of the power structure in their countries. Local police forces often sided with Mussolini's *squadristi*, and Hitler's Brownshirt toughs enjoyed lenient treatment by the conservative Weimar judiciary.

The third stage, and the final one as far as we are concerned, involves the "seizure of power" by which the fascist movement achieves unrestrained rule. But in order to achieve this, *the fascist leaders must first be appointed into government by conservative elites*, who typically wish to make use of their popular following in order to bolster their own legitimacy. The 1922 March on Rome was nearly thwarted by the Italian government — trains carrying the majority of Blackshirts were stopped by police, and the government possessed the military force to repulse the nine thousand who turned up at the gates of the city — but King Victor Emmanuel III, fearing the consequences of open bloodshed, declined to impose martial law and instead offered the prime ministry to Mussolini. After trying and failing to imitate this gambit in 1923, Hitler sought power through the political system instead, and was eventually appointed to the chancellorship by a conservative elite that had been ruling without a parliamentary majority and wished to return to popular rule. Had the intention been to lock him out at all costs, this could have been done, as the NSDAP's large electoral support was beginning to drop off at the time.

In summary, successful fascist movements must cultivate not only the masses but also the vested interests of society. They must be encouraged, or at least tolerated, by an established ruling elite focused on the greater threat from Leftist revolution. Eventually, they must make a bid for power, and find conservative patrons who are both willing to cooperate with them and obliged by their own crisis of legitimacy to do so. Where no such opportunities existed in the 1920s and 1930s, fascism got nowhere; and where it directly confronted conservative authoritarian regimes, it typically ended up being repressed as one more phenomenon of public disorder.

The fascist experience can teach us many things. It illustrates the importance, yet also the limitations, of metapolitical action. It tells us that anyone attempting to follow the route to power walked by the fascists must appeal to a vast array of classes and interests and must work with national sentiment instead of offending it, which rules out anyone who chooses to marginalize himself by waving the flag of a defeated foreign enemy. It also reminds intellectuals that the angry young men attracted to the Right, who often egg each other on into unwise patterns of behavior, are in fact indispensable to the cause — what matters is to put them to good use defending the people being bullied by the Left, instead of wasting them in pointless street parading or noxious infighting.

However, the most important thing that fascism teaches us is that *it cannot be recreated in the present era*. The ruling power structure was founded on fascism's defeat and is watching out for its revival at every turn. The modern avatar of Leftist revolution is not a military threat from beyond the frontier, but a political enemy ensconced in every official institution, and it is now the "antifa" and "SJWs" who enjoy judicial leniency and elite patronage. The managerial revolution in industry, and the abandonment of white proletarian interests in favor of foreign immigrants by the Left, has neutralized a great deal of the old opposition between Bolshevism and big business. Perhaps most importantly in the long run, the West is no longer made up of sovereign states based on the rights of a fighting citizenry but consists of the territories of a *de facto* US Empire that pursues its expansionist goals through manipulation and subversion. And while there are still "conservatives" in office, these are no longer the anti-liberal traditionalists who used that name before 1945, but right-liberal "loyal opposition" who pride themselves on keeping the real Right out of power.

Of the three stages of fascist pathbreaking, the only one available to us right now is *metapolitics*. Thanks to the internet, a true "free press," the savagery and hypocrisy of the liberal oligarchy can be communicated every day to ever-increasing masses of people outside the official media structure. This can never induce the masses to rise up and replace that oligarchy of their own accord, but it can ensure that they become convinced of its illegitimacy and unwilling to react strongly against threats to its power. That is the first step from which all others must follow.

FROM FOURTH TO SECOND GENERATION WARFARE

As regards political action, in a situation where previous roads to power have been closed to us, there is only one model that can offer any hope for success. This is the *guerrilla war* — or, more precisely, the Fourth Generation War (4GW) described by William S. Lind in his works *On War* and *Fourth Generation War Handbook*.

It goes without saying that I am not suggesting a physical war with the managerial state, and anyone who does so is either a fool or an enemy shill. But it should be clear to us by now that politics is war by other means, and that we are in the strategic position of "non-state actors," prevented from fighting in the open against enemies who enjoy official backing. Non-state actors are no exception to everything that I have said about power and patronage, and the most effective ones are aided and financed by sympathetic states. However, we know that patronage is not required for the creation of a political guerrilla movement, as we ourselves have witnessed the creation of just such a movement out of absolutely nothing.

I am referring, of course, to the Alt Right, which *in its original form* showed a promising application of guerrilla methods to political warfare. As a diverse collection of autonomous Rightist groups operating under a loose brand name, it presented no single target for the enemy to attack. The movement had no single leader who could be vilified, co-opted, hyped up as the "big bad guy" indispensable to all Hollywood narratives, or harassed and made to look stupid in public. In the absence of such a hate figure, it was Hillary Clinton and her offi-cial media backers who made themselves look ridiculous by declaring war on Pepe the Frog.

Online trolls associated with the Alt Right used Nazi image-ry to publicly flout the speech restrictions imposed by the Left and transform the "Brown Menace" — the justification for every foreign imperial war and domestic repression campaign, treat-ed with due reverence by Leftists and fake conservatives — into a big stupid joke. It is impossible to say whether the majority of those using this imagery were consciously doing so as a means to these ends, although expressions such as "Great Meme Wars" imply that this was actually the case. The point is that it was done by rank-and-filers sniping from the undergrowth of anonymity, and when the shrieking volunteer commissars wanted to hit back at Alt Right public figures, they found none who were foolish enough to present themselves as targets by endorsing Nazi imagery.

By extending its branding to milder strains of conservatism as well as ethnonationalists and reactionaries, the original Alt Right conformed to the 4GW principle of "hugging the civil-ians," forcing the enemy to infuriate ordinary people by attack-ing them in order to get to the guerrillas. In the physical 4GWs of Iraq and Afghanistan, American forces sowed dragon's teeth among the local populations every time they shot at a guerrilla fighter and hit an innocent bystander. In the political 4GW against the Left, the same effect was achieved when Clinton dismissed half the American electorate as "deplorables" in re-sponse to the rise of the Alt Right. When this sort of thing hap-pens, and the guerrillas (Alt Right) shoot back while the client-rulers (cuckservatives) wring their hands, the loyalties of the people begin to shift in a new direction.

After finding an informal patron in Donald Trump, the Alt Right acquired the ability to go on the offensive. The election of Trump, which offered the chance to substitute a real conserva-tive political class for the professional losers of the loyal oppo-sition, should have been understood as the first step towards reopening a road to patronage that has been closed to the radi-cal Right ever since the defeat of fascism. However, many Alt

Righters in the US—who had been happy to castigate democracy as a rigged game during the years of Obama's rule—treated this event not as the capture of a bridgehead but as the crowning victory of a war. They had Cast Their Votes, Thrown the Bastards Out, and Put Their Man into Office, and some of them really started to say things like "We are the establishment now." They forgot the prudence learned by everybody who lives under a totalitarian regime, and blissfully reverted to the liberal faith of their hearts, discarding hard-won knowledge under the pretext of taking action.

This set the stage for the regression of the Alt Right into conventional tactics, or Second-Generation War (2GW), the tactics of the state forces that tend to lose Fourth Generation wars despite massive superiority in money and muscle. This began with rank-and-filers shaming people for exercising basic prudence, but it was formalized by Richard Spencer's Hailgate stunt in November 2016. Spencer, who had created the original *Alternative Right* website in 2010 and shut it down three years later,[2] almost certainly regretted publicly discarding the Alt Right brand just before it exploded in popularity. In the old Rockwellian tradition, he decided to raise his name by using Nazi symbolism to play the enemy media, forgetting that this strategy always entails being played right back. By sparking a media outcry and winning over the large audiences flocking to the increasingly Nazi-themed outlets of Andrew Anglin and Mike Enoch, Hailgate succeeded in its covert goal of presenting Spencer as the leader of the Alt Right.

However, the wider effect of the stunt upon the Alt Right was disastrous. It drove a wedge into the loose alliance between radicals and populists, negating the 4GW strategy of "hugging the citizens" and allowing the core of the movement to be isolated as a target. The Alt Right quickly reformed into a small alliance of edgy White Nationalist groups revolving around Spencer, and promptly isolated itself further by declaring war on the "Alt Liters" who had broken off to form the

---

[2] https://affirmativeright.blogspot.com/2013/12/looking-back-forging-forward.html

New Right. At the same time, a plan was unveiled to redefine
the new Alt Right as a centralized coalition, commanded by an
eponymous corporate entity under Spencer's leadership. This
threatened the organic unity of the original Alt Right, by making it harder for diverse groups to coexist within the same
movement—and sure enough, ever since the change from "rhi-
zome" to "tree" was made, the result has been a bitter fruit of
obnoxious internal crusades against homosexuals, women, insufficiently edgy people, and other targets.

If the methods of the decentralized Alt Right can be compared to guerrilla warfare, centralization was equivalent to
crawling out from the undergrowth and forming up as conventional battalions in the open field. And at Charlottesville, the
Alt Right marched directly into one of the strongpoints of the
enemy, with no plan other than to triumph by muscle and will.
Although the men present showed great bravery against the
antifa scum and politicized police sent against them, how could
they have hoped to win against the weight of media, judicial,
corporate, and political power stacked against them? Needless
to say, it is the failure of the Alt Right to keep up these costly
frontal attacks has brought us to the present state of affairs, in
which the enemy media demoralizes our people by gloating
over the humiliation of the Spencers and Heimbachs they
themselves elevated into place.

How, in retrospect, could things have been done differently?
And how can things yet be done differently?

We have to admit that the pre-Hailgate structure of the
movement could not have survived forever, and certainly not
outside of cyberspace. The fact that rank-and-filers in the Alt
Right felt the need to out-edge each other in order to gain status is proof enough of the need for formal leadership and hierarchy. But if the contours of the original movement had been
respected, the natural development would have been towards
the creation of several real-life organizations within the overarching brand of the Alt Right, which would have tried out
various approaches until one of them gained the strength and
momentum to absorb the others.

Ideally, these organizations would have carried the guerrilla tactics of the online movement into real life: harrying the enemy and luring him into overplaying his hand against ordinary people, instead of isolating ourselves from those people and courting their hatred by signaling as a threat to social order. Instead of rushing to usurp the brand name of the entire movement, the leaders—again, ideally—would have been wise enough to maintain a degree of plausible deniability between real-life activity and online discourse, making it less likely that political action will backfire on metapolitical work by inviting corporate-antifa censorship.

Although spent political capital cannot be recovered, there is nothing stopping us from taking this course in the present day. Organizations like Identity Evropa in the US (apparently modelled on Europe's Generation Identity) are using political guerrilla tactics such as flash demos and leaflet bombing. Antifa, who feel vindicated by recent events, continue to push conservatives towards radicalization by violently harassing them.[3] The political bridgehead in the US established by the Trump election is still intact, though much beleaguered, and the fight against impeachment may offer an issue around which the Rightist elements sundered by Hailgate can be reunited.

It may be that we shall have to discard the name of the original movement in order to recover its ethos. The centralized Alt Right exists mainly as an idea, which may serve to funnel donation money up to the handful of outlets that follow its rigid orthodoxy but exacts an intolerable price in strategic uselessness and internal friction. Distancing ourselves from the Alt Right brand name cannot make it go away—we are stuck with it for the foreseeable future—but it may dispel the illusion of unification and allow the decentralized substance of the movement to reassert itself. And if we should require another catch-all name that can be used for the purpose of "hugging the civilians," there is always the New Right brand currently being used by civic nationalists, who would be powerless to prevent its repossession by ethnonationalists and reactionaries.

---

[3] https://www.express.co.uk/news/politics/910975/jacob-reed-mogg-queen-mary-university-london-protest-left-wing-activists

Perhaps the long-term success of our struggle will hinge upon future tectonic shifts in the Western power structure. However, at the very least, we can reject the patronage of the only power actor willing to support insane strategy and neo-Nazi stupidity: the enemy media. As Greg Johnson has observed,[4] the media and certain Jewish organizations exert a great deal of control over the selection of leaders in the radical Right, simply by hyping up anyone who confirms their stereotypes as a serious threat and channeling credibility in his direction. It is no accident that the fifty-year-long cautionary tale of "WN 1.0" began when George Rockwell thought he could manipulate the enemy media and resurrected itself for a second act when Richard Spencer fell into the same trap. The fact that both men were, in my estimation, generally sincere in their motives did not prevent the media from making use of their antics in order to discredit the wider movement.

The maxim *no enemies to the Right* can only hold true in the context of *no alliances with the Left*. This precludes courting the attention of the enemy media, just as it precludes selling our principles out to the Left and trying to win mainstream "respectability." Those who want to lead this movement to victory have no serious choice other than to pursue steady, organic growth through meritorious action, and give the Fake News nothing but the savor of a door in the face.

Counter-Currents, June 28, 2018

---

[4] Greg Johnson, "In Bed with the Press," *Toward a New Nationalism*.

BEYOND THE ALT RIGHT:
TOWARD A NEW NATIONALISM

GREG JOHNSON

The Alt Right is dead. But the Alt Right was so useful—and so much fun—that we need to create a replacement for it, the sooner the better. By the Alt Right, I mean the online movement of White Nationalist podcasters, bloggers, and social media trolls that emerged in 2014, coalesced around the Trump candidacy in 2015, then began to change the parameters of political debate with stinging memes like the "cuckservative" barb, becoming an international media phenomenon in 2016.

As I argue in my essay "What is the Alternative Right?" (above) this new Alt Right was quite different from the original Alt Right that took its name from the *Alternative Right* webzine which Richard Spencer founded in 2010 and edited until 2012. The two Alt Rights differed in terms of ethos, intellectual influences, and preferred platforms and media, although they did come to share an ideology and a name. By the beginning of 2015, the new Alt Right was increasingly comfortable with White Nationalism as an ideology and the Alt Right as a brand.

Aside from the fact that #AltRight made a good hashtag, the main utility of the term was its vagueness. It allowed people to signal their dissent from mainstream Republicanism without embracing such stigmatized labels as National Socialism and White Nationalism. The Alt Right was thus an ideal "discursive space" in which White Nationalists could interact with, influence, and convert people who were closer to the political mainstream.

White Nationalists should always remember how we came to our views. We should never lose sight of the fact that it takes an inner struggle, ended by an act of courage, to seriously consider heretical and highly stigmatized ideas, even online, in the privacy of one's own home. Thus we need safe spaces for trying on new ideas and building new relationships. The Alt Right provided that. It allowed people to experiment with being radical and edgy without being one of "those people" or burning one's bridges to the mainstream.

The result was a grassroots online insurgency mobilizing a vast network of highly creative individuals and injecting their memes and talking points into the mainstream, where they began shifting popular consciousness and political debates.

But, as I also argued in "What Is the Alternative Right?," the Alt Right's success in attracting people led to a crisis. Both versions of the Alt Right were always, at core, White Nationalist outreach projects. But there was a perennial battle in the Alt Right between the people who advocated a "big tent" movement and the "purity spiralers" and Right-wing sectarians who wanted to enforce one ideological orthodoxy or another.

I was in the big tent camp. I argued that outreach projects by their nature attract people who do not (yet) agree with us. But you can only convert people who don't already agree with you. The whole point of the movement was to convert rather than repel people who disagreed with us.

But the new Alt Right was such a successful outreach project that it was being flooded with large numbers of Trumpian civic nationalists, including non-whites, who rejected White Nationalism. I thought this was more of an opportunity than a crisis, and that we needed to take a deep breath, remind ourselves that truth is on our side, and then get back to the battle of ideas. Others, however, became concerned that the Alt Right brand would be hijacked or coopted by civic nationalists like Milo Yiannopoulos. This was the Alt Right "brand war" of the fall of 2016.

The brand war came to an end with the Hailgate incident of November 21, 2016, when, before the cameras of the enemy media, Richard Spencer raised his glass with the words "Hail Trump, Hail our People, Hail Victory!" and people in the audience responded with Nazi salutes. This stunt indelibly identified the Alt Right not just with White Nationalism but with neo-Nazism in the minds of the whole world.

This led to a split between White Nationalists and civic nationalists, who came to be called the Alt Lite. To differentiate itself from the Alt Right, the Alt Lite dug in its heels on the one issue that White Nationalists most urgently need to destroy: the moral taboo against white identity politics. The great big beautiful tent, where civic nationalism and ethnonationalism could be debated—an argument that White Nationalists always win—was replaced by a great big ugly wall, over which only venomous Tweet barrages were exchanged.

The expanding discursive space in which White Nationalists could influence the mainstream was replaced by a self-marginalizing political sect which in 2017 began to focus on street activism, even though they were vastly outnumbered and outgunned by the Left, which could count on collaborators in the media and all levels of government, as well as armies of lawyers and effectively unlimited funds. White Nationalists have none of these advantages. Thus a movement that had grown by attacking the system's moral and intellectual weaknesses from a position of strength was replaced by a movement that attacked the system's institutional power centers from a position of weakness. Catastrophic failure was inevitable.

By the end of 2017, much of the American White Nationalist movement was simply exhausted from the wave of doxings, deplatforming, and lawfare that followed the Unite the Right rally in Charlottesville, Virginia, on August 12, 2017. In the days following Unite the Right, more than one hundred people disappeared from my social media sphere alone. They obviously did not change their political convictions, but they clearly believed that the movement was going the wrong direction. Nevertheless, the rallies and college speaking events continued, hemorrhaging people and money—which were in short supply to begin with—until they finally bled out.

The post-mortem of the activist phase of the Alt Right led to a healthy debate about "optics" and whether it is better for American White Nationalists to embrace American political traditions and symbols or imported ones.[1] There was also a growing consensus that the movement needed to return to our strengths, namely the war of ideas. Even activist events needed to be re-

---

[1] See Greg Johnson, "Is White Nationalism Un-American?" and "What is American Nationalism?" in *Toward a New Nationalism*.

configured along the lines of the European Identitarian movement, which does not battle antifa but engages in low-risk, high-reward publicity stunts, i.e., "propaganda of the deed."[2]

But for many in the American movement, 2018 has simply been a year of watching and waiting. People hunkered down to let the storm pass. Now that it is dying down, they are surveying the damage and wondering what comes next.

Wouldn't it be nice to have a common cause to rally around again? Wouldn't it be nice to have a new discursive space in which we could again interface with and perhaps influence the political mainstream?

Some people are hoping that Trump's re-election campaign might provide a rallying point, but most of us have lost our enthusiasm for Trump. Thankfully, there's something bigger and better than Trump. While there will always be a place for defending Trump's National Populist policies from critics and detractors, we can't lose sight of the big picture. We need to look beyond Trump to the forces that made Trump possible.

These are the same forces behind the Brexit victory; behind the rise of politicians like Viktor Orbán, Matteo Salvini, and Sebastian Kurz; behind the success of parties like Alternative for Germany, Poland's Law and Justice, and the Sweden Democrats; and behind the Yellow Vests insurgency in France.

All of these are manifestations of what is called National Populism or the New Nationalism. We need to understand the forces driving the rise of the New Nationalism. Then we need to add our impetus to these forces and try to steer them toward White Nationalism. The New Nationalism should be our new rallying point, our new discursive space in which we can inject our ideas into mainstream discussions.

For starters, I urge every White Nationalist to read *National Populism: The Revolt Against Liberal Democracy* by Roger Eatwell and Matthew Goodwin,[3] two British political scientists specializ-

---

[2] See Greg Johnson, "Interview on Unite the Right 1 and 2," in *Toward a New Nationalism*.

[3] Roger Eatwell and Matthew Goodwin, *National Populism: The Revolt Against Liberal Democracy* (New York: Pelican, 2018).

ing in populism and political extremism.

Eatwell and Goodwin are evidently men of the Left, but they do not seem to be liberals or globalists. Indeed, they relish demolishing liberal and globalist illusions about National Populism, arguing that it cannot be dismissed as mere fascism or racism; nor can it be dismissed as simply a flash in the pan, the product of ephemeral events like the 2008 recession or the migrant crisis; nor is it the last hurrah of "old white males" who will soon die off and be replaced by tolerant Millennials; nor, finally, is it merely the product of charismatic politicians.

Instead, Eatwell and Goodwin argue that National Populism is the product of deep social and political trends which they call the four Ds: Distrust, Destruction, Deprivation, and De-Alignment. *Distrust* refers to the breakdown of popular trust in political elites. *Destruction* primarily means destruction of identity, i.e., the destruction of peoples and cultures by immigration and multiculturalism. National Populism is, therefore, a form of white identity politics. *Deprivation* means the erosion of First World middle-class and working-class living standards due to globalization and neoliberalism. *De-Alignment* is the breakdown of voter identification with dominant political parties.

Eatwell and Goodwin marshal impressive empirical studies that indicate that these trends are pervasive in white countries. These trends are also deep-seated rather than ephemeral. Not only are they going to continue on into the future, they are likely to grow stronger before they abate. Thus, National Populism is here to stay. National Populism is the wave of the future, not just a ripple in the news cycle (hence the great wave on the cover of their book). Eatwell and Goodwin are so confident of this that in their final chapter, "Towards Post-Populism," the only post-populist scenario they can imagine is the political establishment adopting National Populist policies. In other words, they think National Populism will likely become the hegemonic political outlook. This is an astonishing concession, since it means that the hegemony of globalism is drawing to a close.

I find this analysis deeply encouraging, and it puts to rest a fear that has been gnawing at me for the last two years. I believe that nothing less than White Nationalism can save our race, thus the success of our movement is the supreme moral imperative. Whites are in a state of emergency. This is *serious*. This is *urgent*. Thus in 2015 and 2016, I was thrilled to see forces in the broader political realm aligning with White Nationalist ideas and goals, specifically Brexit and the Trump phenomenon.

But I also thought it likely that this historical moment would be fleeting. Thus we had to capitalize on it while it was still possible. This is why I was so horrified at Hailgate, when instead of giving a statesmanlike speech outlining how the National Policy Institute would serve as the intellectual vanguard for National Populism—a move that would have secured Spencer's bid for movement leadership and attracted significant resources—he instead chose the path of juvenile buffoonery, hoping to ingratiate himself with the cool kids at *The Right Stuff* and on the chans.

But that was just the beginning of months of sectarianism, schisms, purges, and purity spirals. In 2017, we saw the birth of toxic, self-marginalizing memes like "white *sharia*" and the return of the worst ideas and attitudes of White Nationalism 1.0. We had arrived at a moment of decision, and our "leaders" had chosen juvenility and irrelevance. They were not ready for prime time. As I explained in my essay "Against Right-Wing Sectarianism,"[4] this could only lead to a smaller, weaker, poorer, and dumber movement. Such a movement would be unable to halt white genocide.

By May of 2017, I started thinking that we needed a new "brand." The term "New Nationalism" was already being used to describe National Populism. The term was broad and vague enough to encompass everyone from White Nationalists to sitting presidents and ruling parties. I even went so far as to reserve the domain name newnationalism.net. In keeping with my essay "Redefining the Mainstream,"[5] I envisioned a discursive space that was the exact opposite of Right-wing sectarianism. Our movement must prefigure the hegemony we want to create in the broader society, encompassing the full diversity of whites, united only by the central principle of white identity politics and

---

[4] In *Toward a New Nationalism*.

[5] In *Toward a New Nationalism*.

free to differ on all other matters.

The most important intellectual battle is over the *legitimacy* of white identity politics. The greatest political taboo of our times is the idea that identity politics is immoral for white people—and *only* for white people. This taboo unites the whole political establishment against us. The political establishment knows this, but many National Populists don't. This is why the establishment attacks National Populists as fascists, nativists, and racists.

But many National Populists don't challenge the idea that white identity politics is immoral. Instead, they insist that they are color-blind civic nationalists, concerned only with a common culture. Then they try to turn the tables on Leftism, accusing it of being *the real identity politics*.

But, of course, the Left is not going to drop identity politics. Why would they drop a winning strategy? Foreswearing identity politics is a losing strategy for the Right, akin to unilateral disarmament, taking a knife to a gunfight, or allowing one's opponents a trump card but refusing to use it oneself.[6]

Thus, the New Nationalism platform needed to be a space where one could argue about virtually anything *except* the moral legitimacy of white identity politics. Instead, our overriding editorial agenda would be to establish that white identity politics is inevitable, necessary, and moral—and to expose the moral illegitimacy of the system.

I shared this idea with a number of writers, podcasters, and video bloggers who also believed the Alt Right was spiraling into irrelevance. They were uniformly enthusiastic. But there were things I had to take care of first, like finishing *The White Nationalist Manifesto*. I also sensed that it would be some time before the Alt Right would finally exhaust itself and people would be ready for something new. Eventually, though, I decided that I want to stick with *Counter-Currents*. I still think that a New Nationalism webzine is a good idea. But somebody else needs to create it.

---

[6] See Greg Johnson, "Why Conservatives Conserve Nothing," in *Toward a New Nationalism*, and "In the Short Run," in *The White Nationalist Manifesto*.

Of course White Nationalists do not need a new platform to contribute to the rise of National Populism. In fact, we have been contributing to it for quite some time. Furthermore, if Eatwell and Goodwin are right, we will be contributing to it well into the future, for white nations will be receptive to National Populism for some time to come. And although nothing has greater *moral urgency* than stopping white genocide, we've got time to get our message and our strategies right. (And if we don't have time to do it right, doing it wrong won't save us, anyway.)

So, how can White Nationalists insert ourselves into the broader National Populist phenomenon? Let's look at Eatwell and Goodwin's four Ds again.

Distrust: when people distrust their rulers, the system loses legitimacy and power. White Nationalists are masterful at mocking the lies, hypocrisy, sanctimony, cowardice, and degeneracy of our rulers. Furthermore, nothing destroys trust in the establishment quite like learning that its ultimate agenda is the genocide of the white race.[7]

But our propaganda needs to be truthful as well, because we want people to trust us. For if distrust becomes pervasive throughout society, then the people cannot unite against the establishment. Our goal is to promote a high-trust society. We cannot accomplish that if we cynically resort to lies because "That's what the establishment does to us." If we want to replace the establishment, we have to be better than the establishment.

Destruction: White Nationalists have been raising awareness of the destruction of white nations and cultures through immigration and multiculturalism for decades. Even so, our educational efforts have awakened far fewer people than the negative consequences of immigration and multiculturalism themselves. The system is doing far more to *push* people toward white identity politics than we are doing to *pull* them. Thus, white racial consciousness will continue to rise even if our movement is completely censored.

We should, of course, do everything we can to raise aware-

---

[7] See Greg Johnson, "White Genocide," in *The White Nationalist Manifesto*.

ness. But I think we have a much more important role to play, namely *deepening* awareness.

First, we need to help people understand *why* multiculturalism is a failure—namely, racial and ethnic diversity in the same state is always a source of weakness[8]—so we don't waste our time with half-measures like "conservative" multicultural civic nationalism. Moreover, only White Nationalists fully understand the forces promoting mass migrations and multiculturalism and how they fit into the overall agenda of white genocide.

Second, and most importantly, we need to defend the *moral legitimacy* of white identity politics. Vast numbers of whites are in thrall to the establishment because they believe there is something immoral about taking their own side in ethnic conflicts. This taboo is like a dam, holding back the floodwaters of National Populism. Once we break that dam, the wave of National Populism will sweep away the whole rotten system.

Deprivation: basic economics predicts that globalization will lead to the collapse of middle-class and working-class living standards throughout the First World, although First World elites will benefit quite a lot. Obviously, the masses in any First World society never consented to such policies. Genuine Leftists recognize that globalization has undermined the gains of the Left in the First World. But global socialism is not the answer to global capitalism. Only National Populists understand the natural limit of globalization: the nation-state.[9]

De-Alignment: when voters begin to distrust the establishment, they begin to distrust establishment political parties as well. White Nationalists are masterful at showing that electoral politics, in which voters take sides in the battles between mainstream political parties, is only a superficial distraction from real politics. Political power does not lie in voters choosing between Coke and Diet Coke. That's an election that the Coca-Cola Corporation can't lose. Real power lies in framing all political de-

---

[8] See Greg Johnson, "What's Wrong with Diversity?," in *The White Nationalist Manifesto*.

[9] See Greg Johnson, "The End of Globalization," in *Truth, Justice, & a Nice White Country*.

bates so that, no matter which party ends up in power, the establishment always wins. Real power lies in establishing the things about which political parties *agree rather than fight* and about which the voters are *never given a choice*.[10] The political establishment, center-Left and center-Right, is of one mind on the goodness of globalization, immigration, and multiculturalism—the very things that National Populists oppose.

What white people want is essentially a socially conservative, interventionist state. We want National Populism. What the establishment wants is socially liberal global capitalism, what Jonathan Bowden called Left-wing oligarchy. The people are never allowed to vote for National Populism straight up. The center-Right packages social conservatism with neoliberal globalization. The center-Left packages the interventionist state with social degeneracy. When the center-Right is in power, they only give the establishment what it wants: lower taxes and freer trade for the oligarchs. When the center-Left is in power, they only give the establishment what it wants: more degeneracy. The parties blame their failures on the opposition and assure their voters that the *next time* their party is at the helm, the voters will finally get what they want. The people are placated with the illusion of political representation in elections where the establishment parties trade power. But no matter who is elected, the outcomes always drift father and farther from what the people want, namely National Populism—and closer to what the degenerate global elites want.

White Nationalists are also highly aware of how the establishment works to co-opt National Populist uprisings like the Tea Party and now, sadly, Donald Trump. For Trump has fallen into the center-Right establishment pattern of giving the oligarchs what they want (tax cuts), failing to do what the people want (a border wall), and blaming his failure on his opponents (first the establishment Republicans, now the Democrats).

In sum, White Nationalists can intensify National Populist forces and steer them toward White Nationalism by deepening the people's *Distrust* of the establishment; broadening and deep-

---

[10] See Greg Johnson, "Hegemony," in *New Right vs. Old Right*.

ening the people's awareness of how and why globalization, immigration, and multiculturalism are leading them to *Destruction* and *Deprivation;* and creating new political possibilities by encouraging *De-Alignment* with the establishment's sham political debates and contests.

But to ride the National Populist wave, White Nationalists have to jettison certain incompatible ideological fixations.

First and foremost, we actually have to be populists. Eatwell and Goodwin also show that National Populism is not anti-democratic. National Populists want more democracy, not less. They also argue that National Populism is not fascist in its inspirations or goals, although the establishment loves nothing more than to stigmatize National Populism with such labels. We shouldn't help them. Thus those among us who sneer at populism and democracy,[11] make fetishes out of elitism and hierarchy,[12] and try to resurrect inter-war fascist movements[13] are not helping.

Second, National Populists really are economic interventionists. Old habits die hard, but those among us who still think in terms of "free market" economics are not helping. Eatwell and Goodwin point out that in the United States, Republican voters are significantly more interventionist than Republican legislators. Which means that Koch-funded free-market fundamentalism has simply produced a party headed by ideologues who are out of touch with their constituency. Don't be one of them.

Where do we go from here? The most important thing to keep in mind is that National Populism is arising out of the *breakdown* of the political system. Just like shattering an atom, the breakdown of a system releases immense energies. It also creates radical new possibilities, "holes in being" where new actions can take place and new orders can emerge.

---

[11] Greg Johnson, "Notes on Populism, Elitism, & Democracy" in *New Right vs. Old Right.*

[12] Greg Johnson, Introduction, in *Truth, Justice, & a Nice White Country.*

[13] Greg Johnson, "The Relevance of the Old Right," in *The White Nationalist Manifesto.*

But the breakdown of systems also creates uncertainty and surprises. It is not an environment in which one can expect to unfold grand plans. Thus, the more our movement is tied to long-term plans and fixed ideas, the less adapted we are to the climate we wish to create, and the more brittle and susceptible to catastrophic failure we become. Accordingly, at the present moment, the best overall strategy is not to get ahead of ourselves. We simply need to *promote chaos, but also plant the seeds of a new order.* Then we need to wait.

The Yellow Vests insurgency is a genuine grassroots National Populist movement. But it was nobody's grand design. It emerged spontaneously, and it surprised everyone. But spontaneous movements of large numbers of people are only possible because the participants share common views and values. Such movements also propagate through existing social networks. Thus, if we want more National Populist insurgencies, we need to promote chaos in the system, seed people's minds with models of genuine National Populist alternatives, and build real-world social networks through which we can propagate ideas and influence. Beyond that, we simply need to adopt an attitude of maximum openness and flexibility in the face of new possibilities so we can react with fresh provocations.

In short, we need more New Right metapolitics. But this is second-nature to us. We've been doing it for years now. We have the best ideas, the best memes, and the best people. But we need a new focus. If Eatwell and Goodwin are right, though, we now know that we have a vast audience, strong historical winds at our back, and time enough to turn the world around. Let's make this the age of the New Nationalism.

Counter-Currents, December 21, 2018

INDEX

Numbers in bold refer to a whole chapter or section devoted to a particular topic.

ABOUT THE CONTRIBUTORS

Michael Bell writes for *Counter-Currents*.

Aedon Cassiel blogs at *Zombie Meditations* and writes for *Counter-Currents*.

F. Roger Devlin, Ph.D., is the author of *Sexual Utopia in Power* (Counter-Currents, 2015) and *Alexandre Kojève and the Outcome of Modern Thought* (2004), as well as many essays and reviews.

Émile Durand writes for *Counter-Currents*.

Gregory Hood is the author of *Waking Up from the American Dream* (Counter-Currents, 2015) and many essays and reviews.

Wolfie James is a wife, a mother, and a pro-white activist.

Greg Johnson, Ph.D., is the Editor-in-Chief of Counter-Currents Publishing and the author of *Confessions of a Reluctant Hater* (Counter-Currents, 2010; second, expanded ed., 2016), *New Right vs. Old Right* (Counter-Currents, 2013), *Truth, Justice, & a Nice White Country* (Counter-Currents, 2015), *In Defense of Prejudice* (Counter-Currents, 2017), *You Asked for It: Selected Interviews*, vol. 1 (Counter-Currents, 2017), *The White Nationalist Manifesto* (Counter-Currents, 2018), and *Toward a New Nationalism* (Counter-Currents, 2018).

Ruuben Kaalep is the leader of the Estonian identitarian youth movement Blue Awakening (Sinine Äratus).

Patrick Le Brun writes and podcasts for *Counter-Currents*.

James Lawrence writes for *Affirmative Right*, formerly *Alternative Right*.

Colin Liddell is Editor with Andy Nowicki of *Affirmative Right*, https://affirmativeright.blogspot.com/

Kevin MacDonald, Ph.D., was Professor of Psychology at California State University, Long Beach, and author of *The Culture of Critique* (1998) and many other books and articles.

Spencer J. Quinn is the author of *White Like You* (Counter-Currents, 2018) and *Reframing White Nationalism* (Counter-Currents, 2018).

John B. Morgan IV is the Book Editor of Counter-Currents Publishing and writes for *Counter-Currents*.

Lawrence Murray writes for *Counter-Currents* and *The Right Stuff*.

F. C. Stoughton writes for *Counter-Currents*.

Donald Thoresen writes for *Counter-Currents*.

Jared Taylor is editor of *American Renaissance*, https://www.amren.com/, and the author of *White Identity: Racial Consciousness in the 21st Century* (2011), *If We Do Nothing: Essays & Reviews from 25 Years of White Advocacy* (2015), and Paved with *Good Intentions: The Failure of Race Relations in Contemporary America* (1993), as well as many essays and reviews.

Adam Wallace is an English writer and commentator.

Hunter Wallace is the editor of *Occidental Dissent*, http://www.occidentaldissent.com

David Yorkshire is the editor of *Mjolnir Magazine*, https://mjolnirmagazine.blogspot.com, and the author of many essays and reviews.